D1624926

Getting New Clients

Books by Dick Connor

Marketing Your Consulting and Professional Services by Dick Connor and Jeff Davidson (Wiley, 1990)

Increasing Revenue from Your Clients

Books by Jeff Davidson

Breathing Space: Living & Working at a Comfortable Pace in a Sped-Up Society (MasterMedia, 1992)

Cash Traps: Small Business Secrets for Reducing Costs and Improving Cash Flow (Wiley, 1992)

Your Bank—How to Get Better Service (Consumer Reports Books, 1992)

The Domino Effect: How to Grow Sales, Profits, and Market Share through Super Vision by Don Vlcek and Jeff Davidson (BusinessOne-Irwin, 1992)

Marketing to Home-Based Businesses (BusinessOne-Irwin, 1991)

Power and Protocol for Getting to the Top (Shapolsky, 1991)

Avoiding the Pitfalls of Starting Your Own Business (Shapolsky, 1991)

Blow Your Own Horn: How to Get Noticed—And Get Ahead (Berkley, 1991)

Selling to the Giants: How to Become a Key Supplier to Large Corporations (Tab/McGraw-Hill, 1991)

How to Have a Good Year Every Year by Dave Yoho and Jeff Davidson (Berkley, 1991)

Marketing Your Consulting and Professional Services by Dick Connor and Jeff Davidson (Wiley, 1990)

Marketing for the Home-Based Business (Bob Adams, Inc., 1990)

The Marketing Sourcebook for Small Business (Wiley, 1989)

Marketing on a Shoestring (Wiley, 1988)

Getting New Clients

Second Edition

Dick Connor
Certified Management Consultant
Springfield, Virginia

Jeff Davidson
Certified Management Consultant
Chapel Hill, North Carolina

John Wiley & Sons, Inc.
New York • Chichester • Brisbane • Toronto • Singapore

Library of Congress Cataloging-in-Publication Data
Connor
    Getting new clients / Dick Connor, Jeff Davidson.—2nd ed.
      p.   cm.
    Includes index.
    ISBN 0-471-55528-2
    1. Professions—Marketing. I. Davidson, Jeffrey P. II. Title.
HD8038.A1C665 1993
658.8—dc20   92-20197

Printed in the United States of America

10 9 8 7 6 5 4 3 2

To Susan

Acknowledgments

We'd like to thank several people for helping with preparation of the book. Dave Alan Yoho's expertise on telephone techniques and Ernie Kosty's valuable tips on proposal writing were invaluable.

We would like to thank our editor, John B. Mahaney, for his enthusiasm, vision, support, and expertise, and John's assistant, Gloria Fuzia, for her patience and professionalism. Thanks also to W. Bradford Wiley, Deborah E. Wiley, Charles R. Ellis, Steven Kippur, PhD, and Karl Weber, among many others at Wiley, for operating such a fine publishing company and professional and trade books division, in an era when most book publishing operations leave much to be desired.

A hearty thanks also to Joyce Kreiger, Lynn McElroy, Stephanie Joel, Lauren Fransen, Joseph Grosso, Peter Clifton, and Teresa Hartnett, who are all very skilled at what they do and help increase the size of an author's royalties!

D.C.
J.D.

About the Authors

Dick Connor is a Certified Management Consultant. He consults internationally with services providers in designing and installing Client-Centered Niche programs. He also provides classroom training and infield coaching on personal selling skills. The originator of the Client-Centered Marketing System® he has written numerous books and articles.

Jeff Davidson, MBA, CMC, based in Chapel Hill, North Carolina, has developed an international reputation for offering high-content keynote speeches. A certified management consultant, Jeff specializes in helping people live and work at a comfortable pace.

Jeff is the author of 18 books. Jeff's books have been selected by major book clubs 19 times and have been translated into eight languages including Chinese, Japanese, Indonesian, Dutch, and Spanish.

Foreword

Getting new clients." The phrase is both exhilarating and frightening to professional service providers who have spent years honing their functional talents to a fine edge but still have considerable concern over how and when and to whom to market.

In 1988, Dick Connor and Jeff Davidson produced an extra ordinary book to help service providers just like you reap the rewards of all the extra hours at the office and with clients. They called their book *Getting New Clients,* an apt title.

Out of the starting gate, the book was an instant winner. It was endorsed by the executive director of the prestigious Institute of Management Consultants; the vice president of the American Marketing Association; the publisher of *Consultant's News* (one of the world's key resources for consultants); the broadcast division of the U.S. Chamber of Commerce; and many other organizations.

Getting New Clients was selected by no less than four book clubs, including the Macmillan Executive Program (now Newbridge Executive Program), and attracted the attention of publishers in France, Germany, and Israel. The book was produced as a double cassette by Wiley Sound Business. The *Library Journal* included *Getting New Clients* among its exclusive list of recommended business books. The authors were asked to speak at conventions and annual meetings across North America and in Australia.

The first edition went to four printings and became a mainstay in the business book section of book stores from Fifth Avenue, in Manhattan, to Manhattan Beach, California.

Quite obviously, you're now holding the revised edition of *Getting New Clients,* and it's a humdinger. This book is no mere glossover of the first edition. Once again, Connor and Davidson have pulled out stops in describing point by point what it takes to become a superior marketer of professional services.

While the authors have streamlined the text and made it more reader friendly, this book is not light reading. Get your yellow highlighter ready and a pocket dictator, and give yourself plenty of time for in-depth *study* of the system. In a sentence, it's the key to your future prosperity!

Dr. Tony Alessandra

La Jolla, California
December 1992

Preface

Getting profitable new clients in targeted niches is the key to both survival and profitable growth in the turbulent times facing professional-service providers.

The competition for virtually every type of professional service is increasing due to a new set of dynamics including (1) the removal of restrictions on all forms of commercialism in the professions; (2) corporate downsizing resulting in an unprecedented influx of new consultants; (3) the increased propensity of clients to change the professional-service providers with whom they work; (4) the effects of technology, particularly the personal computer, on the ability of clients to handle more tasks in-house; (5) an uneven, rapidly shifting economy; (6) new vehicles for reaching clients, such as event marketing, automated telemarketing, and one-stop service centers; (7) further stratification of targeted niche areas as a direct function of society's increasing complexity.

We've rewritten *Getting New Clients* to meet the needs of the busy practitioner who wants to survive and thrive in the 1990s and beyond. It contains principle-based practices and strategies forged by over 35 years' experience in the trenches serving more than 800 firms worldwide, and converts theory into practical reality. It is for busy professionals who want to know what to do and how. Indeed, *Getting New Clients* is a highly detailed how-to-do-it book.

Clearly, the 1990s are proving not to be a straight-line extension of the 1980s. This edition dramatically extends and broadens the client-centered marketing approach we previously introduced. The approach has evolved into a practical "deliverables-driven" marketing *system* for penetrating a targeted niche. You can systematically analyze your existing practice to determine much more precisely the targets of opportunity and targets of attention that deserve the attention of client-centered marketing principles and techniques.

Hereafter, the narrative will be written in the first person, reflecting the voice of Dick Connor. I will talk directly to you, just as if you and I were face to face, focusing our time and attention on improving your ability to attract and acquire new clients.

Throughout the text, I will stress that a "client-centered," industry-specific, new client acquisition program is the only appropriate marketing strategy for professional-service providers. In 1969, when I became the first full-time professional services marketing consultant, I developed and introduced the Client-Centered Marketing™ system. Client-Centered Marketing is a trademark for a marketing orientation that puts the needs and expectations of clients and prospective clients first in the client–firm relationship. Need satisfaction, not the selling of a service, is the primary focus of the professional.

The client-centered marketing approach positions the client and qualified prospective clients as the targets and beneficiaries of your time, talents, and focused expertise.

I will also refer to the principles of leveraging and concentration. As a busy professional, you must leverage the available, often discretionary, time by concentrating on the smallest number of actions to produce the largest result. A niche approach enables the busy service provider to *leverage* his or her own time, talents, and experience to sense, sell, serve, and satisfy the needs of targeted clients and prospects in a niche.

The techniques and tips presented in *Getting New Clients* have been field tested with thousands of service providers worldwide in virtually every type of service firm. Companies providing business services also report excellent results in serving their customers and clients. I am confident that you, too, will prosper through their application, and will receive a disproportionate return on your investment, a hallmark of value-added services.

Unquestionably, it is difficult to put your performance under a microscope. It takes resilience to put the status quo on trial and scrutinize your patterns of behavior, which, after all, have been based on your assumptions, experience, and conventional wisdom.

To assist you in your efforts to generate profitable new clients, I have presented the material in this book in an action sequence. You will know what to do, when to do it, and why.

Even if you are a novice in marketing of any sort, you'll find that everything is explained in a logical step-by-step approach. For readers who have had some experience in services marketing, this book will fill in any gaps and make it easier to explore and use sophisticated approaches you may not yet have employed in your practice. For the "seasoned pro," *Getting New Clients* provides a manual to use in training others in a logical manner.

Dick Connor, CMC
Jeff Davidson, CMC

Springfield, Virginia
Chapel Hill, North Carolina

Contents

Getting New Clients

Introduction

This book answers the key question facing today's professional-service providers. Consultants, accountants, attorneys, communication specialists, EDP and systems consultants, as well as a wide variety of other professional service providers in the fields of finance, real estate, investments, training, engineering, and advertising, ask this question daily.

The megaquestion is, "How can I obtain profitable, high potential, new clients that will enable me to meet my practice-development objectives without having to be a professional salesperson or use distasteful, unprofessional methods such as advertising and discounting?" The answer to this question is presented here.

We're in an era where professional service providers are called on to play an increasingly larger role in the affairs of our clients. Concurrently, the competition faced by service providers across the board has never been more intense. Today the pressure to produce profits is forcing new thinking in firms of all sizes.

There are three keys to survival and profitable growth in the 1990s and beyond. The first is developing a clear focus of your business priorities. This involves such measures as choosing your basis for competing in your chosen niche: Are you product-driven, technology-driven, or *solutions-driven* when it comes to meeting needs? Are you willing to slough off excess costs and energy draining activities in favor of what actually works?

The second key is to develop a skill base that is different from and/or better than the offerings of others in your profession. If you swim with the pack, some days you get to eat, and some days you don't.

1

Third, are you willing and able to outexecute the other players serving your chosen niche? Today, continual reinventing of marketing approaches is mandatory for continuing success in marketing professional services. In addition, do your policies support superior performance? Do you continually refine your practice and its delivery systems? Do you leverage your available resources and tools for optimal gain; for example, is your computer system configured to serve you and enable you quickly and easily to do whatever will totally support your efforts? Or, are you willing to keep settling for the same limited uses of your system.

Computer-assisted communication is one of the most revolutionary marketing developments of the century. Any firm that can afford an advanced desktop computer and a laser printer can compete with the best and the brightest, by profiling the positive characteristics of the best clients; maintaining and adding to powerful but simple-to-use data-base software; making custom contact packages with each target; developing newsletters, card deck, telemarketing programs, and video presentations; and undertaking systematic follow-up in ways that retain and enhance relationships.

To assist you in achieving profitable growth throughout this decade, this book provides an insider's guide to the use of a client-centered approach for developing a new client acquisition program.

The client-centered approach to getting new clients has been acid tested in the field by intelligent, practical, and often skeptical professionals.

The Client-centered niche marketing system™, which includes the application of the Platinum Rule™ and the development of specialized databases, is, in short, a universal approach you can employ to help your professional services flourish. It provides an analytical frame of reference and a foundation for tailoring a marketing program. Moreover, the ideas in this book will enable you to survive and prosper well into the 1990s.

I have had the opportunity to present these ideas and techniques in a three-day workshop, also called "Getting New Clients," to thousands of professionals around the globe. In most instances, these professionals readily accepted the client-centered marketing approach and recognized the importance of focusing on a targeted industry-market niche.

A *niche approach* enables busy professionals to leverage their available time, existing relationships, and resources for the purpose of attracting and acquiring high-potential, new clients in the niche. The niche approach is based on experiences you'll gain in providing value-perceived services to existing high-potential clients in the niche. This allows the professional-service provider to work from a comfort zone, that area of professional behavior where the individual is productive, confident, and forthright.

A service professional is able to work from her* personal *comfort zone* when she can propose effective solutions already developed for and used successfully by the best high-potential existing clients in the niche. Thus, the professional is able to use similar vocabulary, skills, and solution statements that yield success.

Rather than trying to sell a service, a situation in which most professionals find themselves when using traditional marketing approaches, the client-centered-niche approach offers a perspective from which the professional is able to suggest ways the prospect can improve *his* business. Thus, the professional is able to raise the level of exploratory discussion from one of selling services to one of offering value-perceived solutions to the current needs of high-potential prospects in the targeted niche. This is a superior marketing approach. The client-centered-niche approach enables the busy service professional to leverage her time, talents, and experience to sense, sell, serve, and satisfy the needs of target prospects in a target industry or market segment.

In 1985, John Wiley & Sons published our best-selling book, *Marketing Your Consulting and Professional Services*. This book, which reached its eighth printing before being published in a second edition in 1990, offers a by-the-numbers introduction to the broad scope of marketing professional services. This new edition of *Getting New Clients* is the logical extension of that earlier book and focuses on the art and science of obtaining profitable new clients. Many of the terms used throughout this book have been defined and discussed in *Marketing Your Consulting and Professional Services* and are included here for your convenience in the glossary that follows the text.

Years ago, as the material for this book began to take shape, a seasoned professional said to me, "If I can get an appointment with a prospect, my experience and basic problem-solving and communications skills will usually see me through. But getting an appointment with Mr. Right Guy is my Achilles' heel. I don't have a consistent way to open up a contact's door and mind to me. If my referral sources ever dry up, I am dead!"

This book is about opening the door to qualified prospects in targeted organizations. It is also about the art and science of planning and

---

* We will alternate use of *he* and *she* to avoid sexism in the book.

conducting effective new-business discussions with the right contact(s) after you have succeeded in obtaining an appointment.

The goal of the successful professional-service marketer is to promote and produce a value-perceived service solution to an important need faced by prospective clients in a targeted niche. To do this, you need to know what drives the niche: What are the success factors? What are the profit factors? Successful use of the client-centered niche approach involves a transformation from providing services to answering the question, "How many different ways can I help the client to be profitable as it applies to my resources?"

Prospective clients are reluctant to meet with sellers of services who want them to reveal needs during potentially stressful sessions. This book recognizes that the most difficult part of new-client development is finding a prospective client who will meet with the professional. Determining needs is relatively easy for the professional; developing solutions is the stock-in-trade of professional-service providers.

Getting New Clients will show you how to identify the unmet or poorly met needs of prospective clients in the targeted niches. It will show you how to prepare and mail an initial contact package to selected, prospective clients that will be received favorably. It will also discuss how to telephone decision makers in the targeted organization to obtain an appointment to discuss the need identified in the contact package. *Getting New Clients* will show you how to prepare for and conduct an effective new-business interview and an effective follow-up. You will be presented with the essential skills, knowledge, and insights, as well as lessons learned, to make the client-centered marketing approach work for you.

Gone are the days when a client gained was a client retained. Client "churn" is a fact of life even in the best run practices. *Getting New Clients* is of particular interest in the following cases: (1) When you want to or have to change the nature and scope of your practice; (2) when your practice growth from cross-selling additional services to existing clients is not sufficient to provide the profit required for your practice (i.e., sometimes you mine all the gold in your own backyard and it is time to find a new vein); and (3) when you need to replace the revenue from clients known to be lost and clients suspected to be lost.

Not everyone has the same orientation and level of experience. A popular way of describing the levels of experience in a professional-service firm is with the terms *finder, minder,* and *grinder.* This book will serve all three types of readers:

1. For the finder who is proficient in generating new business from existing clients and wants to develop the capability and confidence required to attract profitable new clients.

2. For the minder, often a partner-in-training, who recognizes that the ability to bring in profitable new clients is always recognized and rewarded.

3. For the grinder, who recognizes that transition from "business doer" to "business getter" is the make-or-break activity for most talented professionals, and who wants to accelerate his progress on the path to partnership.

Getting New Clients contains everything you need to obtain profitable new clients, including checklists, sample letters, and new-business discussion guides. You will learn how to develop an insider's understanding and reputation within a targeted industry-market niche. You'll also learn how to develop a database and library for your niche that will provide you with a competitive edge and position you as an insider among those you want most eagerly to know of your services.

Developing Your Client-Centered and New Client Acquisition Program

1

The Client-Centered Marketing System

Getting profitable new clients has never been more important to the services provider and, in today's rapidly changing environment, never more difficult—if you are still using the traditional marketing approaches. Yet, it need not be a painful, identity-rattling venture. In this chapter, we'll lay the foundation of the Client-Centered Marketing System (CCMS), which is designed to help you attract profitable new clients in your targeted industry-market niches.

As defined in our book *Marketing Your Consulting and Professional Services:*[*]

> Client-centered marketing is the development of a special type of client–firm relationship with your most desirable clients, prospective clients, and referral relationships within targeted industry-market niches. Once the special relationship is established, the primary and continuing task is to *sense, sell, serve,* and *satisfy* the needs and expectations of these clients and others in ways that are mutually profitable.

[*] Dick Connor and Jeffrey P. Davidson, *Marketing Your Consulting and Professional Services*, 2nd ed. (New York: John Wiley & Sons, Inc., 1990).

A WORKING DEFINITION

Client-centered marketing is a strategic decision to:

1. Select a targeted industry-market niche for special attention.

2. Develop and enhance relationships with high-potential clients, prospective clients, and influential members of the niche's infrastructure.

3. Prepare, position, promote, and provide value-perceived solution systems for selected hot-button needs of targeted clients and prospective clients in the niche.

4. Leverage the time, talents, technology, and other resources available to you.

5. Serve in ways that result in mutual satisfaction and retention of the client–firm relationship.

In putting client-centered marketing into practice, your goal is relationship and revenue enhancement. Ultimately revenue enhancement is intimately tied to client satisfaction. The cultivation of a satisfied client requires much more than a job well done. It requires building a value-perceived relationship. To build this relationship, you need to understand your clients' industry and target markets, their business goals, needs, restraints, and areas of potential growth. In addition, you need to create opportunities to put this specialized knowledge into practice.

A client-centered marketing approach cuts straight to the hard reality of the business world: marketing and client service are interdependent and mutually reinforcing. One without the other is insufficient. Our CCMS provides a balanced marketing–client service approach.

A client-centered marketing and client service approach is not appropriate for all clients. Rather, it is reserved for the 20 to 40 percent of your existing clients who represent the upper crust. We hope you will also use this approach for the 60 to 80 percent of your targeted prospective clients who represent lucrative long-term contacts. In the CCMS, the targeted prospective clients are the clones of your best existing clients.

Client-centered marketing helps you increase the number and dollar value of high-potential clients and prospective clients you contact and serve in your targeted niche. The remaining 60 to 80 percent of your current clients need only be served in a business-as-usual manner. Since you are a busy professional who struggles daily with finding and allocating time for new business development, we stress the principle of leveraging your time, talents, and technology. This essential principle will be discussed in Chapter 2.

SOME OTHER ESSENTIAL DEFINITIONS

Choosing an industry-market niche for concentration is one of the most important strategic decisions you will make regarding the long-term viability of your practice. You can't be all things to all people, and you certainly can't be all things to all clients. To survive and thrive in today's business environment you must direct your attention to niches that you can penetrate and where you can most readily serve prosperously.

The term *industry* here refers to a specific four-digit Standard Industry Code (SIC) classification as defined by the U.S. Department of Commerce. *Market* is synonymous with the postal zip codes that constitute your practice area for a specific SIC. *Niche* is used as an abbreviation for industry-market niche and includes clients, prospective clients, suspects, nonclient influentials, competitors, and others who serve and interact with the niche in some way.

MARKETING OBJECTIVES

You can achieve nine major marketing objectives by using the CCMS:

1. Generating controlled, profitable practice growth.
2. Expanding services to existing clients.
3. Retaining desirable clients.
4. Upgrading or replacing undesirable clients.
5. Capitalizing on the potential within your existing practice.
6. Managing your image with targeted clients and prospective clients.
7. Attracting desirable prospective clients.

8. Becoming a dominant force in your targeted industry-market niche.

9. Transforming your current practice into a desired future practice.

CLIENT-CENTERED MARKETING VERSUS OTHER APPROACHES

To understand why we stress using the CCMS, let's contrast it with two other marketing approaches that service providers routinely offer—the traditional and the hard sell.

The *traditional* approach is reactive. The underlying assumption is that growth is the result of providing good technical services to meet the existing demands of the marketplace. Little strategy or coordination of effort is invested in stimulating growth. Client problems are addressed only when the client brings them to the attention of the consultant! Frequently, it is too late to correct these problems. In today's competitive market, disappointed clients tend to replace service providers who disappoint them, or are not seen as being proactively responsive to their needs. Firms following a reactive approach seldom have plans or programs for attracting eligible potential clients. Referrals are expected solely as the result of doing good technical work. Increasingly, in today's competitive market, these assumptions can become very costly.

Those following the *hard-sell* marketing approach focus on getting known in their practice area. Instead of focusing on solutions to the needs of their high-potential clients and prospective clients, they put emphasis on communicating about the firm, its services, and its people. They assume that growth is largely the result of being known in the community or region as providers of good service at reasonable prices. "Buying new business" is part of this approach. The assumption is that once the client is hooked on the low bid, profit will be made on subsequent services.

The hard-sell approach may be successful in the short run, since it will attract the price-sensitive prospect who is looking for a good deal. This approach has several major drawbacks, however. Price-sensitive clients tend to migrate to the current lowest bidders; also, quality clients eventually tire of an approach that is not sensitive to their needs. In addition, the majority of professional service providers are uncomfortable with a "pitch-the-product-at-a-price" approach.

An audit services firm learned this lesson the hard way. A hard-sell partner in charge instituted such a program. Monthly goals for the number of contacts with referral sources were set for each of the partners and managers. Training or coaching for success in this activity was not provided. After several months, the program withered and died. Resentment on the part of the participants still lingers. The partner in charge is still wondering why his troops didn't get with the program.

MARKETING IN PERSPECTIVE

Our experience in working with or speaking before professional service firms in all 50 states and 7 countries indicates that without major program status, even the CCMS will not be effective and long lasting. A successful professional practice can be compared with a balanced four-legged stool:

- *Leg 1.* Technical quality: consistent, superb service delivered on a timely, cost-effective basis
- *Leg 2.* Personnel management: selecting, training, developing, motivating, and retaining the best staff available
- *Leg 3.* Financial administration: billing and collecting fees on a timely basis, while controlling marketing and service delivery costs
- *Leg 4.* Client-centered marketing: sensing, selling, serving, and satisfying the needs and expectations of high-potential clients and others in mutually profitable ways

Client-centered marketing is essentially relationship development. The relationship is based on a complex array of technical and personal factors that create a high degree of interdependence. The client is the target and the beneficiary of all the professional's experience, planning, and actions.

Professionals who are effective in marketing have learned along the way to develop relationships with those clients and others who are ready, willing, and able to assist them in their various marketing and selling activities. They search constantly for the relatively few contacts who facilitate the leveraging of their time, talents, and technology.

INSIGHTS AND LESSONS TO BE LEARNED

Effective client-centered marketing requires acknowledgment that:

1. Value is always defined by the recipient, not the provider. Value is in the eyes and emotions of receivers, and is always rooted in their personal and organizational needs systems. Value is a function of needs being identified and satisfied in ways that meet expectations.

2. Clients don't purchase your services and products. They buy your promise to produce a more favorable future for them on schedule, within budget, and in a manner that meets their expectations.

   One exceptionally able professional made it a practice to surface the client's expectations regarding the final result or "deliverable" by asking the question: "How will you and I know when I'm doing the job you expect me to do?" The answer to this question invariably reveals both reasonable and unrealistic expectations that need to be negotiated and agreed on.

3. Services are really bought or rejected in the "gut" by clients. They then justify the buy/no-buy decision to themselves and others by the use of "hard copy," such as competitive proposals and testimonials from others who make the desired point.

We turn next to a detailed discussion of the Client-Centered Marketing System model.

2

The Client-Centered
Marketing System Model

This chapter expands the discussion of the Client-Centered Marketing approach by explaining the content, flow, and use of the four-element CCMS Model. We also illustrate the principle of leveraging your time, introduce the notion of marketing comfort zones, and describe the use of the AIDA model to complete the chapter.

The CCMS Model, shown in Figure 2.1, comprises four basic elements. Carefully examine each of these elements to develop an understanding of the model, and to devise a workable plan for sensing the needs of your targeted clients.

The four elements include:

1. Existing practice factors

2. Existing referral sources

3. Targets of opportunity, attention, and influence

4. New business development factors

I'll discuss the contents of each of these four elements, and show their flow and relationship to each other so you can see how each element can be used in developing and installing your new client program.

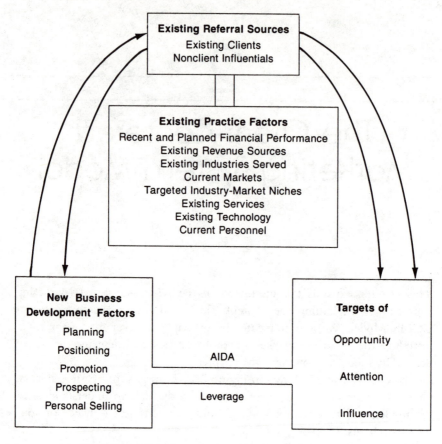

FIGURE 2.1.   The Client-Centered Marketing System Model

EXISTING PRACTICE FACTORS ─────────────

This element comprises eight variables. Each variable impacts on your current ability to provide client service, while simultaneously imposing limits on your potential for growth.

These eight variables are (1) recent and planned financial performance, (2) existing revenue sources, (3) existing industries served, (4) current markets, (5) targeted industry-market niches, (6) existing services, (7) existing technology, and (8) current personnel.

A working definition for each of these eight variables is provided in the following sections.

Recent and Planned Financial Performance ──────────────

Your key measurements include fee volume, net profit, billable hours, managed hours, your revenue targets for the next planning period, and the known or suspected revenue surplus or gap for the next planning period.

Existing Revenue Sources ──────────────────────

There are three revenue sources you need to monitor:

1. *Existing clients.* Typically, your most important source of revenue. They can be broadly classified as "desirable," "unclassified or unknown at this time," and "undesirable." Figure 2.2 shows additional levels of detail in each client class.

Desirable Clients

1. "A" Clients: Clients that make referrals to others in your behalf, have strong potential for fee growth, are receptive to additional constructive service ideas, and frequently provide you with excellent opportunities to develop your skills and information base. Also include here "B" clients you hope will develop into "A" clients. They willingly pay their fees, are generally receptive to additional service discussions, and may be educated into making referrals at a later date.
2. "B" Clients: These clients are your bread and butter clients. They pay their bills, don't give you too much grief, but do not represent potential for good fee growth.

Unknown at This Time—"U" Clients

1. Clients whom you are now serving for the first time
2. Newly acquired clients whom you are yet to begin serving
3. Other existing clients not yet classified

Undesirable Clients

1. "C" Clients: These clients seek discounts and additional free services, and are frequently slow in paying invoices.
2. "D" Clients: These are the clients you wish you had never accepted in the first place. They often operate on the margin of ethical performance and are not adverse to pressuring you to compromise your personal and professional standards.
3. "X" Clients: "A" clients with warning signals.

FIGURE 2.2. Criteria for Classifying Your Existing Clients

2. *Existing prospective clients.* Listings in your "pending new client" file. A prospective client is a nonclient with whom you have had a business discussion and proposed a service solution. You are now waiting to proceed with the engagement.

3. *Existing suspects.* Should be contacted to determine their readiness to become a prospective client. A suspect is a nonclient in your practice area whom you have not yet contacted. You suspect that they have potential, but you will not know this until you contact them.

Existing Industries Served

An industry is a group of similar organizations and individuals you serve that address the same general needs of their customers through their goods and services. These organizations have the same four-digit Standard Industry Code SIC number. The SIC is a classification system used to identify businesses within a common-industry grouping. An industry is composed of existing clients, prospective clients, "suspects," and current and targeted referral sources.

Current Markets

We define *market* as the geographical areas (zip codes) in which you choose to promote and provide a particular service solution system.

Targeted Industry-Market Niches

A *niche* is a selected industry-market area on which you consciously choose to focus your attention and invest your expensive time, talent, and technology. Your purpose is to penetrate, deepen, and eventually dominate the niche. This requires focus, determination, and specialization. The remainder of this book will provide you with the information and tools to do this.

Existing Services

Services refers to the activities and products you deliver for which you receive revenue.

Existing Technology

Technology refers to the databases, service delivery system, service promotion system, software applications, support systems, and so on, used both in marketing and providing client service. Properly developed and used, technology support systems reduce costs, increase productivity, and provide a competitive edge while strengthening your marketing comfort zone.

Current Personnel ————————————————————————

You can classify your staff professionals in terms of "Finder," "Minder," or "Grinder" status. Finders are the professionals who have a talent for uncovering needs and who willingly contact clients and prospective clients to discuss services that meet a need or solve a problem. Minders are good at maintaining and enhancing relationships with existing clients. They also contribute to the development of value-perceived solutions by ensuring that the technical aspects of the solution are in place. Grinders refer to the remainder of professionals who are more comfortable in the engagement-completion aspects of their profession. One of the beauties of the client-centered marketing approach is that the grinder is able to participate in marketing on his terms. Using the client-centered approach, various marketing tools can be used by these talented technical-oriented professionals. In the traditional or hard-sell marketing approaches, "grinder" is a negative term.

EXISTING REFERRAL SOURCES ————————————————

This element contains two classes of referral sources, existing clients and nonclient influentials.

1. *Existing Clients.* Those "A" clients who are especially satisfied with the way you serve them and who provide you with leads, give you written testimonials, and involve you in their professional and trade association activities.

2. *Nonclient Influentials.* Attorneys, bankers, editors, executive directors of industry associations, community leaders, and others who serve your clients in noncompetitive ways, or influence their decisions regarding your services. These professionals are familiar with your firm and will frequently provide you with leads and introductions to prospective clients and other nonclient influentials.

Of the four major elements in the client-centered marketing system, existing practice factors and existing referral sources form the bedrock of your current practice. It is here that you live and work and generate your current and short-term billable hours.

Both elements reside within your current marketing comfort zone—that area in which you can *comfortably* and *confidently* initiate new business discussions with existing clients who need and want your services.

TARGETS OF OPPORTUNITY, ATTENTION, AND INFLUENCE

The third element includes the lesser, concentrated number of clients, prospective clients, suspects, and additional referral sources in which you wish to leverage your time. Note that not every client will receive a target classification. The goal of targeting is to enable you to leverage your time by identifying individuals and organizations that warrant your special attention. There are three separate categories:

1. *Targets of Opportunity.* Existing desirable clients with unmet needs, prospects, and suspects in your new business pipeline, all active referral sources, and targeted industry-market niches. Figure 2.3 summarizes the characteristics of targets of opportunity and targets of attention.
2. *Targets of Attention.* All existing practice factors that warrant your focused attention in the next marketing period. The factors included would be inactive referral sources, currently unclassified clients, and suspects and leads for follow-up.
3. *Targets of Influence.* Additional nonclient influentials that you wish to develop into referral sources. These targets of influence could include additional attorneys, executive directors of trade associations, and so on.

NEW BUSINESS DEVELOPMENT FACTORS

The fourth element, new business development factors, includes five interrelated activities:

Targets of Opportunity

1. Existing "A" and "B" clients with needs for additional services who possess a budget for your services and are willing to discuss their needs with you
2. Existing prospective clients

Targets of Attention

1. "B" clients with potential for upgrading to "A"
2. "Unknown" clients who need to be classified
3. Undesirable "C" clients who can be upgraded by reducing discounts or speeding up payment of invoices
4. Other potential clients in your geographic area needing to be contacted
5. "A" clients with warning signals:
   - Known/suspected to be dissatisfied with your services
   - Targeted by other firms
   - Key clients no longer making referrals
   - No longer receptive to discussing additional services
   - Engagements are no longer profitable
   - May be merger candidates
   - Quality of relationship is 1 or 2
6. Undesirable clients with warning signals:
   - "C" clients for whom discounts or receivables are growing
   - "D" clients who are becoming more troublesome or risky to retain

---

FIGURE 2.3. Current Target Categories

1. *Planning.* The strategic plans that guide the future development of the firm, annual marketing plans that allocate the resources directed to targets, and niche planning that converts the broad goals into specific objectives and action steps.

2. *Positioning.* The determination of how you want your services to be perceived by your targets. It is also a process by which you identify the distinctive roles you choose to play with all who are influential in your new business development activities.

3. *Promotion.* The activities involved in managing your business image and reputation to maximize the impact on your targets of opportunity, attention, and influence.

4. *Prospecting.* The process of identifying high-potential "suspect" organizations in your markets and niches, and then contacting

decision makers within those organizations to discuss solutions for a need they have. The goal of client-centered professional service marketers is to "clone" their most profitable desirable clients. Effective prospecting enables you to find and target nonclients who may ultimately become your most desirable new clients. Once a decision maker in a targeted suspect firm agrees to meet with you, she becomes a prospect.

5. *Personal Selling.* The face-to-face new business discussions you plan for and conduct with the targets of opportunity in your market.

LEVERAGING

Leveraging refers to the process of identifying and capitalizing on the *fewest* targeted actions, resources, and relationships that produce the *greatest* results. Leverage is a "multiplier" activity that produces a cascade effect. For example, you are using leverage when you obtain, from a friendly bank lending officer, the names of attorneys who serve your types of client.

Often, the service practitioner who markets his services is also the one who provides the service, hence the inevitable double bind of selling an engagement and then delivering the service. Mastering the art of leveraging enables solo practitioners to stretch their available time and resources to an optimum degree.

YOUR MARKETING COMFORT ZONE

I mentioned this term earlier and now will explain it in detail. When undertaking new business development activities, such as identifying targets of opportunity, most people find that they are effective when calling on clones of their existing key and A clients. As used here, working from your comfort zone means calling on prospects and suspects with whom you have some type of affinity. You feel comfortable calling on them, and you can speak their business language. Any anxieties you may feel remain at an acceptable level.

The unspoken goal of professional service marketers is to clone their best existing client! This is achieved by getting more suspects and prospective clients who have the same characteristics of that client. Working from the comfort zone enables you to undertake effective self-initiated marketing behavior.

Many professionals are very comfortable talking with referrals, but not in making self-initiated phone calls. Your comfort zone will not be uniform throughout the marketing and selling process. You need to become familiar with the boundaries of your comfort zone and remain within close proximity of its boundaries, while systematically working to expand it.

Frequently, when speaking before groups, I share with them that I am a scuba diver. My current comfort zone in diving is about 50 to 60 feet. I could dive to 90 and 100 feet, and on occasion have done it, but I have not been comfortable. I get no joy out of it, and I can't wait to get out of the water. So it is with your comfort zone when seeking new clients. If you move outside it too quickly, the discomfort may be so great that you withdraw entirely. To increase the size of your comfort zone effectively, you must do so slowly.

THE AIDA MINIMODEL

The AIDA model (attention–interest–desire–action) has traditionally been used in product and consumer marketing to describe the phases involved in the capture of a new customer. However, the model lends itself well to adaptation for services marketing. The model has four phases that you must plan for and execute if your new business development activities are to be effective:

1. The first "A" represents the goal of obtaining the attention and favorable awareness of targets of opportunity and targets of influence.
2. The "I" represents information that you send to targets. This information is designed to interest targets so that they agree to meet with you after you have successfully completed a telephone contact.
3. The "D" represents directed new business discussions with members of the decision-making unit in the targeted organization. These new business discussions are designed to define the gap between what *is* and what is *desired* or *required* by the prospective client. Showing

how your proposed solution will decrease the deviation between what currently is and what is desired by the prospective client is at the heart of the new business discussion.

4. The second "A" represents the agreed-on actions you and the prospective client will take to meet a mutually defined need. Actions may include the preparation and presentation of a proposal or the execution of a survey whereby the client allows you to interview additional key people.

An examination of the individual components of new business development shows that promotion involves obtaining attention and generating interest (AI). Prospecting involves generating interest and obtaining appointments for new business discussions (ID). Personal selling contacts involve managing the discussions with contacts and moving toward agreed-on actions (DA).

Next, we will focus on selecting your targeted industry-market niche.

3

Getting New Clients by Targeting an Industry-Market Niche

The essence of client-centered marketing is satisfying the selected needs of high-potential targets of opportunity. It is also developing relationships with influentials who can serve as resources for achieving your marketing and new-business development goals. In this chapter, we will expand on the definition of client-centered marketing. Specifically, our definition will be in terms of a targeted-niche approach for obtaining profitable new clients.

Client-centered niche-marketing is the process of leveraging the time, technology, and resources available to you to sense, sell, serve, and satisfy the selected needs of high-potential clients and prospective clients. It is important that your service offering be perceived as valuable by *all* involved. Perceptions about your service occur at all times during the client-centered marketing process, including the promotion, delivery, and application of the service.

To penetrate a targeted niche successfully, you must offer "silver bullets." These are solutions to the "hot buttons," issues, or concerns that suspects have and for which they will readily meet with you to discuss how you can be of assistance.

A partner in a Big Six accounting firm developed just such a silver bullet. He capitalized on the uncertainty surrounding the Gramm-Rudman-

Hollings Act by providing workshops and individual counsel to anxious service providers to the U.S. government. *Time* magazine reported that this one partner was responsible for generating in excess of $800,000 in less than a year.

Client-centered niche-marketing is a results-driven, continuing process designed to focus and leverage the relationships and resources available to you. You then use these relationships and invest the resources in developing value-perceived solutions to the important needs of your existing high-potential clients and prospective clients in your targeted niche. The key question that effective client-centered marketers ask themselves is, "How many different ways can I assist my clients and targets to better their business?" (Or, "To better their personal situation?")

If you are an attorney preparing a will for a client, from your perspective you could say you are simply preparing a will. However, from the more important perspective of the receiver, you could be seen as providing the following:

- Peace of mind
- Orderly transfer of assets
- Education funding for offspring
- Financial security for the widow

The effective client-centered marketer provides value-perceived solutions in ways that generate mutual benefits. Value-perceived means that the client perceives great value for his or her dollar. I discovered a way to avoid having a down market with my accounting clients during their busy season. I carefully developed, marketed, and conducted a 3-hour course, "Developing New Business during the 'Too-Busy-to-Market Season.'" Recognizing the firm's needs to keep staff accountants on engagements during the clients' normal business hours, I conducted the course from 9:00 A.M. until noon or 2:00 P.M. until 5:00 P.M. on Saturdays.

The service practitioner who generates large fees doesn't do so because she is providing a specific service per se. She generates large fees because of her ability to recognize a client's needs and to provide solutions in such a manner that the clients recognize the value of such solutions. To put it another way, you get no credit for developing an ingenious way of solving a problem unless you are able to convince a client that your ingenuity in meeting his or her needs will have an economic and/or personal payoff.

MARKETING IS EXPENSIVE AND EGO BRUISING ———

Let's face it—marketing is an expensive function that must be carefully planned and managed. Properly executed, a client-centered marketing program requires a substantial investment of time and out-of-pocket costs to properly develop and promote value-perceived services. Yet, as you proceed through this book, you will see that client-centered niche-marketing, on balance, is far less costly than traditional marketing approaches.

Client-centered marketing begins when you sense, sell, serve, and satisfy important needs of your targeted, high-potential prospects in ways in which they perceive the value; it ends when you acquire new, prompt-paying clients.

This niche-marketing process enables you to work from your comfort zone in virtually all the marketing and selling activities involved in the client-centered marketing approach. Your targets in the niche, the suspects and prospective clients, should be clones of your best existing clients. It is a continuing process, because the approach is structured to enable you to engage in some targeted marketing and selling every day as you serve your existing high-potential clients; develop and strengthen relationships with key influentials in the infrastructure of the targeted niche; and promote, prospect, and sell to your targeted prospective clients in the niche.

Client-centered marketing is a self-initiated, proactive approach. I describe it as the marketing approach that pays homage to what I call the Platinum Rule™: Serve others as they need and want you to. You must strive continuously to deliver value-perceived solutions by providing cutting-edge services, maintaining an image and reputation that you are different from and/or better than the competition, and developing the resources to stay in the forefront of your profession.

NOT WITH ALL CLIENTS ———

A client-centered marketing approach should be used only with approximately 20 percent of your existing clients and 60 to 80 percent of targeted prospective clients. The reason is that only with your Key and A clients and prospective clients will there be a vibrant, dynamic atmosphere in which *continuing* and *additional* opportunities exist for you. The client-centered marketer continuously seeks ways to:

- Assist targets better in *doing what they are in business to do*
- Serve as a conduit to the resources available to deliver value-added solutions
- Ensure quality control and delivery of agreed-upon services
- Deliver value-perceived services

TARGETING A NICHE

The client-centered marketing approach works best when used to focus on targets of opportunity and targets of influence that are members of a specific industry (SIC) and are in the geographical location (zip codes) comprising the practitioner's primary market area. Thus, the primary targets of opportunity become those high-potential suspect and prospective firms and individuals in the industry-market niche.

Secondary targets of opportunity represent those B-level potential clients (suspects) that are part of the industry and are located in the practice area. Contacting B-level suspects requires a lot of time because there are more of them. The best way to handle secondary targets is to use your insider's reputation and promotions (Chapter 11) to create sufficient interest for them to contact you.

Targets of influence are the additional nonclient influentials that are located or reside in the niche, and others throughout the region or nation who can interact with and influence members of the niche infrastructure with whom you have yet to develop a relationship. For example, I leverage my time by developing relationships with influential members of each niche's infrastructure. My targets of influence in the accounting profession are the editors of publications read by my best clients and targets of opportunity.

There are numerous steps involved in generating new clients by targeting a niche. I will summarize these steps, each of which will be explained in detail in Chapters 4 through 23.

ESTABLISHING OBJECTIVES FOR YOUR
NEW-CLIENT PROGRAM

Your immediate goal as a professional is to ensure that your practice survives. Ultimately, your goal shifts to changing the nature and scope of the practice (1) to obtain larger, more profitable clients, (2) to enhance the image and reputation of the firm, and (3) to develop an industry specialization. A number of decisions need to be made. (See Chapter 4.)

Selecting Your Target Niche

Selecting your target niche is the first and most important step in the process of client-centered marketing. Most professionals find they must gather a substantial body of information to decide which niche to penetrate. Fortunately, much of this information already exists within the practice. During this stage, selection criteria must also be established. (See Chapter 5.)

Developing an Insider's Understanding of the Niche

Several key steps are involved in acquiring an insider's understanding. You must first identify industry success factors and the needs and wants of members of the industry. In addition, you must identify targets of opportunity, targets of influence, and members of the industry infrastructure with whom you have a relationship. Finally, you must develop a data base that supports your efforts in marketing to the niche. (See Chapters 7 and 8.)

Tailoring Your Services-Delivery Program

Although a client-centered marketing approach places the client's wants and needs at the forefront of your program, there are still many aspects of service delivery that you will want to standardize. In terms of clients, it is difficult to be everything to everyone. You must also consider in what form your deliverables will be packaged. (See Chapters 9 and 10.)

Developing an Insider's Reputation in the Niche

How does a person create a favorable awareness within the niche and develop relationships with its key members? Some of the strategies involved include writing and speaking to your targets and leveraging memberships within key organizations. (See Chapter 11.)

THE FIRST APPOINTMENT

All of the foregoing lay the groundwork for face-to-face encounters with prospective clients. The next set of activities focuses specifically on getting and preparing for appointments with prospective clients.

Selecting the Needs and Prospect Organizations

This involves selecting a critical need known as a *hot button,* and finding supporting evidence to help you hook prospective clients. The needs you uncover should be ones you can and want to solve, at a good profit margin. Prospective clients with needs in this category become your current targets of opportunity. (See Chapter 12.)

Developing and Managing Your Mailing Program

Your major tasks here will be to develop and write initial contact letters, to prepare a telephone-interview guide, and to test and fine-tune the program. (See Chapter 13.)

Making the Appointment-Getting Telephone Call

What are the secrets of getting through to the appropriate contact person for prospective clients? Key activities in this area include handling resistance, stalls, and put-offs; turning the conversation your way; and securing an appointment. (See Chapter 14.)

Preparing for the New Business Discussion

The importance of preparation cannot be overstated. Your tasks will include preparing a discussion guide and personal-contact kit. Your responsibilities will include arriving on time, alert and relaxed. (See Chapter 15.)

The next steps in getting new clients through a client-centered marketing approach involve the conduct of successful new-business discussions, which includes opening the discussion in a way that builds trust and rapport, defining existing-needs situations, defining the desired or required future situation of the prospective client, presenting your proposed solution, handling concerns and information needs, closing the discussion, and moving to action.

Opening the Discussion

Though you may not have considered it before, it is your responsibility to manage the introductions at the commencement of a new-business discussion. Your goals will be to reduce tension, build trust and rapport, and establish an atmosphere of openness and cooperation. At the same time you will be sizing up the contact and making mental notes for use later in the discussion. You then move on to the body of discussion. (See Chapter 16.)

Defining the Existing-Need Situation

This is a pivotal area and involves numerous steps, including (1) verifying and determining the nature of the need, (2) defining the scope of the need, (3) determining its urgency, and (4) identifying the buying motive(s) of the contact person(s). It also involves determining costs to date, verifying your mutual understanding, and moving to the next phase. (See Chapter 17.)

Defining the Desired or Required Future Situation

What will the prospective client get when you have completed what you have promised? Your task is to define the scope of the future situation and establish a realistic timetable. Other tasks include pinpointing your expectations and the prospect's, determining solution criteria, and specifying the products or services that will be produced or offered.

The second half of conducting winning new-business presentations involves presenting your proposed solution, handling concerns and information needs, closing the discussion, and taking action. (See Chapter 18.)

Presenting Your Proposed Solution

How do you effectively present the proposed strategy and goals that meet a client's needs? When is it appropriate to present a range of solutions? Your tasks include determining the best solution and making an effective verbal proposal that stresses the benefits of your method of handling the prospect's need. (See Chapter 19.)

Handling Concerns and Information Needs

Client objections are a predictable and normal occurrence during new-business discussions. The effective client-centered marketer must understand the anatomy of an objection and, subsequently, welcome objections and use them to her advantage. (See Chapter 20.)

Closing the Discussion and Moving to Action

Your task is to recognize when to close the discussion and debrief the contact person using client-centered scenarios. You must then deliver the closing statement and complete the administrative details. (See Chapter 21.)

Having laid the groundwork for the client-centered marketing approach, prepared for appointments with prospective clients, and conducted winning new-business discussions, you are almost home free. Next, we will discuss the importance of follow-through, which includes preparing a winning proposal (if necessary in your practice) and reinforcing your client's buy decision.

Preparing a Winning Proposal

What does a winning proposal look like? What does it contain, and what does it offer? Your task is to prepare a proposal that meets the needs and expectations of the client while avoiding some of the common pitfalls of proposal writing. (See Chapter 22.)

Reinforcing Your Client's Choice

The effective client-centered marketer understands the importance of handling postpurchase concerns of the client. Touchdowns are not scored until the ball is over the goal line and the official's hands are raised. (See Chapter 23.)

4

Establishing Objectives for Your New Client Program

Management's task is to translate the firm's purpose into a set of clearly defined objectives and related goals that will goad and guide the realization of this purpose. The objectives indicate specific spheres of aim, activity, and accomplishment. Objectives are action commitments you make. They give direction and provide for measurement.

Establishing objectives for your new client program involves determining what you are trying to accomplish in acquiring new clients. Objectives, when fortified by action, lead to a measurable result. Another term for measurable results is "goal." The nature, scope, and potential of your new client program, indeed, its very thrust, will depend on the objectives you establish. In addition, your long-term success will depend on your ability to use leveraging to accomplish the chosen objectives.

REQUIRED AND DESIRED OBJECTIVES

Required objectives must be accomplished for the firm to survive. In other words, you have no choice in the matter. Objectives in this category tend to be immediate, urgent, and serious in nature. Examples of required objectives include:

1. Replace known/suspected revenue shortfall during the next period.
2. Replace high-potential existing clients known/suspected to be lost during the next period.
3. Lower fees for services without sacrificing profit margins.

Desired objectives differ from required objectives in that they may be something that you strongly want, but they are not necessary for survival. Examples of desired objectives include better utilization of existing resources, the ability to attract larger and higher paying clients, or the replacement of marginal clients. You should act on only those desired objectives that are very important. Put other desired objectives on hold and review them periodically. (See Figure 4.1.)

Due to changes in the prevailing environment, in time, these objectives may need to be reclassified as either: required, desired and very important, desired but not important, or not worth maintaining. I made a commitment to promote and teach the client-centered niche-marketing method to the providers of professional services in the English speaking countries of

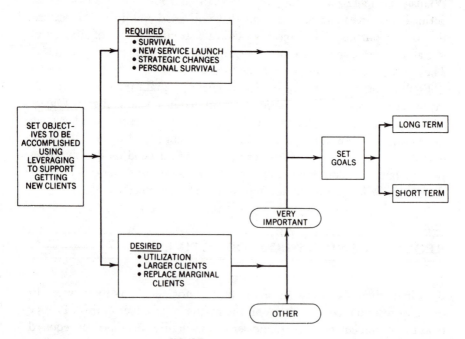

FIGURE 4.1. Setting Goals

the world. A highly desired goal is to be invited to present this method at international and national conferences attended by targets. The appearance at such forums lets me leverage my time and resources.

ESTABLISHING YOUR OBJECTIVES

In developing a prosperous practice, you could establish many classes of objectives. The seven most frequently used classes are:

1. *Strategic Objectives.* Always focused on tomorrow's practice. Such objectives involve a change in the nature and scope of the practice.
2. *Operating Objectives.* Aimed at improving productivity.
3. *Financial Objectives.* Activities that improve profitability or loss of revenue.
4. *Client-Related Objectives.* Factors affecting client service, size, and profitability.
5. *Industry Niche Objectives.* Goals for achieving penetration, specialization, and relationships within the infrastructure.
6. *Personal Objectives.* May be as basic as surviving as a professional in public practice, or generating more work.
7. *Staff Objectives.* Focused on actions dealing with the people you have available for new client activities.

Figure 4.2 shows a number of objectives you may want to accomplish as part of your new client program. Scan through the list and check off no more than five or six objectives at first. You may also want to add objectives in each category. More is not necessarily better when you are establishing objectives. It is better to focus on a few and achieve them than to scatter your energy and resources and do a poor job on a number of them.

Now that you have selected your possible objectives, compare them to see if any oppose each other. Be realistic in selecting objectives because you are going to have to accomplish them on top of an already lengthening "to-do" list.

Any of the preceding objectives, as well as those you add, can be viewed as required or desired based on your particular situation.

Strategic Objectives	Required	Desired
To change the nature and scope of the practice.	_____	_____
To develop and provide more high fee services.	_____	_____
To develop a different industry mix.	_____	_____
To create conditions for service-industry specialization.	_____	_____
To enhance the image and reputation of the firm.	_____	_____
To _____	_____	_____

Operating Objectives		
To obtain better utilization of existing capabilities.	_____	_____
To reduce peaks and valleys by developing an industry-market niche with a business cycle different from others.	_____	_____
To maintain or increase profitability by providing more high-priced services to better clients.	_____	_____
To expand present client base.	_____	_____
To _____	_____	_____

Financial Objectives		
To improve net profit.	_____	_____
To ensure the survival or profitability of the office/firm.	_____	_____
To offset the loss of good clients from attrition.	_____	_____
To replace revenue lost by pruning poor clients.	_____	_____
To provide more recurring sources of new business.	_____	_____
To replace revenue lost from recently terminated/lost clients.	_____	_____
To _____	_____	_____

FIGURE 4.2. Getting New Clients' Objectives

Client-Related Objectives

To acquire larger fee clients.   _____   _____

To expand the base of high-potential
clients.   _____   _____

To transform the client base from a
volume to a cluster practice.   _____   _____

To establish a new industry-market niche
to offset a slump with clients in an existing
niche.   _____   _____

To obtain larger, more profitable clients.   _____   _____

To _____   _____   _____

Industry-Related Objectives

To develop specialization opportunities.   _____   _____

To transform the market mix from
diversified to concentrated.   _____   _____

To _____   _____   _____

Personal Objectives

To survive as a professional in a public
practice.   _____   _____

To determine if I have the temperament
to say in public practice.   _____   _____

To obtain favorable visibility among
others in my firm as a condition for
advancement and election to the
partnership.   _____   _____

To begin building my confidence and
capability so that I can be effective when
I need to be.   _____   _____

To _____   _____   _____

Staff Objectives

To provide more interesting work for
partners and high-potential nonpartners.   _____   _____

To develop more specialists.   _____   _____

FIGURE 4.2. Continued

Establishing objectives, on first reading, appears deceptively simple. Yet, this task cannot be taken lightly. The most successful firms choose, at best, no more than a handful of objectives. Because these objectives literally define and shape the future practice, they should receive careful consideration.

SETTING GOALS TO ACHIEVE YOUR OBJECTIVES

Setting goals, synonymous with achieving measurable results, is essential in accomplishing desired objectives. The goals that you choose must be challenging yet reachable. It is no use to you or your firm to set goals that only lead to frustration, misallocation of resources, or diminished spirits. Peter Drucker says you must ask yourself, "What are my goals? What should they be?" As with establishing objectives, goal setting appears simple. Let's lay the groundwork for setting realistic, achievable goals.

1. You must set goals that enable you to work from your comfort zone. Remember the illustration about scuba diving in an earlier chapter? You don't want to dive into waters that are too deep because you may do damage to your psyche; then you'll become ineffectual even within your comfort zone.

2. Set some goals that let you win "early and often." A win is getting an appointment with a decision maker or influential. Getting early wins bolsters your confidence while you are still learning and gathering information about the niche. It also serves as a springboard for your attempts to achieve more challenging goals.

3. Set goals that are achievable on a "bits and pieces" basis unless you have large blocks of time available. Look for ways to divide up goals into divisible steps so that you can make continuing progress.

5

How to Select
Your Target Niche

Unless your marketing comfort zone is large enough to handle the inevitable rejections that accompany wide-angle, horizontal prospecting, selecting an industry-market niche for analysis and action is a much easier way to conduct your prospecting activities. The key to fairly predictable, significant growth is to be "somebody special to a special group of bodies." You must be perceived as being different and better.

This chapter will help you select an industry-market niche for analysis and action, and it will introduce key ideas for organizing to serve the niche.

SOME KEY DEFINITIONS

So that we are talking the same game, here's a review of some working definitions.

Industry. All clients, prospects, and suspects, with the same 4-digit SIC-code number, offering the same basic type of product or service, and therefore competing with one another. Some of the industries you presently serve, or will be examining, are more appropriately termed professions. For example, I work with many firms in the accounting profession, although the phrase "accounting industry" probably conveys a similar meaning.

Market. The postal zip codes that make up your practice area(s).

Niche. The clients, prospective clients, and nonclient influentials in the SIC-zip code area.

Prospects. Former suspects who have met with you to discuss a need situation and have not yet purchased your proposed solution program.

Suspects. Nonclients who meet your minimum selection criteria, but who haven't been contacted by you or agreed to meet with you yet.

Nonclient influentials. Individuals who have influence within the niche, such as editors and association executives. They may also be government officials with national status. Nonclient influentials may or may not be located within the niche; the determining factor is their degree of influence.

Infrastructure. The players in the niche: the clients, prospective clients, suspects, nonclient influentials, and organizations serving or affecting the niche.

A STRATEGIC DECISION

Choosing an industry-market niche is one of the most important, strategic decisions you can make regarding the long-term viability of your practice. You can't be all things to all people, and you certainly can't be all things to all clients. You must direct your attention to industry-market niche(s) where you can most readily serve and most prosperously penetrate. As I mentioned earlier, it is likely that your task of getting new clients must be done with limited resources. Even if you had unlimited resources, you would want to allocate them wisely and appropriately.

Selecting a niche is called an "Intensive Growth Strategy" by marketing theorists. The primary strategy is that of *market penetration*. The goal is to increase the market share of current services in the niche by attracting more high-potential new clients.

Niches change concurrently with, and in reaction to, changes in technology, competition, regulations, social trends, and so on. Change provides you with opportunities to develop and take advantage of leverage. You can best capitalize on leveraging opportunities by earning an insider's understanding of and reputation with members in a high-potential niche.

Previously, you may not have given much thought to the types of clients you should be acquiring. Wrong choices, however, can be costly. If you settle for C and D clients, you will not enjoy your work because you'll have fee problems and collection problems. While muddling through the problems of marginal clients, you will also miss the leveraging opportunities created by your interaction with key and A clients.

THE SELECTION PROCESS

Choosing an industry-market niche on which to concentrate is an evolutionary process. It starts with examining appropriate industries (by 4-digit SIC code number) and ends with getting new clients from commitments supported by realistic time and dollar budgets and time-phased work schedules.

As a rule of thumb, you want to select a relatively stable niche(s) not dominated by one or more of your competitors. It is helpful if your technological capability is perceived as state-of-the-art at least (leading edge would be better). If you already have some clients in the niche you ultimately select, or if you have relationships with niche influentials, these are certainly plus factors. Likewise, if you or your staff is experienced and enjoys working in the niche, this is a big plus.

As we discuss the steps involved in selecting your niche, keep an eye out for leveraging opportunities. Can your services be specialized and delivered profitably? Can you reach prospective clients relatively easily? Is there an established infrastructure that you can identify and penetrate without too much time and cost? If so, you may be tapping into a gold mine. Figure 5.1 shows the steps involved in selecting a niche.

Identify the Industries You Presently Serve

This step is easy to complete if you have classified your clients by the industry in which they serve and compete. If you have not done this analysis, you will need to organize your information using the following format:

Figure 5.2 is a convenient form for your use in making niching decisions. To use this form to its fullest:

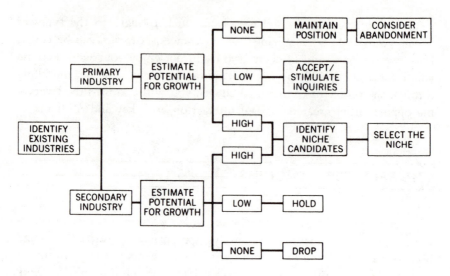

FIGURE 5.1.   Selecting Your Industry-Market Niche

1. Enter the four-digit SIC number of your current niches from the largest percentage of total revenue to the smallest. Place the SICs with largest percentages in the primary niche section.

2. Define the niche (paving and roofing materials, for example) on the line calling for a description of the niche.

3. Estimate the potential for growth for your firm both in the short term, within 12 months, and long term, beyond 12 months, using an "H" for high potential, an "M" for moderate potential, and "L" for low potential.

Determine Your Primary and Secondary Industries

A primary industry is one that constitutes a relatively large percentage of your total revenue. A secondary industry is one that currently generates a relatively small percentage of total revenue.

Estimate the Potential for Growth in Each Niche

In assessing industries, ask yourself, "Are my primary industries the ones I should or want to be in?" If not, examine secondary industries that warrant further attention and that may be shifted to the primary status. The

Current Primary

	Sic Number	% Total Revenue	Description of Niche	Potential for Growth*	
				Short-Term**	Long-Term***
1.	( )	_____	_____	_____	_____
2.	( )	_____	_____	_____	_____
3.	( )	_____	_____	_____	_____
4.	( )	_____	_____	_____	_____
5.	( )	_____	_____	_____	_____
6.	( )	_____	_____	_____	_____
7.	( )	_____	_____	_____	_____
8.	( )	_____	_____	_____	_____

Current Secondary

	Sic Number	% Total Revenue	Description of Niche	Potential for Growth*	
				Short-Term**	Long-Term***
1.	( )	_____	_____	_____	_____
2.	( )	_____	_____	_____	_____
3.	( )	_____	_____	_____	_____
4.	( )	_____	_____	_____	_____
5.	( )	_____	_____	_____	_____
6.	( )	_____	_____	_____	_____
7.	( )	_____	_____	_____	_____
8.	( )	_____	_____	_____	_____

* List an H (high), M (moderate), or L (low).
** Short-term = now up to 12 months.
*** Long-term = beyond 12 months.

FIGURE 5.2. Current Primary and Secondary Industries

industry or industries that you primarily serve should be ones that constitute a relatively large percentage of your total revenue. Your secondary industry is represented by clients who represent a smaller, though significant percentage of your total revenue and who you can readily serve.

In choosing your industry-market niche, it is important to estimate the potential for future growth among primary and secondary-industry candidates. Past trends are one thing. If the estimates for potential growth within a primary industry are poor, either abandon further action within that industry or maintain your current level of effort in serving it.

Even if the potential for growth is low, you can elect to accept all inquiries regarding your services. You may even choose to follow through if you are in a survival mode. Your goal, however, is to focus on primary industries that have a high potential growth estimate. Examining these industries in relationship to their geographic representation, including proximity and accessibility, aids in identifying niche candidates.

One source of information for estimating potential growth is *Predicasts,* by F&S Publications. It forecasts growth of all industries by SIC number and is a useful tool to accelerate your understanding of the growth and future direction of the niche. *Predicasts* is available in the business reference section of any major city library, university library, or federal-government-related library. Industry and professional trade associations also contain a wealth of information regarding trends in their respective industries.

Another excellent source is the trade association serving the industry. Association directories can be found at any library and offer the names, addresses, and telephone numbers of industry, trade, and professional associations. Two directories in particular—*Gales Encyclopedia of Associations* and *National Trade and Professional Associations*—collectively offer more than 10,000 association listings. The associations themselves can provide industry trend information, surveys, publications, and many other services.

The Department of Commerce produces the *U.S. Industrial Outlook,* which traces the growth of 200 industries and provides five-year forecasts for each industry. This publication is available by mail. Write to:

Superintendent of Documents
U.S. Government Printing Office
Washington, DC 20401

Build the Forms for Producing the Records

To manage and maintain the data you will be collecting, you will need to design carefully the form used to enter the information for each record. Figure 5.3(a, b) shows examples of forms used to prepare records for various files. They should provide you with some ideas.

Determine the Size of the Niche

You will need to obtain all the relevant information to make your final decision regarding which niche(s) to select. Among the basic information

```
FORM USED IN ENTERING PUBLICATION DATA

Publication:
Publisher:
Editor:
   Last:                              First:
   Gender:
Address:
Suite:
City:                     State:              Zip:
Area Code:        Number:
Subscription $:
Type:
Circulation:
Frequency:
```

FIGURE 5.3(a).   Form Used in Entering Publication Data

```
FORM USED IN ENTERING DATA ABOUT STATE
SOCIETIES AND PROFESSIONAL ASSOCIATIONS

Last Name:                      First Name:
Title:
State Society:

Address:
Suite:
City:                     State:              Zip:
Area Code:        Number:
Publications:
            a:
            b:
Conferences:
         1:
         2:
Number of Members:          Membership Directory:
```

FIGURE 5.3(b).   Form Used for Entering Data about State Societies and Professional Associations

you need are the *raw numbers* of prospects within the niches being examined. Several excellent national mailing list companies offer free catalogs with this type of information. Additionally, these companies can provide you with actual target lists, including the name, address, and phone number of companies by SIC number, zip code, and other selection criteria.

American Business Lists, Inc.
5707 South 86th Circle
P.O. Box 27347
Omaha, NE 68127
402-331-7169

R. L. Polk and Company
6400 Monroe Boulevard
Taylor, MI 48180
313-292-3200

Hugo Dunhill Mailing List, Inc.
630 Third Avenue
New York, NY 10017
212-682-8030
800-223-6454, outside NY State

Dun's National Business List
16 Progress Drive
Shelton, CT 06484
800-654-7834
800-435-3742, in Connecticut

Market Data Retrieval
16 Progress Drive
Shelton, CT 06484
800-243-5538

All these companies can assist you in identifying nearly every suspect in any particular industry-market niche.

Develop Your Preferred Prospective-Client Profile

An effective way to select your niche is to develop a preferred prospective-client profile. In other words, you put the cart before the horse. What would you like your new clients to look like? Act like? What makes them desirable? To develop the profile, define the characteristics of your desired new clients in the targeted niche.

First copy and fill in the chart shown in Figure 5.4. You will want to keep these profiles and refer to them for a visible record of your practice needs and preferences. Then you can monitor your needs and assumptions.

Next, think about the best clients you now have in the niche—the clients you really enjoy working with and serving. What are their characteristics? Are their size, management style, habit of prompt payments, stage in the growth cycle, and so on, attractive to you? List these characteristics on lines 1 through 9, using more space if necessary. Though you may not have realized it, the positive characteristics of key and A clients help to define your comfort zone. Now, attempt to identify the two or three factors that really set these clients apart from all others, and put an asterisk after them.

Favorable characteristics of A clients that might be listed include the following:

- Make referrals to you
- Pay on time
- Have potential for growth
- Are highly visible within their industry
- Manage with integrity
- Have a year-end in an off-peak season for you
- Have streamlined management
- Have experienced relatively rapid growth
- Are a prestige client
- Pay the full per-diem rate
- Easily won—no costly proposals required

In addition, any A client with whom you enjoy working, who offers challenging work, or who you simply wouldn't want to be without, we'll term a "key" client. Your key and A clients represent the backbone of your firm.

Now, think about the worst clients you have served in the niche. These are the ones you would like to eliminate from, or avoid bringing into, your practice. What are the characteristics of these C and D firms? What among their attitudes, management styles, or operating procedures turns

Date ___ / ___ / ___

PREFERRED PROSPECTIVE CLIENT PROFILE IN:

_____

(INDUSTRY SIC# AND NAME)

POSITIVE CHARACTERISTICS OF KEY AND A CLIENTS

1. _____
2. _____
3. _____
4. _____
5. _____
6. _____
7. _____
8. _____
9. _____

KNOCK-OUT FACTORS—C AND D CLIENTS

1. _____
2. _____
3. _____
4. _____
5. _____
6. _____
7. _____

FIGURE 5.4.   Preferred Client Profile

you off? List these knock-out factors on lines 1 through 7 in Figure 5.4, page 48, using more space if necessary.

Some knock-out factors could include:

- Not following your advice
- Lagging behind their industry
- Haggling over your fee
- Unchallenging work
- Clients so large you are seen as an extension of their work force
- Seek unreasonable or unethical services

You will want to limit the number of absolute knock-out factors that can cause a no-go decision. If a prospect has any one of these factors, say to yourself, "This one does not come aboard." Remember, you are shaping your future practice right now with every client you accept. Re-examine these lists to be sure you included all the positive characteristics and the knock-out factors.

You have now prepared a very valuable profile. You have a current picture of the type of client you want to attract. In a sense you will be seeking clones of your best clients. You will be able to use this profile to educate your referral sources, brief your staff, focus your prospecting time and efforts on preferred targets, and develop new-client acceptance guidelines.

If you have done a good job of analyzing your practice or maintaining up-to-date client engagement summaries, the task of producing a preferred prospective-client profile need not be difficult. If you have never undertaken any kind of analysis of this sort, then you must gather some basic information before you can proceed.

Frequently, professionals seek referrals and leads for new clients by telling their clients and influentials, "If you have any leads, send them my way." This is not a sound practice. Too often you'll end up with C and D clients. Specify the type of new clients you are seeking. When you have this knowledge, generating new leads by referral becomes much easier. You can then say to your A clients, "I would like to 'clone' you. I am looking for additional clients just like you that have the same management style and orientation." This is the highest compliment you can pay to a client; consequently, it opens many new doors.

Establish Selection Criteria ———————————————————

Ideally you serve at least two industry-market niches that have counterbalancing business-activity cycles, which enables you to level your workload and offset any unexpected variances. Many criteria could be used for selecting your niche. Over the years, I have found that the following are among the most important:

- The number of existing key and A clients in the niche
- The nature of your competition
- Existing and expected growth patterns
- The interests of you and your key staff
- The ability to transfer your technology developed from serving clients in a closely related industry
- The number and strengths of your nonclient influentials
- The estimated costs of identifying and contacting the target
- The costs of developing sufficient insider's understanding
- The costs of developing appropriate technologies required to provide support services
- The support and cooperation of partners with relative experience in the niche

The existing and expected growth patterns in targeted industries should be examined further. For example, is the industry growing at a rapid pace or is it relatively stable?

Identify the Resources on Hand and Experience in Serving the Niche ———————————————————

Were you to select this particular niche, what specific experience do you have in serving it? What resources would you use, including existing relationships, industry data, or other inside information or competitive advantages? What is your current image and reputation within the niche? What promotion techniques could you use to stimulate interest? Are the organizations and memberships you currently maintain sufficient for meeting prospects and nonclient influentials? Or would you have to join other organizations?

Make the Go/No-Go Decision

Now comes the moment of truth, the time in which a go/no-go decision must be made regarding the industry-market niche you have been analyzing. It would be nice to use a simple formula to make the most appropriate choice. Unfortunately, there isn't one; at least, I haven't encountered it. Niche decisions are of a qualitative, subjective nature.

Your decision to go with a particular niche must feel right. By now, you have done your analysis and determined the areas in which you want to specialize. Hopefully, you have identified something different and better about your services so that you can attract those "special bodies." The niche that you choose must be one in which you are willing to commit and invest your time, technology, and resources, so that you can stand out from the herd.

Making the niche decision involves taking calculated risks. The analysis you have undertaken provides you with more informed decision-making capabilities. You must have confidence in your capabilities to enter and successfully penetrate the niche that you define. This will involve dropping what does not fit, unless it is needed for short-term survival. If you have any doubts about selecting a particular niche, don't select it.

A "gut check" is in order: Is your niche dominated by a few companies? Are the needs of typical prospective clients in this industry such that any work you do for them will be challenging to your staff and transferable to other clients?

Check it out and analyze it further. A bad choice can be very costly. Remember, your decision sets strategic practice decisions. It's similar to steering a huge ocean liner. If you choose in haste—spin the navigation wheel around too quickly—you will capsize or take a long time to right the ship and resume a smooth voyage.

As with any decision, there are always costs involved. Perhaps the hardest decision to make is to abandon a niche that you had previously penetrated. After all, you have already invested time and resources. Abandoning the niche would force you to acknowledge time and money lost and engender feelings of guilt and second guessing.

6

Organizing to
Serve the Niche

You must effectively undertake several organizational tasks to serve the niche. These include preparing your niche data base, organizing your library, assembling and codifying your experience in serving the niche, and developing your service delivery system for the niche.

In this chapter, we will focus primarily on preparing your niche data base and library. Subsequent chapters will discuss the other tasks.

Developing your data base and organizing your library involve asking the fundamental question, "What information do I need to sense, serve, and satisfy the needs of this niche?" This information must be *organized* and maintained on a regular basis so that it supports you in your continuing client-centered marketing efforts. Barbara Hemphill, an organizing consultant, points out that organization helps to reduce costs. "Research shows that the average white-collar professional is responsible for eight file drawers of paper—18,000 documents," Hemphill emphasizes. "The average professional spends 20 percent of his time looking for misplaced information."

It is absolutely critical that you handle the nuts-and-bolts side of getting new clients. You must keep your data base and library in superb condition. They are as much a part of your overall marketing efforts as the clothes you wear and your in-person presentations. In fact, as we will see in subsequent chapters, you must also keep your presentation materials, traveling files, appointment books, expense records, client correspondence, and briefcase in the same exemplary condition in which you keep your office prospect files.

PREPARING YOUR DATA BASE

To manage and maintain the data you will be collecting, and to capitalize on the information contained in the library you will be assembling, you will need to choose an appropriate data base software package. This software must have the capability to do word processing and mail merges. When contacting the niche, your ability to immediately turn out custom-tailored computer-assisted hard copy such as a promotion letter, an engagement letter, and a proposal will help you win more clients quickly and keep your marketing costs at a minimum.

Seven steps are involved in preparing your data base, four of which are discussed in this chapter; others are covered in later chapters.

1. Determine the files you need.
2. Determine the nature and number of fields to be used in each record.
3. Build the form for producing each record.
4. Enter information already on hand.
5. Identify additional data needed and the best source(s).
6. Acquire and enter the data.
7. Maintain and update the data base.

Determine the Files You Need

A file is a collection of information that is related to a single subject or topic. Three files must be created:

1. Existing clients
2. Prospective/potential clients
3. Nonclient influentials

Determine the Nature and Number of Fields to Be Used in Each Record

A field refers to a single-entry item of data, such as name, classification, SIC, and so forth. A record is composed of related fields. Experts who design data bases caution against using too many fields. More is not always better. Your goal is to enter only the information you need to accomplish your objective.

For your existing clients, the minimum fields should be:

Name

Address

Zip code

Telephone number(s)

Name(s) of contact person(s)

Firm's internal identification number (if used)

Class of client—Key/A/B/C/D

Past three years' revenue

Services provided past 12 months

Major needs, problems, and opportunities

Proposals outstanding

Essential background information

For your prospective/potential clients in the niche, the following fields should be sufficient:

Name

Address

Zip Code

Telephone number(s)

Name(s) of contact person(s)

Probable potential class of client—Key/A/B/C/D

Major needs, problems, and opportunities

Services to suggest

Proposals outstanding

Essential background information

Preparing records for the nonclient influentials (NCIs) file requires a bit of thought.

There are three broad classes of NCIs:

- *Multipliers.* Individuals who, because of their responsibilities, have the potential to provide you with multiple promotion and prospecting opportunities. Included in this group would be:

    Executive directors of industry/trade/professional associations in the niche

    Editors of key publications read by your clients and prospective clients

    Academics who interact with members of the niche

    Sponsors of conferences and other educational events

- *Reciprocals.* Others who serve your type of clients and prospective clients. These people expect you to provide them with leads in return for leads they give you. Included in this group would be:

    Advertising agencies

    Attorneys

    Bankers

- *Others* who are or can be influential to you.

Because this is such an individual matter, I've summarized a number of possible NCIs in Figure 6.1.

Build the Forms for Producing the Records

An important aspect of building your form is determining the fields you will use in sorting the information entered in the records making up each file. If you are building a data base from scratch, consult a data-base expert in your community. You may be able to find one at the computer store where you purchased the software package. If not, hook into the user groups for your type of computer. You often can get the names of such groups from the computer stores or "hackers" in your community. I have successfully used a high school computer whiz as my consultant both in designing my forms and handling the data-entry task.

Enter the Information on Hand

Your goal is to get an early win by entering the data on hand. This gives you a feeling of satisfaction and provides the basis for subsequent steps. It will also help you determine what is needed.

Alumni of your college

Alumni of your firm who speak well of it

Association executives in niches you serve or are targeting

Attorneys

Bankers

Civic officials

Clubs frequented by your clients

Convention and tourism bureaus

Economic development department personnel

Editors of publications read by your clients and targets of opportunity

Former executives of clients who have moved to nonclient/suspect organizations in your niche

Government officials

Insurance agents/CLUs

Management companies

Neighbors

Other professionals serving your client and targets

Politicians

Real estate salespersons

Stockbrokers

Trust companies

Universities

FIGURE 6.1. Possible Nonclient Influentials

A quick and easy way to gain and enter information on nonclient influentials is to trade business card files with noncompeting professionals who also serve your niche. It is becoming increasingly possible to trade data disks containing such names with others. One consultant in New York City is a master of exchanging names. His goal is to develop name awareness and relationships with everyone who is and can be influential to him in reaching his marketing objectives.

ORGANIZING YOUR LIBRARY ———————————————

Much of the data gathering you will undertake to develop your computerized data base will also support the development of your library. Here are some of the basic items to gather.

1. *The "Bibles" Used in the Niche.* Every industry or profession has certain key manuals or handbooks that are used by the members in their daily operations. These insider books contain vital information about the industry. The next time you are at a client's office, find out what the key reference handbooks are.

2. *Major Publications Read by Clients and Prospects.* Virtually all publications are cited in one or more of the following directories, located in your public library:

Writer's Market

Working Press of the Nation

Bacon's Publicity Checker

Oxbridge Directory of Newsletters

Hudson's Newsletter Directory

Gebbie's All-in-One Directory

Magazine Industry Marketplace

3. *Engagement-Related Materials.* Assemble materials you will use and refer to frequently. There are four major categories:

Proposals—to analyze and enter into the word processor for rapid turnaround

Engagement letters—to use with proposals

Final reports—to use in new-business discussions as evidence of accomplishment

Work programs, budgets, and so on—to use in estimating the fees involved in proposed solutions to needs

4. *Competitor Information.* This includes brochures, Statements of Capability, copies of their proposals, news clippings, and so on.

5. *Niche Data.* These include legislation, trends, and economic studies.

6. *Other Materials.* These include materials about your prospective clients and influentials. As you get more deeply into an understanding of the niche (Chapter 8), undoubtedly you will uncover other key directories, reference materials, and insider's reference materials.

Organizing to serve the target niche will pay off in spades when developing your niche service-delivery system. You will be able to tailor and/or routinize your systems as the situation demands (Chapter 6). Being organized will also accelerate the rate at which you can develop an insider's reputation in the niche (Chapter 11) and specifically:

- Help you generate greater name awareness of your firm among targets
- Facilitate your handling of inquiries and enable you to develop them further
- Bolster your programs for prospecting and promotion

In Chapter 7, we will examine those factors that assist you in developing an insider's understanding of the niche. Then you can appropriately tailor your service-delivery system and develop an insider's reputation, a coveted position among service providers.

7

Developing an Insider's Understanding of the Niche's Industry

This chapter presents a system for developing an insider's understanding of the industry in your selected niche. The combination of industry analysis and market analysis adds up to a niche analysis. The next chapter will discuss the procedures involved in completing and analyzing the market in your niche.

Your continuing goal is to identify high-potential niches and to develop and execute effective action programs designed to penetrate them by offering solution programs that meet hot button needs with high-margin service solutions. The ability to develop and convey services that are perceived as both different and better than your competitors can only be done by developing an insider's understanding of the niche. When you have an insider's knowledge, all the remaining steps to obtaining new clients become easier.

A MICRO LOOK AT THE INDUSTRY

Up to this point, we have taken a broad, or "macro," look at the niche in which you will be competing. In this chapter, we will be taking a detailed, or "micro," look at the industry in your selected niche.

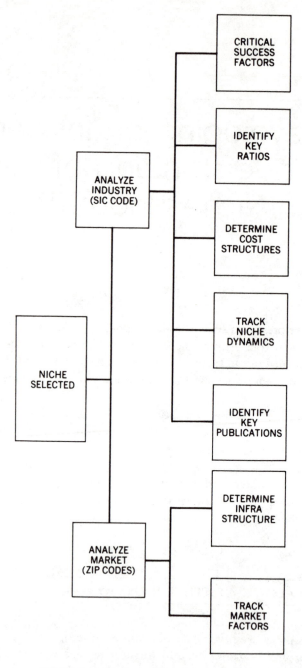

FIGURE 7.1.   Understanding Selected Niches

Figure 7.1 is a graphic description of the tasks involved in developing an insider's understanding of the niche.

An industry analysis involves the identification of critical success factors, key ratios, the industry cost structure, typical gross-profit margins, net profitability; the factors improving the industry-technology changes; and economic, social, and governmental factors. Using today's terminology, we can say that we are developing an understanding of the *infrastructure* of the niche.

The market analysis side of understanding your niche involves determining the infrastructure and the factors affecting the market. Often, the term infrastructure is tossed about but not really understood. The infrastructure on a zip code basis consists of the clients, prospects, suspects, nonclient influentials (local), competitors, and all others who serve or impact the niche. This also includes the trade and professional associations and organizations in which these "players" belong. Factors affecting the market include current economic conditions and the density of clients and prospects within the targeted industry, by zip code.

DETERMINING THE CRITICAL SUCCESS FACTORS OF THE INDUSTRY

John F. Rockart, writing in the *Harvard Business Review,* observes that "Critical success factors for any business are the limited number of areas in which results, if they are satisfactory, will ensure successful competitive performance for the organization." Stated differently, they are the few key areas in which things must go right for a business to prosper. Rockart contends that the critical success factors are areas of activity that should receive "constant and careful attention from management." Your ability to identify these factors and their prime measurements will put you at the head of the class of potential service providers on whom your clients and prospective clients will rely.

Critical success factors (CSFs) consist of the three to eight factors or performance areas that must function successfully for a business to flourish, given its location, stage of growth, mission, and growth strategies. There are two major classes of CSF. The first consists of all-encompassing, industry-based factors. In the automotive industry, for example, this would include styling, a high-quality dealer system, cost control, and meeting industry-based energy standards. In the supermarket industry, this would include the product mix, inventory turnover, and sales promotion.

The second class of CSF contains organizational-based factors. In the home entertainment industry, for example, Motorola has chosen not to engage in research and development. Thus, a CSF for Motorola would be the rapid replication of new developments made by others in the industry.

IDENTIFYING THE CSFs IN YOUR NICHE

In today's information-rich environment, it's relatively easy to identify the CSFs in your selected industry. There are nine sources you will want to tap:

1. *Your Current Clients.* Speak first with your clients in the niche and ask them what industry and organizational factors are important and why. Ask them how they measure each factor. Later in the chapter, we discuss the prime measure for each CSF.

2. *Annual Reports.* Visit the reference section of your library to read annual reports for companies in the industry, and any other information that profiles the industry.

3. *Red Herrings.* The prospectuses issued by organizations in the industry that wish to go public contain valuable information. Pay particular attention to risk factors spelled out in the analysis section.

4. *U.S. Industrial Outlook.* Published annually by the Bureau of Economic Analysis of the Department of Commerce, this book predicts the growth profile of development for the next five years in more than 200 domestic industries, arranged by SIC number.

5. *Stockbrokers.* Stockbrokers who specialize in the industry can be tapped for information you need. It is their business to know the CSF of their respective industries and which companies are adept at meeting them head-on.

6. *Business Magazines.* Publications such as *Business Week* and *Fortune* frequently carry articles discussing the strategy of industry leaders and challengers. For example, a recent story in *Business Week* discussed the marketing strategy of a financial services firm's "bold

decision to buck the conventional wisdom in serving the industry." The conventional wisdom discussed the industry-based factors.

7. *Others Consulting to the Industry.* Discussion with noncompeting consultants can yield insights for your penetration programs. Piggyback on their ideas while you share your ideas.

8. *Industry Trade Association.* Many associations publish studies regarding the growth potential of the industry as well as information about pending legislation that may impact the member organizations.

9. *Commercial Bankers.* Bankers serving the industry can share the criteria they use in evaluating business plans and other funding requests.

The same process that is used in examining an entire industry can be used to examine individual clients. Figure 7.2 shows the industry-based CSF for trade associations.

Next, for each of the CSFs within an industry, there is a measurement that can be used to track the performance of individual companies. Figure 7.3 indicates the corresponding measurement, *prime measures,* that are used to determine the health and vitality of trade associations. Following this, Figure 7.4 provides an example of critical success factors and prime measures for a construction firm. A blank form follows (Figure 7.5) for your use in determining the prime measures for your industry.

IDENTIFYING THE KEY RATIOS USED IN MANAGING THE INDUSTRY

Numerous sources of ratios can be consulted to form a composite profile of a firm:

- Dun & Bradstreet. This company annually publishes *Key Business Ratios,* which presents 14 ratios for 125 lines of business.

- Robert Morris Associates. This firm publishes an annual financial statement study.

- Accounting Corporation of America, 1929 First Avenue, San Diego, CA 92101. This organization publishes *Parameter of Small Businesses,* which classifies its operating ratios for various industry groups on the basis of gross volume.

IDENTIFYING INDUSTRY-BASED CRITICAL SUCCESS FACTORS

SIC # <u>8611</u>   Description of Industry <u>TRADE ASSOCIATIONS</u>

List the five to eight most important industry-based CSFs below:

1. Legislation

2. Member communication

3. Membership

4. Economic indicators

5. Financial resources

6. Competitive environment

7. Lobbying effrots

8.

IDENTIFYING INDUSTRY-BASED CRITICAL SUCCESS FACTORS

SIC # _____   Description of Industry _____

List the five to eight most important industry-based CSFs below:

1.

2.

3.

4.

5.

6.

7.

8.

FIGURE 7.2.   Identifying Industry-Based Critical Success Factors

IDENTIFYING PRIME MEASURES FOR A CLIENT'S CSFs

Name of Key Client _____

SIC # __8611__   Description of Industry __TRADE ASSOCIATIONS__

Critical Success Factors	Prime Measures
1. LEGISLATION	Pending Bills Voting Records of Politicians
2. MEMBER COMMUNICATION	Participation Level at Conventions Time Lag Between "News" and Communication to Members Amount of Feedback from Members Communication Costs vs. Other Associations
3. MEMBERSHIP	Ratio Members to Non-members in Industry Dues Structure Advertising & P/R $$ to Total Members & Revenues versus Other Associations
4. ECONOMIC INDICATORS	Insurance Rates GNP Unemployment Rate Interest Rates Balance of Trade
5. FINANCIAL RESOURCES	Member Dues Government Aid to Members
6. COMPETITIVE ENVIRONMENT	# Of Competing Associations & Membership # Of Non-members in the Industry Services Provided by Non-association Providers (For example, Consultants or Educators)
7. LOBBYING EFFORT	Bills Enacted vs. Association Position $$ Spent vs. Other Assoc. # of Lobbyists

FIGURE 7.3. Identifying Prime Measures for a Client's CSFs

CRITICAL SUCCESS FACTORS AND PRIME MEASURES

Industry: Construction firm

Critical Success Factors	Prime Measures
1. Image in financial markets	Price/earning ratio
2. Technological reputation with customers	Number of contracts won versus number of bids made Customer "perception" interview results
3. Market success	Changes in market share Growth rates of company
4. Risk recognition in major bids and contracts	Length of company's experience with similar products "New" or "old" customer Prior customer relationship
5. Profit margin on jobs	Bid profit margin as ratio of profit on similar jobs
6. Company morale	Turnover, absenteeism, etc. Informal feedback (Management discussions with employees)
7. Performance to budget on major jobs	Job cost budgeted/actual

FIGURE 7.4. Critical Success Factors and Prime Measures

- National Cash Register Company, Marketing Services Department, Dayton, OH 45409. This firm publishes *Expenses in Retail Businesses,* which examines the cost of operations in more than 50 kinds of businesses obtained from primary sources, most of which are trade associations.

- The Small Business Administration. The SBA has a new series of reports that provide expenses as a percentage of sales for many industries. While the reports do not provide strict ratio information, a comparison of percentage expenses will be very useful for your financial management.

IDENTIFYING PRIME MEASURES FOR A CLIENT'S CSFs

Name of Key Client _____

SIC # _____   Description of Industry _____

CRITICAL SUCCESS FACTORS	PRIME MEASURES
1.	
2.	
3.	
4.	
5.	
6.	
7.	
8.	

FIGURE 7.5. Identifying Prime Measures for a Client's CSFs (Blank Form)

- Trade Associations. Many national trade associations publish ratio studies.

Talk with commercial bankers serving targets, and read the annual reports and prospectuses in the niche. Ratio analysis does nothing to correct a weakness in business operations, but diagnosis is a critical first step.

DETERMINING THE COST STRUCTURE OF THE INDUSTRY

I use the term *costs* to mean the financial resources that are used in the development and/or the acquisition of other resources used in the performance of a business function or operating process.

A business function could be marketing, advertising, sales, and so forth. A business process would be manufacturing, administration, and the like. Mack Hanan, author of *Key Account Selling,* says that ". . . you must know the location of significant cost centers that are susceptible to reduction." Implied in this statement is the tag: through the use of resources available in you.

Every business function and business process is a cost center. Your goal is to identify the cost points in each business function that you can affect positively. If you're an accountant, the job is easier because you have ready access to the key financial data. If you do not have such access, you need to discuss costs with your clients in the niche, talk with others who serve the niche, and become a student of the cost structure for the niche.

TRACKING THE DYNAMICS OF THE NICHE

Tracking the changes, trends, legislation and other factors affecting the niche is a continuing responsibility. The easiest way to do this is to identify the major publications serving the niche and monitor the dynamics. As mentioned in Chapter 8, these industry-specific publications can be used in a variety of ways.

I shall complete our discussion of publications in this section.

IDENTIFYING THE PUBLICATIONS

Identifying the publications read by niche members is relatively easy. The directories presented in Chapter 6 collectively list over 10,000 publications in every topic area. You will be able literally to identify 90 percent or more of all publications serving your target niche.

Now let's examine the wealth of information available from these publications that can be used to support your client-centered marketing efforts.

1. *Readership Demographics.* All publications maintain information on their readership, including average age, income, sex, job title, and other valuable data.

The key to obtaining such information is to write to the advertising department and ask for a copy of the advertising rate card and readership demographics. The advertising rate card will explain the various costs and procedures for placing a single or continuous ad within the publication. You can also use *Standard Rate and Data,* which contains information on all major U.S. publications and a directory of advertising rate cards.

2. *Editorial Guidelines.* Those who regularly write for magazines know that most editors maintain a published set of editorial or author's guidelines. Available to anyone who asks, these guidelines define the nature and scope of the material the editor is seeking to serve the interests of the readers.

3. *Special Issues.* Many publications periodically offer a special issue that highlights developments and trends in the industry. For example, in November 1991, *Purchasing* produced a special issue entitled the "Top 100" that "told the purchasing story as it has never been told before." According to the publishers, the issue added a totally new dimension to the collective knowledge of the U.S. industrial marketplace. Other publications such as *Forbes, Fortune, Business Week, Inc.,* and *Venture* are noted for their special directory and industry-focused issues.

The editorial calendar will pinpoint when a special issue will be published.

The calendar from *Business Marketing* outlines the topics and issues for a 12-month period.

4. *Subscriber Mailing Lists.* Most publications have subscriber mailing lists for sale. Although some publications sell their entire list of subscribers

(representing overkill to you if you only want subscribers in a particular locality), others offer a more targeted list. In addition, many publications sell their subscriber lists to the direct-mail catalog houses (a partial list appears in Chapter 5), which often can offer them to you at a lower cost than the publisher because of high-volume sales.

INSIDE THE MAGAZINE ITSELF

In reviewing any particular publication read by your targeted niche, pay close attention to the following:

1. *The Masthead.* Who publishes, edits, advertises, and circulates the publication? How often is it distributed? Who owns the publication? Is it published in affiliation with some association or other organization? The masthead provides this information.

2. *Table of Contents.* In addition to the normal feature articles, considering your new strategic focus, look for the following:

Book reports

Washington watch

Trend watch

Columnist

Reader surveys

Letters to the editor

"My say" or opinion pieces

Names in the news

New products and services

Advertising index

3. *Classified Ads.* This section, particularly if there is a job mart, is often a giveaway as to the needs of the industry. Yet, I bet you rarely read these even in your own industry publications.

Other things you will find inside publications are fairly obvious. Who writes the articles and what kind of bylines are printed? Are articles accompanied by pictures, charts, or art work?

The publications read by your targets are among the least expensive, the most effective way to gain inside information—all while seated at your desk.

IDENTIFYING OTHER DATA SOURCES

Selling to the Giants, by Jeffrey P. Davidson (Tab/McGraw-Hill, 1991), contains a wealth of information and data sources on industrial markets. Here are a few that will hasten your ability to develop an insider's understanding:

National Technical Information Service
  4285 Port Royal Road
  Springfield, VA 22161

American Management Associations
  135 West 50th Street
  New York, NY 10020

Directory of Conventions *Successful Meetings*
  1633 Third Avenue
  New York, NY 10017

U.S. Statistical Abstract
  Superintendent of Documents
  Government Printing Office
  Washington, DC 20402

U.S. Industrial Outlook
  Bureau of Economic Analysis
  Department of Commerce
  Washington, DC 20230

Special Libraries Association
  1700 18th Street, NW
  Washington, DC 20009

There are also numerous data base vendors and services that will provide you with information via your PC or computer-system terminal. Some of the major vendors include:

Dialogue
   3460 Hillview Avenue
   Palo Alto, CA 94304

CompuServe
   500 Arlington Center Boulevard
   Columbus, OH 43220

Bibliographic Retrieval Services
   1200 Route 7
   Latham, NY 12110

Other key directories, such as *Ward's Business Directory,* are available in most public libraries.

This concludes our analysis on the industry level. By now, your confidence in your ability to call on suspects should be building.

8

Developing an Insider's Understanding of the Niche's Market

This chapter completes the insider's analysis begun in the previous chapter. We will be taking a detailed micro look at determining the infrastructure and the factors affecting the market.

Remember, the term infrastructure on a zip code basis consists of the clients, client referral sources, prospects in your new business pipeline, suspects, nonclient influentials (local), competitors, and all others who serve or impact the niche.

Factors affecting the market include current economic conditions, and the density of clients and prospects within the targeted industry by zip code.

Let's now examine each of the elements involved in the market analysis. You may want to refer back to Figure 7.1 before you start.

IDENTIFYING THE NICHE INFRASTRUCTURE IN THE MARKET

Identifying Clients

Identifying existing clients in the niche is an easy task if you have entered their primary SIC number in your client file. If you have not yet done this, now is an excellent time to do so. Round up all the names of all the clients you serve in the industry. Ideally, you have classified them in terms of their potential for growth, as mentioned in Chapter 5.

Identifying Your Referral Sources

A targeted referrals program is the backbone of a successful new business development program. Building and maintaining an active referral program enables you to make contacts with preconditioned prospects, who are generally more receptive to meeting with you because of their high regard for the referral person.

There are two different classes of referrals: current clients and nonclient influentials. Each referral source has distinct benefits and requirements for development.

1. *Current Client Referral Sources.* Your task now is to identify the current clients in the niche that provide you with referrals. Figure 8.1 illustrates a convenient form you can use to keep track of current clients who provide you with leads and make referrals on your behalf.

1	2 Initiate?		3	4 Potential**		5
Client Executives Name and Affiliation	No	Yes*	Quality of Relationship (1 to 4)	Short- Term	Long- Term	How I Plan to Use This Referral Source

* Level of effort   1 = Poor   ** Potential
A = continuing/recurring   4 = Perfect   H = High
B = sporadic   M = Medium
C = one time only/dormant   L = Low

FIGURE 8.1.   Existing Client Referral Sources

2. *Nonclient Influentials.* Nonclient influentials (NCIs) are attorneys, bankers, noncompeting consultants, editors, and others who both serve and influence your targeted suspects and prospective clients. Your nonclient influentials consist of two groups: those you know and those you need to know. Often your competitors and other nonclient influentials will lead you to them.

There are some disadvantages to using NCIs including their expectation of a reciprocal lead and the possibility that the NCI misrepresented or oversold your capabilities to prospects. Also, an NCI referral may not be as meaningful as a client referral because he or she cannot personally vouch for your services.

Figure 8.2 shows another convenient form you can use in listing your influentials.

Identifying Prospective Clients

Next, identify existing prospective clients. This is not difficult. Inventory prospective clients in your pipeline and indicate the likelihood of converting them to new clients.

1 Names and Affiliations of Influential Contacts	2 Initiate?		3 Quality of Relationship (1 to 4)	4 Potential**		5 How I Plan to Use This Referral Source
	No	Yes*		Short-Term	Long-Term	

* Level of effort   1 = Poor   ** Potential
A = continuing/recurring   4 = Perfect   H = High
B = sporadic   M = Medium
C = one time only/dormant   L = Low

FIGURE 8.2.   Existing Nonclient Influentials

Identifying the Suspects —————————————————————

Identifying the suspects in your niche is made considerably easier if you purchase the subscriber mailing lists for the key publication read by members of the industry. Suspects include both organizations and the names of specific contact persons in the organization: the very information included within subscriber mailing lists. Numerous data sources abound including subscriber-mailing lists of key publications, association-member lists, chamber of commerce directories, and your existing clients.

The business journal serving your local area usually offers theme and other special issues that list the leaders in particular industries and professional areas. In my own area, the *Washington Business Journal* and the *Washington Post Business* frequently provide such lists as "the 100 largest employers in the Washington area," "the 25 largest advertising firms," and a "directory of area couriers." It is not necessary to subscribe to the publications. Often, the first or last issue of the year has an index of articles published in the preceding 12 months. If your local library cannot supply back issues, write or call the publication. They will be able to send you a back issue for a fee, or refer you to a library or repository with their back issues.

The nature and type of information you generate on suspects affects your database design and upkeep considerations. When creating your data files, be generous in the amount of space you allow in each field while limiting the number of fields you include. It is better to have lots of blank space within your files than to be toiling with exotic codes that enable you to cram a lot of information into a small space.

When identifying suspects, the profile you developed in Chapter 5 of your key and A clients becomes a valuable tool. This profile can be used as your "talk piece" in educating your referral sources. To gather information about suspects, the data sheet that you use need not be complicated. (See Figure 8.3.)

While gathering information on suspects, seek the name and title of the decision maker(s) in charge of operations requiring your type of service. Also, who is the most receptive and positive influencer who can get you to the decision maker? The title of the person with whom you wish to make contact might be determined by recalling the most recent discussions you had with new clients or prospects within the niche. Others within your firm, as well as nonclient influentials such as lawyers, bankers, and so forth, may be able to identify the appropriate title.

DATE

NEW SUSPECT DATA SHEET

Name: _____   Industry: _____   SIC: _____

Address: _____

_____

Telephone: _____

Key Names:

_____

_____

_____

Founded: _____   No. employes: _____   Est. Sales/Yr: _____

Remarks:

_____

_____

_____

_____

_____

_____

How identified:

client referral	[ ]	nonclient referral	☐
association directory	☐	industry directory	☐
direct inquiry	☐	magazine article	☐
newspaper	☐	met personally	☐
civic, social org.	☐	trade show	☐
		other	☐

FIGURE 8.3. New Suspect Data Sheet

As you review the directories and information sources highlighted throughout this book, be on the alert for terms particular to the niche. For example, what is termed the personnel department in the insurance industry is called the human resources division within banking.

Another way to get the title of the proper person is to call the organization and ask the receptionist for the name of the person who makes decisions about engaging the type of services you offer. If you have already targeted the title of the person you will call, ask his or her secretary for a name. That way, you can honestly say when calling the officer, "I was told by your office you were the right person to contact." (More on making telephone contact in Chapter 14.)

As you gain more information about suspects in the niche, begin to sort your information by your level of knowledge. The form shown in Figure 8.4 can be used for this purpose. The first column is obvious.

IDENTIFYING SUSPECTS

Name and SIC Code of Suspect	Nature of Services Needed	Next Steps

FIGURE 8.4.   Identifying Suspects

The second column, "Nature of Services Needed," should be filled in to the best of your ability and updated as you gain more information about particular suspects. Ideally, you will have identified the hot buttons needs, issues, and concerns of suspects in your niche. Thus, the nature of services needed may begin to fall into a few categories, making your job that much easier. The third column, "Next Steps," requires that you identify what you do with each suspect on whom you are collecting information.

Suspects become prospects when they agree to meet with you. In most instances, the next step will be to call each suspect, either to get the correct name and title of the contact person, or to make an appointment with that person.

TRACKING THE MARKET-AFFECTING FACTORS

This step involves monitoring the economic conditions affecting your practice area. Included will be such factors as growth rate, unemployment, mergers and divestitures, strikes, and so on. Your goal is to stay current with the happenings in the market that could have an impact on the receptivity and buying ability of prospective clients in your niche.

If the tasks you will need to perform, as laid out in this chapter, seem overly analytical or initially difficult, be comforted. They will minimize the level of sales proficiency you will need in face-to-face discussions. I find that the more technically oriented professional-service providers prefer this approach because it is a logical extension of their technical work-flow process.

Pursuing the steps that follow will place you in front of more prospects faster and easier and provide a simpler way to sense client and prospective client needs.

Distilling Your Knowledge

To distill your knowledge of the niche, prepare the worksheet shown in Figure 8.5. In section 1a, ask yourself, "What are the concerns of clients in this niche?" Then, list those concerns in the space provided. If your targeted niche were the construction industry, SIC code number 1611, your answers might include "cost control," "timely reporting in control of multiple jobs," and "too much overhead."

AN INSIDER'S NICHE ANALYSIS

Niche: _____   __/__/__
            (SIC # and Description)   (Date)

1. Clients in this niche:	2. Current hot buttons are:
a. Are <u>concerned</u>:	
With?	
About?	3. Industry-success factors:
b. Are <u>forced</u> to:	
Do?	
Have?	4. Information sources
c. Would <u>like</u> to:	Include:
Do?	Directories:
Have?	Publications:
d. Are <u>influenced</u> by:	Organizations/
Whom?	Associations:
What?	

FIGURE 8.5. An Insider's Niche Analysis

For item 1b, answer the question, "What are the problems these clients face?" Even if you can't help the clients with these problems, you want to know because it gives you more empathy and opportunities for meaningful discussion. If your clients were in the retail office supply business, SIC code number 5943, your answers might include "compliance with the new tax laws," "employee pilferage," and "price instability among suppliers."

In 1c, ask, "What are clients in the niche vitally interested in that I can assist them in doing or obtaining?" If your client is an EDP-systems installer, the answer might be "to obtain cost-plus contracts versus fixed fee," "to maintain a smooth cash flow," and "to develop more confident junior staff that can service client needs." Practically speaking, your ability to answer 1c-type questions is synonymous with your ability to identify new business opportunities for your firm.

In 1d, ask, "Who and what positively influence clients in this niche?" If your clients are realtors, for example, the answers might include "banks and savings and loan institutions," "corporate relocation officers," and "availability and condition of existing housing."

The top of the second column of the worksheet asks for the current hot buttons in the niche. (This will be discussed in greater detail in

Chapter 12.) Hot buttons consist of any topics, issues, or trends of a contemporary and keen interest to prospects within this niche. If your clients are members of the airline industry, for example, current hot buttons might include "shortages in air traffic controllers," "terrorism," "the effect of discount airfares," and "frequent flyer programs."

For number 3, determine as many of the industry-success factors as you can for this niche. If your clients are industrial launderers, SIC code number 7212, this list might include "efficient use of energy," "maintaining cost control over supplies," "eliminating waste," "passing EPA and OSHA inspections," "securing corporate accounts," and "maintaining schedules" and "customer deadlines."

For number 4, list the best directories for this niche, the ones that give you insider information. If your niche consists of one-to-five person, public-accounting firms, SIC code number 8931, you would certainly want to list the directory of the National Society of Public Accountants, with over 18,000 members. Next, list the publications read by your clients and prospects in the niche. If your target consists of design and product engineers, SIC code number 8911, publications of interest would include *Design News, Machine Design, Product Design and Development,* and *Product Engineering.* As I mentioned earlier, the subscriber lists to these publications can usually be purchased and used to identify targets of opportunity in your market area.

Next, identify the organizations and associations to which your clients and prospects belong. If your clients consist of machine shops, SIC code number 3599, these organizations might include the National Association of Manufacturers, the National Federation of Independent Businesses and the U.S. Department of Commerce. Figure 8.6 is an insider's analysis completed for the construction industry, SIC code number 1611.

A MASTER MENU OF NEEDS

The research and analysis you have done of the targeted industry will enable you to develop and maintain a master menu of needs. This is analogous to the menus in a software program. The main menu lists the major topics or activity areas covered in the software program. Each major topic or activity area is further described or delineated as a submenu. Submenus have a number of tasks or options listed.

AN INSIDER'S NICHE ANALYSIS

Niche: #1611 Construction Industry   /   /
              (SIC # and Description)   (Date)

1. Clients in this niche:

   a. Are concerned with/about:

      Cost controls

      Timely reporting & control of multiple jobs

      Too much overhead

   b. Are forced to:

      Too much executive involvement at lower levels

      Crisis management-reaction

      Customer deadlines and schedules

      Financial pressures of jobs and vendors

   c. Would like to:

      Delegate and still maintain control

      Lower overhead

      Cost plus contracts v. fixed fee

      Adequate financial resources

   d. Are influenced by:

      Banks and S&L's

      Real estate owners and operators

      Economic upturns and downturns

2. Current hot buttons are:

   Microcomputers

   Organizational review

   Personnel resource utilization

   Income tax planning

3. Success factors include:

   Obtaining a line of credit

   Availability of bonding

   The weather

   Front-loaded billing

4. Information sources include:

   Directories:

   List of contractors from state registrar of contractors

   Local homebuilder guides

   GCA Directory

   AB&C Directory

   Publications:

   Builder Contractor

   Construction

   Engineering News Record

   Construction Equipment

   Organizations/Associations:

   Registrar of Contractors

   Associated Builders & Contractors

   National Association of Home Builders

   General Contractors of America

FIGURE 8.6.   An Insider's Niche Analysis

Figure 8.7 is the "*Main Menu of Needs*" that I created for the accounting profession. Figure 8.8 is the submenu of needs for existing clients, item 1 of the main menu. Figure 8.9 is the submenu of needs in industries, item 7 on the main menu.

The main menu and corresponding submenus of needs grow out of the development of an insider's understanding of the niche.

The term *need* refers to something in a suspect's situation that:

- Is present but unwanted, a negative need situation such as excess costs, poor morale, subpar performance of a success factor, and so on.

- Is desired but is missing or in short supply, a positive situation such as marketing expertise, advanced technology, and so on.

- Needs to be done, a short-term task situation that requires the use of resources available to us, such as managing a project for the client, performing a diagnostic analysis, developing a program, and so on.

These needs are grouped in three categories including hot buttons, recurring needs, and emerging/potential needs.

DICK CONNOR, INC.
MAIN MENU OF NEEDS
ACCOUNTING PROFESSION

1. Clients, existing
2. Prospects, existing
3. Suspects
4. Referral Sources
5. Industries
6. Markets
7. Industry-market niches
8. Services
9. Promotion
10. Prospecting
11. New-Business Discussion/Selling
12. Managing the Marketing Function

FIGURE 8.7. Dick Connor, Inc., Main Menu of Needs

```
                    SUBMENU
              1. EXISTING CLIENTS

                                        HB   R   E

1. Determine the nature and potential of existing
   client base.                              X
2. Retention of Key & A clients              X
3. Providing additional services             X
4. Developing referrals                      X
5. Up-grading/replacing marginal clients             X
6. Serving high-potential Key & A clients in client-
   centered fashion                      X

HB = hot button
 R = recurring
 E = emerging
```

FIGURE 8.8.   Dick Connor, CMC Submenu (Existing Clients)

```
                    SUBMENU
             7. EXISTING INDUSTRIES

                                        HB   R   E

1. Identify existing industries (SICs)       X
2. Classify in terms of existing revenues    X
3. Estimate potential for growth         X
4. Monitor the dynamics                      X
5. Develop an "insider's" understanding  X

HB = hot button
 R = recurring
 E = emerging
```

FIGURE 8.9.   Dick Connor, CMC Submenu (Existing Industries)

Hot button needs are those that are on the lips of your targets. They are current and deemed to be important by your targets. These needs will sometimes be one-time needs and thus require a modified or minipromotional system. Frequently, they will have enough staying power to become recurring needs; consequently, they merit a full promotional system.

While hot buttons will get you the appointment, handling recurring needs enables you to make a lasting contribution and earn the revenue that flows from satisfied clients.

PREPARING YOUR NICHE DATABASE

As you complete the tasks involved in working with your market, you'll want to use the data-entry forms discussed in Chapter 7. Remember, more is not necessarily better! List only those names that have potential for your practice.

COMPLETING YOUR LIBRARY

Now is the time to index and file any additional directories, publications, annual reports, and so on that you've encountered in your library. Make readily available those books and materials you need for responding to new-business opportunities and to provide client-centered solutions to the important needs you serve.

In Chapter 9, "Preparing Your Service Promotion and Delivery Systems," we will discuss how to use the insider's understanding of the niche you have developed to showcase your professionalism and create solution packages for recurring services.

9

Preparing Your Service Promotion and Delivery Systems

Throughout this book, we have stressed using a client-centered approach. Client-centered marketing is not a substitute for high-quality service, nor is it a ploy to be used in selling a "plain vanilla" service in a "rocky road" package.

The approach was defined earlier as sensing, serving, selling and satisfying the selected needs of targets of opportunity in the niche. The information you have assembled now can be directed toward successfully promoting your services and profitably delivering your services within the niche.

PREPARING YOUR SERVICE-PROMOTION SYSTEMS ──

The purpose of preparing a service-promotion system is to maximize the efficiency and the effectiveness of your promotional program for the niche. The following goals will guide your activities:

1. To be perceived as a knowledgeable insider by all who receive the promotional materials.

2. To prepare need-specific, initial-contact packages designed to obtain appointments with targeted suspects.

3. To enable you to be cost–effective and highly responsive to opportunities to contact and converse with prospective clients.

4. To showcase your professionalism in the mind and emotions of the targets.

5. To position your services as different from and better than the competition.

6. To be able to respond to needs with what are perceived as value-added solutions by interested prospects.

Figure 9.1 shows the elements of a service-promotion system. With each element, for each prospect, a decision must be made whether to tailor (T) or treat routinely (R). Sometimes a combination of the two is necessary, R/T.

1. *Initial Contact Package.* The preparation of the three elements in the service-promotion system is covered in detail in Chapters 13 and 14. Because the approach is need–driven, the cover letter and enclosure often

SERVICE-PROMOTION SYSTEM	T	R	R/T
1. Initial contact package			
a. Cover letter	X		
b. Need-specific enclosures	X		
c. Telephone contact guide			X
2. New-business discussion package			
a. Question sheet		X	
b. Testimonial letter		X	
c. Problem-approach-result write-ups (PARs)		X	
d. Approved client list		X	
e. Sample final reports and other "deliverables"			X
f. Other firm and promotional materials			X
3. Proposals	X		
4. Client-centered analysis	X		
T = tailored for client			
R = recurring/standard			
R/T = minor tailoring of recurring standard factors			

FIGURE 9.1. Service-Promotion System

must be tailored to each client. Your basic telephone contact guide should be slightly modified to include the contact's name and specific appointment information.

2. *New-Business Discussion Package.* The preparation of the package includes six elements:

a. *The Question Sheet.* Used during the new-business discussion, this helps guide you through the prospect's potential new-business situation. The questions, of course, are different for each service being offered to the niche.

Figure 9.2 shows a question sheet I use with marketers of professional services who want to talk with me about establishing a marketing function in their firm.

b. *Testimonial Letters.* These are statements of praise and commendation from satisfied clients in the niche. The testimonial, since it is in the client's own words, is more believable and convincing than information you've prepared.

QUESTION SHEET FOR DISCUSSING A FIRM'S READINESS TO ESTABLISH A MARKETING FUNCTION

1. Do you have a recognized marketing "champion" in-house who is willing to and capable of heading the function?
2. Do you have a clearly developed and communicated mission statement or vision for the firm or office?
3. To what extent is marketing responsibility assigned, articulated, understood, and accepted?
4. To what extent is marketing built into your performance and reward systems?
5. What percentage of total gross fees has been invested in marketing over the past three years?
6. What is the current and desired nature and scope of the practice in each functional specialty?
7. How often do partners and others meet to discuss marketing?
8. To what extent is a keep-off-my-turf attitude and behavior alive and well in the firm?

FIGURE 9.2. Readiness Question Sheet

One client of mine periodically asks me to meet with a number of his clients for the purpose of acquiring testimonials. While we have a light lunch in a casual atmosphere, I chat with his client representatives to break the ice and make them comfortable. Then, I ask them to share what it is they like and dislike about the firm and the particular service for which I am developing the testimonial. To minimize notetaking and speed up the process, I get their permission to tape record their remarks.

When a particularly good testimonial statement is made, I replay it. We discuss the statement. Then, I ask for permission to quote the person. When this is given, I suggest that I write a letter on his stationery using the exact words as recorded.

During one 2-hour session, I was able to obtain four good statements and agreements. An important by-product of such a meeting is the number of "I wish that . . ." statements made by the clients that provide insights into additional service opportunities.

c. *PAR Reports.* Each time you assist a client in the targeted niche, you can enhance your promotional system. You can document the problem, approach, and results (PAR) related to each client engagement and then use the capsule summaries to favorably influence prospect clients. Most of the well-known consulting firms and Big Six accounting firms, as well as other successful professionals, employ some version of PAR reports. Many firms use these in their marketing literature, including capability statements, brochures, pamphlets, and proposals.

One large accounting firm described in a marketing brochure how it helped a hospital revive its financial management system.

A county-run hospital was facing great financial hardship; its advisory board had no faith in the accuracy of the hospital's financial statements. Worse, its chief financial officer had just been fired. The accounting firm was called in to provide financial management support for three months. This allowed the hospital staff to hire a permanent chief financial officer during the interim.

Within three weeks, patient registration, patient billing, and accounts receivables were analyzed. A 16-page work plan was developed to reduce the backlog in billing and accounts receivables. The accounting firm then began to study cost management and productivity improvement. With a strong foundation in place, the hospital now has a profitable future and strong management guidelines.

The above minicase was adapted from the marketing literature of an established, successful public accounting firm. Figures 9.3 and 9.4 present variations on how PAR reports can be prepared.

There are many advantages to using PAR reports. As mentioned, they can be used in proposals, brochures, and capability statements. They can also be used in newsletters and as exhibits and charts during new-business discussions, and in training new staff. PAR reports are excellent tools for educating your client-referral sources, including your existing clients and nonclient influentials.

If you have not used PAR reports before, go back through your files for the past two or three years and ask the staff on completed engagements to develop PARs for all situations that support your new targeted-niche focused-marketing efforts. Hereafter, develop a PAR report as each new-client engagement is completed. Your PAR reports should be added to your niche data base.

d. *Approved Client List.* Be certain that you maintain a current list of niche clients you have served who have given you approval to use their name. Experienced marketers do not banter this list around freely, but

---

Problem–Approach–Results (PAR) Report

INDUSTRY: Local Government   OFFICE: Milwaukee

PROBLEM SITUATION:

A class-action suit had been filed against a city for releasing untreated sewage into public waters. The class action was for loss of business and punitive damages. Actual damages claimed were $1 billion from over 100 businesses. The client asked us to provide litigation support to substantiate damage losses.

ABC CO. SOLUTION

ABC would provide the professional and technical assistance needed to substantiate the business losses.

RESULTS EXPERIENCED BY CLIENT

The city provided a draft of the documentation request written by in-house legal counsel. This document was modified by ABC because of its expertise in the business environment. As a result of the documentation request, we were informed that all of the suits were dropped except one, and it was not being pursued at this time.

FIGURE 9.3.   Problem–Approach–Results (PAR) Report (Sample 1)

Problem–Approach–Results (PAR) Report

INDUSTRY: Local Government   OFFICE: San Francisco
                                                Bay Area

PROBLEM SITUATION:

A city budget office had not received recognition from the California Society of Finance Officers regarding its financial reporting practices for 20 years.

ABC CO. SOLUTION

ABC assisted the city in (1) changing accounting principles to conform to GAAP, (2) designing a new financial reporting format, (3) typing the financial reports, and (4) resolving review comments regarding reporting deficiencies.

RESULTS EXPERIENCED BY CLIENT

The city received recognition in the form of an award presented to city officials at the Society's annual convention for outstanding financial reporting.

FIGURE 9.4. Problem–Approach–Results (PAR) Report (Sample 2)

rather keep it in ready reserve and show it only if the hot prospect is skeptical of their experience level, and so forth.

e. *Sample Final Reports.* Use these and other sample deliverables to assemble a sample case of your final products involved in the solution program for the need under discussion.

A financial-planning firm in Virginia Beach prepared a montage of management-letter comments made in client reports using graphics to illustrate ratios, trends, and so on. Actual pages from client letters were photocopied and the name and proprietary information blanked out. When the opportunity arises during a discussion with a prospective client, the financial planner says to the prospect, "You may be interested in the way we tailor our reports to reflect our client's needs and interests." He reports that the prospect is usually impressed with the client-centeredness of the document. Subliminally, the professional is also demonstrating that he can keep a confidence!

f. *Other Firm and Promotional Materials.* Other articles that deal with the need you are promoting should also be acquired.

3. *Proposals.* Accumulate several of your proposals that document your approach to delivering the solution program for the need under discussion.

Some of your previous proposals may be reusable. Simply enter the client-specific information gathered during the new business discussion.

PREPARING YOUR SERVICE-DELIVERY SYSTEM ———

When I worked for Booz, Allen, and Hamilton, an international consulting firm, we would distill our experience at the end of each client engagement to obtain the maximum mileage from what we had already done. Figure 9.5 shows the elements of the service-delivery system we used.

SERVICE-DELIVERY SYSTEM	T	R	R/T
1. Client-specific			
a. Engagement confirmation letter			X
b. Progress reports	X		
c. Final report/other deliverable(s)	X		
d. Client satisfaction review			X
2. Engagement Administration			
a. Work plan			X
b. Budget	X		
c. Activity schedules	X		
d. Quality-control procedures			X
e. Invoice preparation		X	
3. Engagement Wrap-up			
a. PAR produced		X	
b. Press release if significant engagement	X		
c. Recommendations for additional services	X		
d. Engagement distillation			
Inputs to standard practice manuals	X		
Purchase detail: trigger for the purchase, title(s) for best contact	X		
Standard patterns, fee ranges appropriate and expected jargon, buzz words	X		

FIGURE 9.5.   Service-Delivery System

Client-Specific Documents

1. The engagement confirmation letter can be prepared by entering the specifics of the engagement in a letter previously drafted and stored in your word-processing system. Remember to emphasize the solution goal, the importance of the engagement, and the benefits to be derived on completion of the engagement.

2. Progress reports must be customized if you are to exhibit a unique approach for the client. You can develop boilerplate progress reports for the recurring aspects of the engagement, however.

3. The final written report or other deliverable(s) must be tailored. Prepare a final product of the engagement that justifies the budget allocated for it. The meeting during which the final product is delivered becomes the vehicle for discussing additional services.

4. The client satisfaction review, a check on the degree to which the client's needs and expectations were met, too often is bypassed by the busy professional. Referrals come from clients who are aware that their needs *and* expectations were met, and that you took the time to bring your service to their attention so they could "vote" on the degree to which they think you met them.

Engagement Administration

1. Preparing a work plan in advance for this type of engagement enables you to estimate a fee quickly during the proposal phase of the new-business development process.

2. Because you have a range of costs associated with each task, you can quickly estimate the cost required to complete the current engagement. Your goal should be to develop and update a standard work plan and time and dollar budgets for completion of the deliverables for each task involved in the need-solution program you are promoting and delivering.

3. Activity schedules, the daily list of subtasks, must be tailored to meet the circumstances of the specific client situation. Having the work plan spelled out enables you to prepare the activity schedules to reflect the uniqueness of the situation.

4. Quality-control procedures can be standardized for most engagements. Your goal is to modify the standard process to reflect any circumstances in this engagement that need to be monitored to ensure quality.

5. Invoice preparation can be routinized. Some engagements require invoicing early and often, even though the actual hours invested lag the amount being invoiced. I do this for engagements with a lot of out-of-pocket expenses or where the final product is going to be delivered far down the pike.

Engagement Wrap-up

1. Finish each engagement with a PAR. The person managing the engagement should be held responsible for generating the report and reviewing it for accuracy and completeness with the engagement team and *the client*. This is a logical extension of the client-satisfaction review. The PAR can be a powerful relationship builder when reviewed with the client. Seize the opportunity of obtaining a testimonial letter at this time. The PAR can be used to prime the pump, to get the client in a responsive, helpful mood.

2. One of my more alert clients generates a press release along with the PAR if the engagement is deemed to be significant. A variation on the press release would be the development of a joint article describing the engagement routine and the benefits the client obtained.

3. Prepare a discussion guide to suggest recommendations for additional services the client should consider at this time. Tailor it to meet the present buying conditions in this client's situation.

4. Engagement distillation is another task that frequently gets short shrift. My experience at Booz Allen taught me the importance of milking each client engagement for its maximum use in upgrading the niche-information base, increasing the experience, capabilities, and value of the staff, and generating new business. This was all done before the popular and widespread use of computers.

SUMMARY

Yes, advance preparation is necessary before calling on new-business prospects. If you can weather the time needed for preparation, you'll experience the most productive marketing period of your firm's existence.

10

Preparing a Client-Centered Analysis of a Service

The services you offer must be perceived as adding value to the operations of the prospective client. As explained in our book, *Marketing Your Consulting and Professional Services* (New York: John Wiley & Sons, 1990), prospective clients are not really seeking to purchase your services; rather, they are focusing on the end results that you will produce. Prospects purchase the expectation of receiving a more favorable future that contains expected benefits.

A benefit is something prospective clients perceive as valuable in their terms. It always relates to the purchaser's needs and expectations and how they will be met. By using the chart shown in Figure 10.1, you will be able to identify benefits that are important to prospective clients and, more importantly, develop descriptions of the service to which the prospect can relate easily.

Your task is to identify a hot button or a recurring need for which you have a service solution. First, enter the name of the service you want to analyze at the top of the chart. Next, move to "Improve or Enhance" and ask yourself, "in what ways does this service enable the prospective client to improve or enhance something they value?" List your answers in the block. For example, sample answers might be competitive capability, internal operations, and so on. The remaining blocks are filled out in the same fashion. You might complete all blocks.

For: _____

                              (Service)

Your task is to identify client needs and problem situations for which your service is appropriate. For each verb listed below, identify how your service applies. For example, under the word "eliminate" you might put "unnecessary forms and procedures."

Improve or Enhance	Reduce, Relieve, or Eliminate
Protect	Restructure
Identify	Restore or Resolve

FIGURE 10.1.   Client-Centered Service Analysis

When finished, you will have developed a set of potential benefits in terms that can be used to promote your services to prospective clients. The service analysis can also be used in new business discussions, proposal writing, and in training your staff. An example of an analysis using my Market Keys software program is presented in Figure 10.2.

Client-Centered Analysis		
For: Service Provider	Need: Unfocused Marketing Efforts	Service: Marketing Keys

Improve or Enhance	Reduce, Relieve, or Eliminate
Client data base Profitability Telephone techniques Operations Internal control Revenues Capability statement	Misdirected efforts Paperwork Implementation bottlenecks Marketing errors Unnecessary expenditures
Protect	Restructure
Market share Credibility Reputation Profit Liquidity	Proposal development system Quality of reporting system Unprofitable operations
Develop or Install	Restore or Resolve

External reporting
Marketing information
  system
Cost systems
Decision-making model
	Prospecting system
	Resolve backlogs, uncertainty
	Inefficiencies, management
	  anxiety

FIGURE 10.2.   Client-Centered Analysis (Accountant)

As you can quickly gauge, some terms can be applied to more than one category. You may have several terms of your own to add. The headings for each category are not etched in stone, almost any action-related verb will work. The exercise will help you to identify specific need situations of your clients and prospective clients; it will also help you relate and discuss relevant client benefits in their terms provided by your service.

Other key service words and phrases that could be used in filling out the client-centered service analysis are as follows:

Improve

Decision-making capability

Profits

Cash flow position

Through-put time

Internal operations

Public product image

Quality, reliability, effectiveness
of software

Usefulness and relevance of
documentation

Operating efficiency and
productivity

Understanding of costs

Appearance

Information for decisions

Credit rating

User service needs

Long-term outlook

Competitive capabilities
Employee morale and motivation

Employee safety
Market position

Use of EOP equipment

Enhance

Credibility of client's role in
community

User orientation of software

Service to particular groups or
users

Inherent advantages

Shareholder value

Competitive edge

Utilization of equipment and
facilities

Employee morale and motivation
Working capital position

Organizational image

Technical understanding of
problem

Existing strengths and image

Status in peer group

Existing skills

Multinational marketing
opportunities

Reduce

Number of internal and external
conflicts

Costs

Deficits

Downtime

Skills levels requirements

Service delays and unreliability

Excess capacity
Idle equipment time

Peaking of demands

Risk

Waste

Inefficiency

Tax liabilities

Relieve

Conflict

Congestion

Public pressure and adverse
   opinions

Recurring problems

Future cost pressures

Pressure and tension

Organization conflicts
Blockages to staff development

Undue workload

Eliminate

Inefficiencies and waste

Bottlenecks

Misappropriation of resources

Conflict

Constraints

Headache

Adverse criticism

Low cost–benefit ratios

Extra paperwork

Deficits

Cumbersome routines

Pilferage and internal security
   problems

Shortsightedness

Unnecessary cost

Note: Not all blocks need to be or will be completed for a given service.

You now have a set of potential benefits that can accrue to a client. The completed chart can be used in proposal writing and face-to-face discussions with clients and training staff.

11

Developing an Insider's Reputation in the Niche

Developing an insider's reputation in the niche provides at least two major benefits. First, it minimizes the amount of rejection you will experience when marketing to the niche. Second, it helps to stimulate new-business inquiries from those who know and trust you. When members of the niche regard you as one of them, it is a clear sign that you have built the trust and rapport necessary to be prosperous.

The strategy for gaining this reputation is to develop and employ a mix of promotional activities that fit your current, promotional comfort zone. This provides you with maximum leveraging opportunities. Such opportunities emerge by being involved in forums—organizations and groups comprising your targets of opportunity and targets of influence—and publications read by these same targets. As with many of the tasks outlined in Part I, the bulk of the work to develop your reputation takes place before and during new-business discussions with targets. Thereafter, the reputation-building activities are executed on a continuing basis.

DEVELOPING OBJECTIVES

Successful firms have at least four basic objectives in developing an insider's reputation:

1. Becoming an active, accepted, visible, working, and serving member of the infrastructure of the niche or profession.

2. Creating, maintaining, and enhancing a favorable awareness of you, your firm, and its services.

3. Stimulating inquiries from high-potential suspects.

4. Paving the way for gaining acceptance from targets of opportunity when you make need-specific mailings and telephone contacts. (See Chapters 13 and 14 for a discussion on this fourth objective.)

To pursue these objectives, your short-term goal is to create a favorable awareness on the part of those whom you "condition," the A and I in the AIDA process mentioned earlier. Your immediate goal is to obtain an appointment with the most appropriate decision maker in suspect organizations, thus creating an initially qualified prospect, the D step in the AIDA process. (See Chapters 12, 13, and 14.) Your final goal is to convert the prospect into a new client and/or referral source, the last A step in the AIDA process.

Let's look at the first two objectives in detail.

Objective 1

To become an active, accepted, visible, working, and serving member of the niche's infrastructure, you will need to obtain a position of leadership in at least one, and hopefully several, targeted organizations. It is of no value to you or your firm to identify and join organizations that comprise targets of opportunity or targets of influence if they do not meet, get to know, and think favorably of you. Thus, your task is to identify and obtain memberships in viable organizations. You can do this by contacting existing high-potential clients to determine which organizations they belong to and recommend joining. At this point you should ask them to sponsor you for membership.

Next, contact the executive director of each target organization to gain further information. Interview him or her by phone to take an initial "gut check" about the organization. If this step is successful, ask for the name of the head of the new-member committee. These steps will help you decide whether to join.

If you previously looked askance at joining targeted organizations, this is an excellent time to reconsider. Involvement in targeted organizations is an important aspect of your professional and personal development as well as the development of new business for the firm. Moreover, you will be able to gain confidence in your ability to deal with influential people from different environments. Quality involvement with targets enhances the image and reputation of your firm and your profession in general.

Preparing for a position of leadership in a targeted organization requires spending several months as an active participant to gain visibility. When you become better known, and develop some relationships within the organization, you can use these contacts to spur your nomination to key positions and committees. Many organizations experience a shortage of high-caliber leadership; don't hesitate to throw your hat in the ring.

Heading up a visible committee will provide you with personal growth and leadership opportunities, perhaps beyond those you could achieve in your own firm. In addition to rubbing elbows with prospective clients and nonclient influentials, membership and involvement in targeted organizations strengthens relationships with your existing clients.

The role of activities chairperson is a high-leverage position because you're highly visible and have unlimited access to key people in the niche. For example, you could call the mayor's office to see if the mayor would be willing to speak to your group members. If the response is no, you could ask for an alternative official. When calling that person, you are able to say, "Mr. X, while speaking with the office of the mayor, it was mentioned that you are very knowledgeable regarding municipal zoning. Would you be willing to address our group?"

Serving on the new-member committee is also a valuable position, especially if the new members represent potential new clients or nonclient influentials who can lead you to new-business contacts. Other by-products of earning a position of leadership include:

- Organizing and managing volunteers who share your interest builds your communication and leadership skills
- Demonstrating the value of knowing your firm's personnel
- Gaining confidence in your ability to interact with community leaders
- Acquiring fundamental leadership and communication skills that further support your marketing efforts

As you become a more active, accepted, and visible member of the niche, there are other, higher level activities that further the accomplishment of the objective. For example, you can entertain clients and non-client influentials, host social functions, and donate the use of your office for a particular organization's events. You can attend conferences and seminars in the niche and conduct your own on-the-spot surveys.

An accounting firm based in Dayton, Ohio, conducts on-the-spot surveys during the annual business-accounting conference held in its city. Each day during the three-day conference, several junior partners poll the attendees on a topic of the day. The results are posted by 8:00 A.M. the next day and copies on the firm's letterhead are distributed.

A Provo, Utah, law firm provides a small conference room for the bi-weekly use of a subcommittee from the United Fund. The partner in charge of practice development says, "This small gesture brings big names into our firm twice a month."

While so far I have focused primarily on membership in local groups, the same strategies and pay-offs apply on a national level. It never hurts to have a national reputation even though the scope of your marketing efforts is currently confined to your local market. Who are the high rollers of your industry? Who counts nationally and is known by most everyone in the industry? Where and when are the national forums held? It is here that you will have the opportunity to meet the leaders of your industry.

Objective 2

You can undertake numerous activities that will create, maintain, and enhance a favorable awareness of you, your firm, and its services. Your goals in undertaking each of the activities are to generate greater name recognition for you and your firm; to educate your targets regarding what your firm is all about, the types of service solutions it offers, and some of its clients; and to have members of your firm and members of target firms become better acquainted.

Speaking to Targeted Groups

Many opportunities exist for speaking to targeted groups, and you can create additional opportunities. Why is it important to speak to targeted groups, and what are some of the benefits? Probably the biggest barrier faced by many professional-service providers is the fear of speaking to groups. Consequently, you can turn this into an advantage. Speaking to targeted groups provides the following benefits. This activity:

- Enhances your communication skills
- Increases your self-esteem and perceived net worth to others
- Enables you to be perceived as an expert in the field
- Identifies you as an individual and firm to seek for professional assistance
- Offers increased exposure, both internally and externally
- Often generates immediate new contacts

If you refuse a speaking engagement, you have lost an opportunity. The seeds you plant today may take a while to bloom. If nothing is planted now, the results will be as expected.

A number of years ago, one of my objectives was to build a client base in Australia. To build name awareness, I accepted speaking assignments in the United States, Canada, and the Caribbean with accounting, consulting, and management groups that had affiliations in Australia. During my speeches, I indicated my interest in Australia and invited visiting "Aussies" to say hello upon conclusion of my talk. Within two years, I was booking four to six weeks of work "down under" per year.

Many leveraging opportunities develop for the service practitioner who speaks to targeted groups. For example, questions from attendees are invaluable. I have frequently held crackerbarrel sessions after the speeches in which attendees ask me questions on hot button and recurring-need areas that were not addressed during my presentation. The issues raised during these sessions served as automatic guideposts for tailoring and enhancing my promotional and services-delivery systems (Chapter 9).

When speaking to a captive audience—and that is exactly what your listeners will be—you can poll them on various issues. In addition to bolstering your understanding of the niches, you can develop these minipolls as news releases. The information and feedback you gain from one presentation can immediately be used in subsequent presentations, rapidly increasing your reputation in the niche.

As you address the hot buttons and recurring needs of the niche, you further multiply your leveraging opportunities. *Marketing Your Consulting and Professional Services* contains an excellent description of how to identify target groups and secure a speaking engagement using excerpts from tape-recorded speeches. Many groups are in a state of perpetual need when it comes to finding speakers.

The amount of time and money you spend preparing and delivering a speech will depend on your goals and the type of organization you will be addressing. Your goals may be simply to practice your delivery, introduce your firm's new program to handle a need, be invited to speak at this group's national convention, or generate qualified leads for new business.

The time, the setting, and the format of the speech are usually set by the host organization. You will usually be requested to speak for 30 to 45 minutes, with 10 or 15 minutes for a question-and-answer session. The group's meeting planner or program host can fill you in on all the details regarding scheduling information. In any event, be sure to provide quality handouts reprinted on your firm's letterhead so that attendees may readily call you in the future. (See Figure 11.1.)

One technique I have used to good advantage is to ask the meeting planner for a copy of the membership directory and list of attendees. I also hold a business card raffle at the conclusion of my presentation. This has several benefits. First, it holds their attention and it enables me to establish personal contact. The prize I offer is an autographed copy of my first book. The prize you offer can be any book of quality, whether or not you wrote it. The recipient instantly becomes your friend and booster.

Jeff Davidson, CMC
2417 Honeysuckle Road
Chapel Hill, NC 27514
(800) 735-1994

MARKETING PROFESSIONAL SERVICES:
JEFF DAVIDSON'S 11 PRINCIPLES OF SUCCESS

1. Write down what it will look like when you're there.
2. Use available help, but allow that you won't find another you.
3. Have many irons in the fire so that you are not depending on any one client.
4. Delegate often, concentrate on those tasks you must do personally.
5. Carefully research the range of available images, choose one, and then cultivate it.
6. Identify the 10 people who could accelerate your plans and then meet them.
7. Stay flexible, roll with the punches, and maintain perspective.
8. Make your work fun, or get out.
9. Ruthlessly discard what doesn't support your quest.
10. Think like your client.
11. Expect the journey to be hard and expect to make it.

FIGURE 11.1.   Handout Example: Jeff Davidson's Principles of Success

Many novice speakers make the mistake of "cutting and running" after their presentation. Stick around for at least 30 minutes and possibly longer. You should take full advantage of the leveraging opportunities that exist when you have a room full of prospective clients and nonclient influentials. There will always be time to rest later.

If you have arranged to have your presentation taped, then you can listen to it following the presentation and critique yourself. Also, by transcribing the tape, you may find that, with a few hours' work, you have a publishable article in the making. If the tape is a good one, get it duplicated. It will be a valuable tool when contacting other meeting planners and will increase the likelihood of your being invited to speak.

Writing for Targeted Publications

All the publications you identified in establishing your niche data base and library are excellent places to send an article. Given all the information you have assembled about the niche, it would not be difficult to determine several interesting topics. Your article need not be more than 750 to 1,000 words (three or four double-spaced typed pages). As long as you simply address one of the hot buttons or recurring needs of readers, the probability of your article being accepted and published will be high. (See Figure 11.2.)

The editor of an association-based publication is what I call a "mega-leverage" nonclient influential (NCI). The editor of *The Practicing CPA*, Graham Goddard, is a case in point. He and I have worked out an agreement whereby I query him about an article topic I have. If he agrees that it's suitable, I send him a draft. He, in turn, edits, tightens, and, if necessary, restructures it to fit the needs of his readers. Graham's philosophy is, "I know best how to present your material for my readers, so give me your best presentation."

Each time you write an article make at least 20 copies of it. On the average, every 20 times you mail out a manuscript, you will ultimately achieve one acceptance. These days editors do not mind receiving simultaneous submissions—in other words, you are also mailing the same article to other editors. You can also mail two or three different articles to one editor at the same time. These mass-mail techniques increase your chances of getting into print.

If you have never had an article published before, take heart. Each year between 800,000 and 1,000,000 people in the United States alone have their first article published.

WHEN SHOULD YOU CALL A CONSULTANT?

It's a plain matter of fact that there is a problem in the company. The quarterly figures show it, or the employees whisper about it. It may be that sales are eroding, or that employee morale is sinking, but you're not exactly sure why. Is it time to call in a consultant?

For any management consultant to do the job well, he first has to know precisely what the problem is that you want investigated. That may be the hardest part. Before hiring a consultant, a management team may want to sit down together and try to define and write out the problem, its effects on the company, its probable causes (as the management sees them), and possible solutions. In doing so, you may find you don't need a consultant.

Yet, certain problems inherently lend themselves to solution by someone from outside the organization, according to Jeff Davidson, a management consultant in Chapel Hill, NC and co-author of *Marketing Your Consulting and Professional Services* (John Wiley & Sons, New York, NY). Following are a few of his suggestions for determining when you need outside assistance:

- The time and talents are not available in house to solve the problem.
- The true state of affairs can be determined only by the objective examination of someone not involved in daily operations.
- Management has already tried, and failed, to solve the problem.
- Unfamiliarity among management with the specialized field.
- A desire for fresh ideas or new techniques.
- A conflict of views within the organization.

Davidson warns that calling a consultant should not be used as a status symbol, to back up an unpopular decision, or as a political weapon to discredit the views of a rival in the corporation.

For more information, write: *Jeff Davidson, 2417 Honeysuckle Road, Chapel Hill, NC 27514. (800) 735-1994.*

FIGURE 11.2. Short Article Example in Industrial Distribution (Vol. 75, No. 1). Reprinted with permission.

Take advantage of the pyramid process when trying to get published. It is far easier to get a small column published in a newsletter than in a major, nationwide magazine serving your targeted industry. Once you get published in a newsletter, make an attractive reprint, write the words "previous publication" in the corner and include that reprint when sending out other manuscripts to editors of larger publications.

Having been already published in any other publication influences editors favorably and multiplies your chances of getting published again. When you have been published several times, you begin to benefit from the "halo effect." As publishers and editors see that you are well published, they automatically read more closely the manuscripts you send them.

Successful firms, those with well-developed systems for getting new clients, seem to have mastered techniques for getting into print. Review the most prominent magazines in the niche, and you undoubtedly will find published articles authored by partners and principals of well-known firms. It is no coincidence that the firms are well known and their key people are in print. Articles written by your competition are must reading. Study them to see how you might use their articles to help you make *your* selling point to suspects in your niche.

Perhaps the greatest obstacle to getting published is the concern that what you have to say is not important or how you say it is unacceptable. Both of these fears are unfounded. If you have done your homework, you *will know* what topics are of concern to the niche. If you are not particularly adept at writing, have others in the firm edit your manuscript; talk the details into a tape recorder and have a junior associate flesh out the article; or hire a ghost writer.

I learned to use ghost writers years ago after I met a respected contributor to the *Harvard Business Review.* I asked him where he found time to research and write the articles. He looked at me incredulously and stated, "Dick, *no one* who is really keen about using their time well writes their own stuff. I use a freelance writer to interview me for a one-expert story. She quickly prepares an outline and draft that she walks me through. I do the final editing before it's submitted." Good writers are available in every location: ask around and you'll find them.

Be on the lookout constantly for ways to extract articles from reports and written materials you have already developed. Transcribe the tapes from your speaking engagements and half the job is already done. Too many professionals who spent years writing compositions and term papers in school have been traumatized by the harsh remarks and comments of their teachers and professors. The editors who receive your manuscripts are not nearly as critical. If they like your basic theme, often they will help edit your manuscript.

Several fine software programs are available that you can use to improve your writing techniques. These include "Right Writer," a Write Soft™ product by Decisionware, Inc., among others.

At all costs, avoid sitting at your desk staring at a blank screen or a blank page and attempting to write an article from scratch. You probably won't do it. Start by listing everything that comes to mind regarding a problem you can solve, a trend in the niche, or an opportunity to be exploited. Since most professionals view article writing as an elective activity, you should set a personal goal of completing one article every three to six months, or whatever time frame you choose.

Once you have actually written your article and had it published, many more leveraging opportunities become available. As mentioned, the article reprint can be used to influence editors and accelerate the process of getting published in the future. Beyond that, the article reprint can be used as a promotional tool when contacting suspects and prospective clients.

Preparing Articles That Promote Your Firm

An advanced strategy in preparing articles to develop an insider's reputation within the niche is to include you, your firm, and its services as the subject of your article. Done skillfully, the article in print and its reprint are effective ways of establishing a reputation and gaining high visibility. Figure 11.3 provides an example of such an article.

If treated as a major feature story, the article should be loaded with illustrative applications of how your clients are better off since being served by you. This type of article often refers to anonymous clients by location but includes enough information so that readers within the niche think that it was a real case with a real company.

A variation on this theme is to prepare the same type of article but much shorter, focusing on a particular problem or portion of the problem-solving process. The PAR report can be used to get the article underway. The short feature presented in Figure 11.3 accomplishes this task.

There are seven steps in the development of the major feature story we have been discussing:

1. Hook the reader into the case history by quantifying the benefits you helped the client achieve. In other words, at the outset of the article summarize what was accomplished and foreshadow what is to follow.

2. Place the story in perspective by describing the client organization and the management objectives, which could include improving sales, improving the quality of its products or services, reducing costs, or accomplishing some other objectives. It is important to state the client's objectives early in the article so readers with the same objectives will immediately identify with the company and other readers can relate more easily to the story.

3. Describe the problem in sufficient detail, providing such information as the prevailing environment, recent client experiences, current sales

PATH FROM FADS TO PRAGMATISM CIRCLES THE GLOBE

FAD ENTREPRENEUR Fred Reinstein has made a name for himself by developing and marketing such products as the "Wacky Wallwalker," "Sydney Slush Muggs," and E.T. posters.

Now, Reinstein has created a practical household product—and a $50 million-plus business—by attaching a one-piece pressure washer to a garden hose.

Called Turbo-Wash and distributed by Reinstein's Turbo-Tek Enterprises, Culver City, Calif., the product features a black tank that holds eight ounces of soap and a tube with a high-pressure nozzle.

Primarily marketed as a device for washing cars, Turbo-Wash can also be used for houses, boats, and other outdoor surfaces.

Reinstein developed the idea for his product with inventor Rudy Proctor in late 1984. By May 1985—with the help of $2.5 million in start-up funds—he was marketing the product throughout the U.S., Canada, Europe, and Japan.

IN JAPAN ALONE, he expects to sell nearly 1 million units in 1986.

"We've created a market for the product and made it so we can sell it anywhere in the world at the same price," he said.

Although advertising and word-of-mouth sales have helped make Turbo-Wash a worldwide success, Reinstein gives the most credit to his company's in-house distribution and marketing division, Distribution Systems International (DSI). All of his previous successes have been merchandised through DSI.

Reinstein said DSI is comprised of a network of people who have contacts in the business world, including manufacturing agents and merchandise brokers, who have the ability to go into any major market area and move a product.

Reinstein refers to them as "bullets," because their contacts at drugstores, discount houses, and supermarkets allow them to get orders—sometimes on a day's notice.

"DSI HAS MADE Turbo-Wash happen," he said. "They'll tell us what to do to a product to make it fit a particular marketplace. We then do what we have to do to make our product fit their distribution needs."

Reinstein said input from DSI allowed his company to change 15 attributes of the Turbo-Wash package to make the product more marketable in Japan. Another plus for sales was the fact that the Japanese are very clean about themselves, their homes, and cars. Reinstein said many found the Turbo-Wash was an efficient tool for accomplishing those tasks.

"Also in Japan, you have a situation where if a product works, fills a need, and is from the U.S., it becomes a fad," he added. "Everybody's got to have one."

Reinstein called Japan "the simplest and most profitable place in the world to do business. They pay up front, they take the product and market it the way they say they are going to, and it's all done on a handshake."

"WITH OUR Turbo-Wash product, we went into Japan and worked with several distributors on a nonexclusive basis until we found one capable of selling our product." Reinstein's company finally chose a distributor who moved 600,000 units of the American-made product, bringing in gross sales of $10 million.

Reinstein sees a continuing market for the Turbo-Wash—unlike "108-day" fad marketing. He is currently planning the introduction of four accessory Turbo-Wash products this year, including a foam wax, a steel cleaner, a mildew cleaner and retardant, and a whitewall tire cleaner.

"We have developed high-gross products which can easily be merchandised and cross-merchandised," Reinstein said. "The bottom line is giving the consumer value for money."

Despite his success with Turbo-Wash, Reinstein has not totally forsaken his career as a fad merchant. He is currently working on a new novelty product he plans to market sometime next year. The only information he would offer is that "it levitates, and kids are going to love it."

FIGURE 11.3. Sample Promotional Article. Reprinted from *Marketing News*, published by the American Marketing Association, December 19, 1986.

figures, and other pertinent data. Tell whether the problem had been an acute or long-standing need.

4. Present the solution in a before-and-after context, such as, "Previously ABC company's problem was XYZ. They found that by applying DEF they are able to achieve GHI. . . ." Discuss the various alternative solutions that your firm produced and how you and the client arrived at the ultimate solution. Next—and this is vital—relate your service's features and capabilities as the solution. This conveys to the reader that what you have to offer is different from and/or better than anything else available. Frequently, firms develop a system that is named based on their acronym, such as LASER. In this manner, readers know that you have something, but there is just enough mystery to make them want to know more.

5. Relate the benefits resulting from your service solution to the results the client was able to achieve. Use quotes or testimonials from the satisfied client. Also cite any statistical measures that support the improvement, such as sales figures, quality-control data, reduction in costs, and so on.

6. Elaborate on how the service you provided continues to be used to master the problem. Bring the reader up to the present. Offer an extended explanation of what the client is presently experiencing and how your system or solution continues to provide benefits. This portion of your article must leave the reader with a good feeling about the case history and your firm in particular.

7. Wrap up your article with a summary of the case history that restates the key benefits. Make this paragraph short, sweet, and uplifting.

The immediate goal of preparing this type of article is to have the reader clip and save it. Look through your own files and examine the articles you have saved. What was it that attracted you to them? What nugget or information gem satisfied your need to know? Now, the $64,000 question—whom have you contacted as a result of something you have read? Chances are it was the firm that had developed a good understanding of the niche and had an ongoing program for developing an insider's reputation.

Capitalizing on Publicity Opportunities

To enhance your firm's image further, you need to identify and capitalize on other available publicity opportunities, such as writing letters to the editor, opinion pieces, and educational flyers. Letters to the editor, particularly in response to controversial issues, generate more exposure than most people are aware of. The magazines, journals, and newsletters in the niche are read eagerly by its members. A reply to the editor or an editorial opinion that reflects your understanding of the niche has a significant impact.

Don't hesitate to be controversial if you have a strong opinion. Figure 11.4 is a copy of a letter that expressed my opinion about an ad in *Advertising Age* that I thought was inappropriate. Fortunately, editors frequently clamor for these contributions, so the probability of having your views published is much higher than having an article published. Be certain to review recently published letters to determine their form and tone.

An educational flyer or brochure is also a useful tool to generate publicity. Many organizations, such as professional and industrial-trade associations, produce such items. At the individual-firm level, successful firms have produced printed material with titles such as:

"Eight Things to Look for in Selecting an Attorney"

"Five Services Your Accountant Should Be Providing"

"How a Management Consultant Can Help You"

Notice that these are not titles that highlight the specific benefits you can provide. Rather, they provide general education about the profession, with the implication being that since your firm is aware of such criteria, it also meets them. The educational flyer can be converted readily into an article with a minimum of effort.

Most professional-service providers with whom I have worked either don't recognize the value of these additional publicity opportunities or never allocate the time to take advantage of them. Please view these activities with a new perspective. Anything that places you and your firm in the eyes of the target niche, and creates a favorable association with lasting benefits, is worth pursuing. To generate publicity you have to get the wheels in motion. The opportunities always exist. Those who have made the commitment to develop an insider's reputation (which includes some of your competitors) look at generating publicity as an ongoing, long-term activity.

All the things I have discussed so far in this book, including name/ service recognition and exposure, creation of an image, and generation

February 5, 1987

Viewpoint: Letters Editor
ADVERTISING AGE
740 Rush Street
Chicago, IL 60611-2591

The nature and tone of the ad for the Trout & Ries War College Workshop (page 23 in the February 2, 1987 edition) troubles me:

> "The true nature of business is not serving the customer . . . [it's] outwitting, outflanking, outfighting the competition." proclaimed the lead statements.

Terrific, guys!

This warfare mentality, and the related strategy and tactics flowing from it, leads to many of the abuses we decry in the profession.

It's the other way around!

Sensing, serving and satisfying the marketing related needs of the client is the *only true reason* for being in business. Forget this fact and the end is soon in sight.

If competition's your game, learn to compete against the outmoded notions of marketing, service, sensitivity and responsiveness that linger in the minds and emotions of your only competitive resource, your people.

I'd welcome the opportunity to debate these two fine fellows in the forum of informed opinion, *Advertising Age.*

Very truly yours,

Richard A. Connor, Jr.
The Client-Centered™
Marketing Mentor

DC:io
Enclo.

FIGURE 11.4. Sample Letter by Dick Connor

of referrals and contacts, can be achieved as a result of capitalizing on publicity opportunities.

Creating the Publicity Event

The creation of a publicity event, such as a national forum, is another advanced publicity strategy for those practitioners who are ready to make a bold statement about their relationship to the target niche.

Hosting events such as national forums makes some powerful declarations to the niche:

"We own the niche."

"We preempted it."

"We are the educational force."

There are many examples of firms that have achieved this position in their respective niches. As part of your task in developing an insider's understanding of your niche, determine which competitors, if any, are hosting such forums. A careful analysis of the brochure will indicate what is involved in staging such a forum. You could consider hosting a forum on a joint-venture basis with a noncompetitor.

Demonstrating Your "D&B"

Another extremely effective way to create, maintain, and enhance a favorable awareness of your firm is to look for ways to demonstrate for your targets your "D&B" manner, or how your services are *different* and/or *better*. Always keep clients apprised of your industry activities, including speeches given, meetings attended, articles written, and so forth. If your firm monitors legislation, pass such information along to your targets. If you are offering some new type of service, issue a news release to the press and your clients. Many firms regularly invite clients and prospective clients to social and sporting events. Some professionals send postcards to key-client executives when traveling for business or pleasure.

Firms that are particularly adept at maintaining favorable awareness contact clients during periods when they are not actively serving them. In addition, the winners make follow-up calls about completed engagements and, if the situation is appropriate, offer incentives to contract for additional business, such as discounts for immediate follow-on work.

Many firms sponsor get-acquainted tours of their company facilities; others host theme or after-work parties with wine and cheese or hors d'oeuvres.

Occasionally, entice prospective clients with free advice over the phone. At social, civic, and professional functions, introduce clients and nonclient influentials to one another, as well as to key professionals they might be interested in knowing. Those who refer business to you appreciate having business referred to them.

Another excellent strategy for demonstrating your D&B manner is to put together a list of those who serve your targeted industry. This list could be as simple as the names and phone numbers of key sources of information, or as involved as a bound directory.

Objective 3

The probability of stimulating inquiries from high-potential suspects in the niche is greatly enhanced by your insider activities. There are several ways to accomplish this objective:

- Plan and conduct niche-centered seminars
- Further leverage the use of speeches and articles
- Develop and place advertisements
- Contact suspects for research purposes
- Distribute need-driven newsletters based on your research
- Distribute niche-specific brochures

Plan and Conduct Niche-Centered Seminars

In any metropolitan area, you can plan and conduct seminars that will provide educational benefits to attendees, generate revenue, and stimulate inquiries for your services. Such a seminar can be advertised through your newspaper, by using direct-mail lists, or in affiliation with a university or association. If you have sufficient space in your own offices, it can be held there or in meeting rooms at local hotels and conference centers.

Most sessions last either a half or full day, and lunch is included in the seminar fees. Much has been written on the seminar business in previous years. Several excellent texts are available, including:

An Executive's Guide to Meetings, Conferences and Seminars by James Jeffrey and Jefferson D. Bates. New York: McGraw-Hill, 1982.

Speak Like a Pro! by Maggie Bedrosian. New York: John Wiley & Sons, 1987.

How to Conduct Training Seminars by Lawrence Munson. New York: McGraw-Hill, 1984.

How to Create and Market a Successful Seminar or Workshop by Howard L. Shenson. Woodland Hills, CA: Howard L. Shenson Publications, 1985.

Further Leverage Use of Speeches and Articles

As previously discussed, any time you give a speech or get an article published you have created a tool that can be leveraged. One organized practitioner gave 14 speeches in the course of a year, and the speeches were in chronological sequence according to a book outline he had developed. At the end of the year, by transcribing his 14 speeches, he was able to assemble a 265-page rough draft of his book manuscript.

In the next six months, working with one of his junior staff members, he was able to complete a 280-page manuscript, which was ultimately published as a hard-cover book. Had he sat down to write a 280-page manuscript from scratch, the book never would have materialized.

A management consultant in Yorkshire, England, was able to convert an article he had previously published into a position paper that got him invited to the most prestigious symposium in his field. As a result of his presentation at the symposium, he generated five inquiries for his services, three of which led to new clients. He also was invited by two editors to submit articles.

One way to leverage your existing resources is to review your files and determine if any previous articles, client reports, outlines, or memos can be spun off into other articles. Make your speeches, articles, and publicity vehicles count two, three, and four times—never just once. That is the way to keep the inquiry pipeline flowing.

Develop and Place Advertisements

Since the Supreme Court ruled that lawyers may advertise as long as their claims are accurate (the Bates decision, 1982), all professions have gained added flexibility in their ability to attract new clients through advertising.

Having researched the niche thoroughly, the probability that you will be able to develop and place an advertisement that will stimulate inquiries is far greater than that of the average practitioner. Developing and placing advertisements is never easy, and usually costly.

Any successful advertising program must be of an ongoing nature. Just one or two ads do not generate the kind of impact necessary to keep the inquiry pipeline open. If you choose to place advertisements, first identify the key publication(s) read by the niche. Then, carefully examine several issues of the publication, noting who advertises, what they offer, and the image they convey.

Next, write to the advertising department of the publication and ask for the rate card, a breakdown of the various prices the publication charges to run an advertisement. Normally, you receive substantial discounts by running an ad several times. To determine whether to place an ad, check the cost per thousand—the cost of reaching 1,000 members of your targeted niche. If you are advertising in a national publication to reach local targets, the cost per thousand may be quite high. Depending on the target group, you may not have a choice; the key publications of the industry could well be national or international in scope. Nevertheless, the cost per thousand is a useful measure of the strength of your advertising dollars.

Contact Suspects for Research Purposes

You can stimulate inquiries by contacting suspects in the niche for research purposes. Those firms that are able to dominate the niche do so in part because they are continuously publishing the results of surveys and inquiries regarding trends, hot buttons, and developments within the niche.

The research conducted can be gathered by mail or phone surveys. Mail surveys have a far lower rate of response than phone surveys but enable you to reach many more targets with far less effort. Moreover, those who don't respond still have received the message that you are conducting research. Calls directly to targets require considerable effort on your part but are likely to yield far more information about the suspect and often result in inquiries. A consultant to the architect-engineering profession uses the research contacts to good advantage. First, he keeps his name in front of the key players in the niche. The calls keep his finger on the pulse of the niche and alert him to immediate and emerging needs. Sometimes he obtains work that he otherwise would not have been considered for. Today, out of mind equals out of pocket.

Distribute Niche-Centered Newsletters

Seven years ago, while preparing *Marketing Your Consulting and Professional Services,* we decided not to include newsletters because the task of developing them, on even a quarterly basis, was seen as prohibitive. With the advent of desktop publishing and other available supporting software, the strategy of offering a quarterly or even monthly newsletter becomes much more viable.

If done properly, a newsletter can be an effective tool for establishing an insider's reputation. If not done properly, you're better off not issuing a newsletter because it will detract from your image. The key to producing and distributing an effective newsletter that stimulates inquiries is to stay on target. The size of the newsletter is relatively unimportant; it can have 1 page or as many as 8 to 12. The information must reflect your insider's understanding of the niche, the recurring needs, the hot buttons, and in general the issues that are on the minds of your targets.

A frequent mistake in distributing a newsletter is reiterating or encapsulating information published by other sources. This can be marginally effective, but fails to demonstrate your insider's understanding of the niche and the different and better aspects of your service(s). It is far better to use your newsletter to convey the results of your own research. Showcasing your own findings effectively conveys your deep understanding and separates you from the competition.

Distribute Niche-Specific Brochures

Your understanding of the niche and the research you have been compiling will also enable you to prepare a brochure that can stimulate inquiries. Refer back to the exercises in Chapter 7 on critical success factors and the client-centered analysis for the terminology and tools to prepare a brochure that hits home the moment it gets into the hands of the target.

The items about your firm that must be contained in the brochure include how long you have been in business, your size and location, and the qualifications of your staff. It is helpful to include information on the quality of your service(s) and your firm's reputation. Most important to the target is information on others who have used your services, and your firm's ability to sense, serve, and satisfy the needs of the niche. Quotes or endorsements from satisfied clients are always helpful. Figure 11.5 depicts a simple, three-panel brochure that typifies what I've been talking about.

Reality versus theory

Business profit depends on a commitment to long term problem solving.

W. L. Nikel and Associates, Management Consultants

Executives attending seminars that we conduct at the American Management Association mention these critical problems in managing:

- Inflation, productivity and governmental pressures.

- Rapid changes in technology and competition; new competitors.

- Too little time to plan because of "alligators."

- Not easy to stay current with latest developments in management.

- Difficulty getting functional units to really work together.

- Too little time to evaluate competitive strengths and weaknesses in current and potential markets.

- Limited rewards for long term profit planning.

FIGURE 11.5. Three-panel brochure. Reprinted by permission of W. L. Nikel and Associates.

William L. Nikel
President

W. L. Nikel and Associates
Management Consultants
28 Harper Terrace
Cedar Grove, New Jersey 07009-2223
201-857-3055

Professional experience:

Mr. Nikel has over 25 years of proven consulting and management experience in consumer and industrial products and markets, retailing and wholesaling. He leads executive seminars and courses with the American Management Association on a wide range of subjects and is a guest lecturer at Columbia University Graduate School.

His consumer marketing experience includes management and internal consulting at Exxon Enterprises and J.C. Penney Company. At Exxon Enterprises he managed dealer and electric utility sales, advertising and marketing programs. At Penney he developed and managed diversification programs and consulted on store and catalog operations, strategic plans, and consumer financial services.

Industrial marketing experience includes Lukens Steel Company and the Noland Company, a Southeastern wholesaler of plumbing, heating, electrical and industrial products. His principal assignments were strategic planning, diversification, marketing research and consulting for key customers.

FIGURE 11.5. Continued

Mr. Nikel received an M.B.A. in Marketing from the Wharton School of the University of Pennsylvania and a B.A. in Economics from Ursinus College. After graduating from the U. S. Naval Intelligence School he served as a Lieutenant (j.g.) during the Korean War.

He is a member of the Association of Management Consultants, Wharton Business School Club of New York, American Marketing Association, New York Organization Development Network and Appalachian Mountain Club. He is a former director of the Virginia Peninsula Homebuilders Association.

Mr. Nikel and his family have lived in Upper Montclair for many years and are active in church and civic affairs. He is an avid jogger, hiker and cross country skier.

Our approach as consultants is to:

Utilize experience from marketing, physical distribution, financial analysis, human resource development and other fields to provide a multi-discipline capability.

Improve cost-effectiveness of client assignments by:

- Clearly defining the opportunity or problem before moving out of the initial phase.
- Summarizing the situation in a written description, to sharpen the focus.
- Moving more quickly to solutions and into implementation.

Use a proven, systematic method to review long range market and competitive trends.

Provide a clear outline of work to be done, with a completion schedule and cost estimate.

Meet scheduled progress reports and completion dates.

We do not accept an assignment unless we believe that the value created by our services will be far greater than the cost to our client.

FIGURE 11.5. Continued

Key areas of management consulting experience:

Our experience and accomplishments include these representative areas:

Market Penetration. Developed a market measurement system that triggered a multimillion dollar expansion and acquisition program by a leading wholesaler.

Profit Improvement. Reduced expense by $600,000 annually through a comprehensive program to control catalog merchandise returns. Program included management information systems, transportation and warehousing, store/catalog operations, merchandise planning and customer service.

Diversification. Saved over $10 million by substantially reducing scope of diversification into building materials. Our evaluation pinpointed much higher distribution costs than projected by our client.

National Advertising and Merchandising. Developed a successful marketing planning and implementation system for 20 nationally advertised consumer product lines.

New Products. Saved an estimated $1.3 million through a conclusive market test that changed market development strategy because of consumer price resistance.

Client evaluations:

Clients' comments about our assignments include:

"Gave us more than we expected."

"Assignments demanded broad experience and skills."

"Excellent reasoning, analysis, planning, writing and oral presentations."

"Contribution was substantial, innovative and thoroughly professional."

"Excellent leadership in developing teams of executives."

References:

Client references can be readily provided.

FIGURE 11.5   Continued

*Reasons for choosing
W. L. Nikel and Associates:*

Our clients include retailers, banking and insurance,
hospitals, manufacturers of home furnishings, sporting goods, heating and electrical equipment, contractors, professional organizations and investor-owned
utilities.

We have found that our clients often choose us for one
or more of these reasons:

Expertise in key businesses. This enables us to be
useful to our clients immediately in specific problem
areas.

Breadth and perspective. A broad perspective
gained from many functional areas avoids overlooking less obvious but important aspects of client opportunities and problems.

**Experience in both planning and implementa-
tion.** This facilitates practical, cost-effective solutions and programs geared to capabilities of an organization and its people.

**Track record in developing teams of execu-
tives.** Our experience with many types and sizes of
organizations permits us to develop and improve
teamwork in key areas.

FIGURE 11.5 Continued

Management consulting services:

- Marketing and strategic planning
- Positioning
- Pricing
- Industry surveys and competitive analyses
- Marketing research
- Diversification
- Marketing audits
- Sales forecasting and financial analysis
- Marketing information and control systems
- Acquisition and divestiture studies
- Sales and merchandising management
- Distribution strategies
- Customer service
- Coordination of marketing and
    physical distribution
- Advertising and sales promotion
- Public relations
- Management development and training

W. L. Nikel and Associates
Management Consultants
28 Harper Terrace
Cedar Grove, New Jersey 07009-2223
201-857-3055

FIGURE 11.5. Continued

A POSITIONING CASE HISTORY

Here is a look at how one accounting firm in Chicago positioned itself to gain an insider's reputation in its chosen niche. The firm decided to develop a series of niche "white papers" aimed specifically at the target market, which would immediately be recognized by the recipient as important information. To produce these papers, the firm hired a market researcher who would periodically gauge the current concerns of trade associations, periodicals, the firm's existing clients, some of its prospects, and other niche influentials. The researcher was specifically instructed to distinguish the very serious issues from the less serious so the papers could attract high-potential prospects with information specifically aimed at their needs.

Numerous steps were taken to carry out the strategy. It was determined that the white papers would be distributed on a monthly basis. Some of them provided how-to information, such as how to avoid problems. Other issues focused on new developments and trends and conveyed the message that the accounting firm understood these changes through its long tradition of being a leader in the field, its current research, and its ongoing surveys.

As the papers evolved, other features were added, such as checklists based on case histories. A perforated reply card for requesting more information was also added, as was a personal cover letter that introduced the philosophy and purpose of the paper. The letter emphasized that this communication was a public service on the part of the firm to maintain and upgrade the standards and sources of information available.

The implied message was that the accounting firm was very concerned with the standards and procedures of firms within the industry and wanted to help them stay up to date by providing current information. Contributory articles by industry leaders, which often focused on an explanation of their positions in dealing with previous problems, were included.

After several months, the paper evolved into a newsletter format. A professional writer/editor was hired to assist the marketing researcher in developing the end product. Each issue of the newsletter was numbered, but not dated, so that issues could be sent to prospects on an individual basis. The publication had a sturdy, substantial, elegant look.

Though the newsletter was only one page, front and back, the back was reserved for a brief description of corporate philosophy, more information, solutions to the problems discussed on the front side, and the firm's return address. Overall, the back page maintained a nonselling stance. The newsletter was positioned as an information service.

For nonclients who had already received three or four mailings, a decision was made to enclose a request card for the firm's other how-to lists, evaluation tools, and mini-manuals. This strategy was undertaken in the realization that the targets wanted to receive this information but were highly selective in reading advertising material.

As more issues were developed, requests from other firms in the niche, but not on the mailing list, started to come in. Using its computerized database system, the accounting firm was able to keep track of which publication each recipient had received and bring them along in measured sequence. All envelopes were typed, rather than labeled, so that no one felt as if they were receiving a mass mailing. In addition, mail was stamped and sent first class rather than by postage meter or bulk mail.

The newsletters were distributed with the goal of creating the need for interaction—something that could not have been achieved if the recipients thought they were receiving an item from another direct-mail campaign by a company that wanted to sell them something. As a follow-up to this story, the firm is still employing these techniques and is generating a healthy percentage of inquiries as a result.

OTHER INSIDER STRATEGIES

A Lake Worth, Florida, firm offering tax preparation assistance decided to reach key decision makers in the niche by joining the most prominent trade association. By establishing a high degree of trust on an interpersonal basis, the firm was able to increase sales and reduce promotion costs.

Several members of the firm joined the association, and they examined the various committees of the association to see which firm members could participate as leaders. Having joined the appropriate committees, the firm's members immediately offered to do research for the committee or help prepare for upcoming events. During this time, they were able to become familiar with the terminology and language used by the target niche. They also were able to gain a fair understanding of the needs of the decision makers in the niche. In this way they became sensitive to the changes taking place sooner than did most of their competitors.

Another firm that provided communications and public-relations services developed joint-venture programs with other types of noncompeting professionals. This enabled them to reduce research costs while maintaining an insider's understanding of their niche. On a periodic basis, staff members from the various firms who were responsible for maintaining the library and niche data base met and traded target lists, loaned key publications, and created reciprocal referral systems. In the course of 18 months, the initiating firm was able to substantially accelerate its understanding of, and reputation in, targeted niches.

A professional training specialist in Canberra, Australia, compiled a press kit consisting of her quarterly newsletter, some article reprints, her firm's brochures, and some endorsement letters from satisfied clients. She then identified five journalists who covered her beat. Every couple of months she sent them a cover letter explaining the latest trends in training and development and her specific experiences. After the first three mailings, a period of about nine months, no one had called. Undaunted, she mailed the next round and about a week later received a call from an international training magazine. This magazine was not on her list to receive her publicity kit. However, it turned out that one of the journalists to whom she had been sending her kit had attended a conference in Sydney with the editor of the training publication. The journalist was asked if he had ever encountered someone who had vast experience using a certain kind of training technique, and he offered her name to the editor. As a result, the trainer was featured in this prominent international industry publication and was able to leverage reprints of that article by favorably influencing a much greater percentage of her prospects and suspects.

MAINTAINING AN INSIDER'S REPUTATION

Figure 11.6 is a composite of what the most progressive, successful professionals do to maintain an insider's reputation in their targeted niche. Relax when reading this list; few firms are able to engage in all the activities listed.

All the suggestions and strategies outlined have required that you work in the trenches. You have had to do much analysis and planning and perhaps rethink some of your basic business objectives. The rest of the chapters in the book flow from what you have learned in Chapters 1 through 11.

MAINTAINING AN INSIDER'S REPUTATION

- ☐ Make speeches
- ☐ Host seminars
- ☐ Publish articles
- ☐ Write brochures
- ☐ Develop newsletters
- ☐ Join trade associations
- ☐ Conduct industry surveys
- ☐ Participate in radio interviews
- ☐ Develop industry manuals
- ☐ Obtain leadership positions in trade organizations
- ☐ Attend industry seminars
- ☐ Develop technological expertise
- ☐ Deliver quality and timely services
- ☐ Maintain contacts with key industry influentials
- ☐ Gain and maintain good name awareness in the industry
- ☐ Maintain a professional appearance
- ☐ Identify recurring needs and hot buttons
- ☐ Build credibility with other service providers in the industry
- ☐ Cultivate a "D&B" manner

FIGURE 11.6. Maintaining an Insider's Reputation

Once you have assembled the information you need, getting new clients will become much easier. You will be able to speak their language and make your firm attractive to targets of opportunity and influence.

The chapters that follow are a bit shorter and represent easier reading and implementation. We begin with Part II: "Getting and Preparing for Appointments with Prospective Clients."

Getting and Preparing for Appointments with Prospective Clients

12

Selecting a Need and the Right Suspects to Contact

Having spent considerable time researching the niche and increasing your insider's understanding, now it's time to obtain appointments with high-potential prospective clients. This involves the following five steps:

1. *Selecting the Need to Be Promoted*. Your goal is to select a current hot button or important recurring need that your targeted suspects have and want solved at this time.

2. *Developing a Preliminary Need Scenario*. Your goal is to visualize the probable need situation of the individuals in the suspect organizations to whom you will send your initial contact package. You want to get in sync quickly with the players in these organizations.

3. *Selecting Suspect Organizations in your Niche for Contact*. Your goal is to target high-potential suspect organizations to contact during this specific promotional-prospecting campaign.

4. *Developing Your Initial-Contact Mailing Package*. This package consists of a "grabber" cover letter and a need-specific enclosure. Your goal is to find an enclosure that makes your selling point and grabs the contact's attention.

5. *Making Telephone Calls to Obtain an Appointment*. Your goal is to obtain an appointment with a member of the decision-making group in the targeted organization to discuss the specifics of their need situation and suggest how you can solve it.

This chapter will discuss the first three steps. Chapter 13 will discuss step 4, and chapter 14 will discuss step 5.

SELECTING THE NEED TO BE PROMOTED

As a general principle, the stronger the need, the easier it is to obtain appointments with the decision maker in the targeted organization. If you offer training programs and workshops on reducing sexual harassment in the workplace and the organizations you call on have been hit by major negative publicity, your chances of being heard have to be good. Remember, however, to focus on a need and the benefits you can provide, rather than to pitch your product or the service you offer. This is one of the best ways to use the Platinum Rule mentioned in Chapter 3.

Find a need that is urgent and important enough to the suspect organization's contact so that he will meet with you. A problem well defined is half solved. This goes doubly for the notion of solving a need. Up to now, I've been using the term *need* generically to describe a situation faced by a targeted suspect. Let's take a few minutes to explore this topic.

1. *Negative Need Situations.* In three need situations, unwanted, negative conditions are present or probable. First, there may be a *deficiency* (yellow-red alerts discussed later in this chapter) in some existing performance factor. Second, there is the *threat* of some unwanted condition occurring; and finally, there is a *decision* to be made that involves uncertainty on the part of the contact.

2. *Positive Need Situations.* There are two positive need situations. One occurs when some positive, desired/required condition is *lacking*. The other occurs when some positive condition (performance, people, system, etc.) exists but is in *short supply.*

3. *Short-Term Task Situations.* These situations require your type of skills, knowledge, and technology. In today's economy, task-driven engagements are increasing as organizations seek to streamline their operations.

Remember, the purpose of all this analysis is to enable you to talk "suspect talk" when you prepare your initial contact package (Chapter 13) and make your telephone contact (Chapter 14). If you think as they do, use their vocabulary, and promise benefits, you can quickly establish yourself as someone who is worth meeting.

A deficiency refers to subpar performance of an existing business function or process; that is, sales are off, scrap is up, morale is poor, or costs are above budget. Each of these unwanted conditions is an enemy of effective organizational management and requires analysis. You know how to do this; and, more importantly, you know how to correct the cause of this deficiency and bring performance up to the desired/required levels. The best deficiency has two essential aspects. First, it will occur in the performance of one of the critical success factors you identified while you were developing your insider's understanding of the niche. In addition, the subpar performance will be approaching the "red-alert" zone of what I call the "yellow-red alert" model.

Yellow-Red Alert

The yellow-red alert is a simple and powerful tool. I learned about it years ago when I was with Booz, Allen, & Hamilton.

Suppose that inventory turnover is an important success factor for suspect organizations in your niche and that your expertise enables you to prevent and solve such problems. Further, assume that nine turns a year for product X is the industry standard. You know this because you did your homework during the industry-understanding phase. (See Figure 12.1.)

You also know from discussing inventory with your key clients that a turnover of between nine and eight for product X is in their tolerance zone. Performance in this range is expected and does not alarm them. Promoting your need-solution program to suspects who are in this operating condition usually generates little interest on their part. However, if your initial contact package is well prepared, they may file it in their "consultants" file.

The next zone, eight to seven turns, is the yellow-alert zone. Management wants to prevent the now subpar performance from falling below seven into the red-alert zone, "where it hits the fan." Promoting your need-solution program to suspect organizations in the yellow-alert zone frequently generates a high degree of interest and acceptance by the executive responsible for managing inventory.

When contact persons are operating in the red-alert zone, they may be more resistant to outside assistance at first, because they are being bombarded from within by superiors and others who have a stake in the operation.

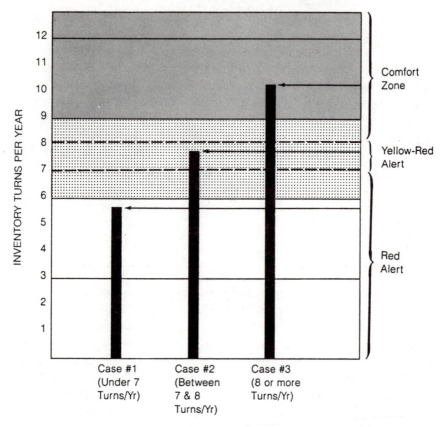

FIGURE 12.1. Comfort Zone Related to Inventory Turnover

Your goal for the deficiency-need situation is to design a solution program to bring the present performance up to the desired/required level of performance specified by the buyer.

A *threat* situation refers to one in which an unwanted occurrence is probable. Your solution should prevent the unwanted condition from occurring or, if it occurs, minimize the adverse effects.

A *decision* situation is one in which the contact is faced with a choice and requires your expertise to make the right one. Alternative courses of action must first be identified and evaluated; then the optimal alternative must be selected and implemented. Your solution should remove the uncertainty in the situation by assisting the contact in selecting and implementing a cost-effective course of action.

Positive Need Situations ————————————————

A *lack* situation is one in which a desired/required positive performance factor, such as a niche data base, compensation plan, and so on, is needed, and you can provide or develop the factor. Your solution should develop and install a new performance factor that produces the desired/required results.

A *short supply* situation is one in which some level of positive performance can be enhanced. For example, some service firms are lucky to have a "rainmaker"—business developer—on board, but have no one to back him or her up.

Short-Term Task Situation ————————————————

In today's economy, many organizations are tightening corporate belts and downsizing the staff by identifying and eliminating nonessential employees. This is creating a huge market for task-driven engagements that require your skills and knowledge.

RECOGNIZING NEEDS ————————————————

Your solution should produce the results sought on a cost-effective basis for the contact and your firm. What are the basic criteria indicating that a need is present and worthy of your pursuit? First, the contact person in the suspect organization must recognize the need as being important enough to discuss at this time. If swift resolution is seen as mandatory or required, so much the better.

On your end, the need is something that you can fill in "D&B" fashion; you have the resources to handle it and you have evidence of past accomplishments, including PAR reports and testimonials. It is also important that you *want* to do this type of work on a constant basis if necessary.

Another key criterion is to make sure the competition is not excessive and that they haven't devised the stake through the heart that kills the vampire (need) once and for all. Finally, the need should be one from which you can make a reasonable profit.

There are several *benefits* in identifying hot button or recurring needs that you will use when making initial contact with suspects. You will be able to increase the probability of obtaining an appointment, thus minimizing the number of false starts. Nothing is more time consuming and mentally or emotionally draining than calling on nonreceptive, uninterested targets. In fact, calling on such targets will cause you to doubt the validity and appropriateness of your services.

Another important benefit is that you maintain and build your self-esteem by minimizing the probability of rejections. Busy decision makers are always interested in discussing a need situation, especially if they think they can obtain some free information enabling them to do the job themselves. When calling them to discuss a hot button, you have already answered the foremost question in their minds, "What can I gain from talking to you?"

By focusing on a specific hot button or recurring need of qualified suspects, you can save time and energy because you will narrow the number of contacts. Thus, those who respond to the hot button you have addressed are much more likely to become your clients. Finally, you continue to build and enhance your insider's reputation with the targeted niche. In essence, you generate marketing points for your firm, even when you perceive that not much has happened.

Hot Button Identification 101

If you have already prepared step 1, refer to your main menu of needs in the backup folder for the niche. (Refer back to the passage on menu of needs in Chapter 7.)

Next, talk with existing clients in the niche. Your mission is to convince them that you have a genuine interest in their well-being and in improving the value of your services to them. You can do this by simply asking them about their operations. Ask nondirective, open-ended questions about specific critical success factors, such as:

"What do you have to concentrate on to ensure survival and profitability?"

"What is the status of the XYZ problem?" (If you know about a problem or objective that is probably important throughout the niche.)

"Where are you focusing your attention during the next six to nine months?"

Their answers will give you keen insights into your potential clients' problems, as well as opportunities to improve their situations.

If you are serving large clients, visit the department heads and ask the same questions. Meanwhile, observe the operations, housekeeping, work flow, and so on. Look out for positive exceptions to industry standards. Also, look for opportunities to review client reports, which may provide clues to the needs of others in the niche.

To stay abreast of industry developments, you must also be able to identify hot buttons. By now, this should be old hat to you. Review key industry publications. Your goal in monitoring publications read by your best clients and your targeted suspects is to obtain appointments by determining their current hot button needs. Review specific industry and professional journals, as well as general business and local business publications.

Reading general business publications, such as *Business Week, Forbes, Fortune,* and *Barron's,* for example, provides you with information about larger trends, such as restructuring, downsizing, foreign competition, and so on. In the case of downsizing, look for ripple effects among suppliers to the major players in the industry. Review help-wanted ads to identify high-growth organizations and those having trouble retaining good employees.

Some professional service firms hire part-time graduate students to review recent literature on the industry. Such reviews help identify recurring problems, people on the move, and key conferences. Monitoring the topics for yearly conferences can provide you with excellent insights on the needs of the niche. Because conference topics and speakers must be selected well in advance, they will be of highest priority to the niche.

- Another good source of industry needs are industry studies published by research organizations such as Frost & Sullivan and Standard & Poor's. While they may cost from $300 to $1,500, the information can be quite useful.

- Check the president's message in the annual reports of larger companies within the niche. These often provide useful insights into the trends and major problems of the niche players. When reading an annual report, look for accounting notes on significant financial changes; they could be clues to the gems that you will use in finding needs to penetrate the niche.

- "Red herring" prospectuses for firms wanting to go public must discuss the risk areas, which translates into opportunity areas for the alert professional. After reading a couple of prospectuses and seeing the same risk areas identified, you will know that you have a hot one.

Tap the Industry Influentials —————————————————————————————

Those who serve, influence, and regulate members of the niche are well positioned to identify hot industry topics and those destined to become hot. Industry influentials can be identified through your A clients, publications, directories, and targeted mailing lists.

Another essential task is to meet the industry influentials and establish relationships with them. This will allow you to find today's hot buttons as well as tomorrow's. There are several basic ways to meet the industry influentials:

1. Call them directly and identify a topic of direct interest to them. Later in the conversation, you can bridge to your interests. You don't get a second chance to make a favorable first impression. Consequently, your call must have something in it for *them*. Remember the Platinum Rule: Do unto others as they would have you do unto them.

2. Attend meetings, conventions, trade shows, civic, charitable, and social functions at which industry influentials will be present. Before attending the event, you will need to identify a topic of direct interest to them.

3. Arrange to meet influentials at lunch using a mutual third party. This form of leveraging your existing relationships can easily double or even triple the number of industry influentials you personally contact.

4. Establish a dialogue with influentials by writing. Send something of interest to them. Even if you get no response following several letters, you still will be in an improved position to set up a face-to-face encounter once you're ready to do so.

5. Schedule your own event that industry influentials would eagerly attend. For example, if you offer brokerage services in the financial district of your town, a well-catered open house could be appealing to bankers and financial planners in surrounding office buildings.

In the months and years that follow, take the necessary time to maintain your relationships with industry influentials by calling them and sending them notes ("I have been thinking of you") and "alert information"—anything you come across that would interest them. This is a small favor that reaps large rewards. People genuinely appreciate receiving items or interesting clippings, which they may have otherwise missed.

DEVELOPING A PRELIMINARY NEED SCENARIO

By now you have identified at least one hot button or recurring need in your preparation for meeting with prospective clients. The purpose of preparing a need scenario (see Figure 12.2) is to get in sync with the target. You want to view the need situation from the contact's vantage point.

Using an example from my practice, let's look at each item on the Need Scenario worksheet.

The Need

State this as simply and powerfully as you can, using the suspect's vocabulary where appropriate. For example: "Improve the new client-getting capability of PITs (partners in training) in local CPA firms in the United States."

Direct Responsibility

Who in the targeted suspect organization is directly responsible for the need you are able to fill? In my example, the managing partner of the local firm is typically responsible for the development of tomorrow's new partners. But not always. Some of the more aggressive local firms now have marketing people responsible for ensuring that the development occurs. This is where your insider understanding pays dividends.

Others Involved

Who else in the suspect organization is involved or concerned and in what ways? Who wants my need solution to succeed? Why? Who will be affected by the solution and in what ways?

Negative Unfulfilled Consequences

What costs and risks are associated with the need? What additional costs and negative consequences are likely to be incurred if the need is not met at this time? What conclusions can you draw as to the nature of the negative consequences—not serious, acceptable risk, serious, critical, unacceptable risk, and so on?

In my example, the costs are both out-of-pocket and opportunity costs. Too often PITs are told to go out and get new clients without being

NEED SCENARIO

The need I will fill is _____

_____.

The need is the *direct* responsibility of _____
Title

_____

Others who are involved in the need are:

Who/title	Their stake in it
1. _____	_____
2. _____	_____
3. _____	_____

The *negative* consequences to the contact of not handling the need include

_____

_____

The *positive* consequences of handling the need include _____

_____

_____

The *solution* goal for this need is _____
Improve

_____

record, protect, build, regain, etc. _____

_____

Evidence I can cite includes _____

_____

_____

FIGURE 12.2. Need Scenario

shown how to go about it. The result is that too many PITs, if they engage in any new-client development at all, invest too much in entertaining without capitalizing on their relationships with influentials in targeted niches. A serious consequence of the lack of PIT training is the risk of turning them off completely regarding marketing.

Positive Consequences

What benefits are likely to accrue if the need solution is installed at this time?

- Will new revenue be generated?
- Will existing revenue be protected?
- What costs will be reduced or eliminated?
- What efficiencies will be introduced?
- Will morale be improved? If so, by how much?

PITs trained in the how-to of client-centered marketing recognize that new-client development is largely the result of leveraging their relationships, problem-solving experience, and insider understanding. Once the PITs are enthusiastic and confident, they know what they must do to obtain new clients.

The Goal

State the goal for the need situation here. If you have done a good job defining the need, the goal will often be a reiteration of the need statement. Frequently, the goal statement changes due to the in-depth analysis required to complete the scenario.

You have taken a giant step closer to being in sync with the targeted suspect organizations. The insights gained through completing the Need Scenario will be useful as you develop your initial-contact package, the subject of the next chapter.

SELECTING SUSPECT ORGANIZATIONS

Now that Steps 1 and 2 are complete, it is time to determine targets for the upcoming contact program. If you delight in keeping your data base current, you need to go no further, simply search your mailing criteria. You may also come across new lists or have traded data bases with another professional. Finally, there will always be newcomers to the niche no matter how much you are on top of things.

Your goal is to select only those organizations and individuals that:

- Are most likely to have the need you are promoting.
- Want the need to be solved at this time.
- Have the necessary funds.

For example, the buying cycle for my CPA suspects does not run between January and April. Because that's their busy season, most communications to them would be shelved. Therefore, likely targets during that period are my other two primary niches—consultants and lawyers—who are not affected by the calendar as much.

Having the funds available implies that these funds will be invested in your type of solution. I long ago quit trying to market to one niche on the more technical side of the professions. This group of firms is experiencing rapid consolidation and many business failures because they are resistant to paying my daily rates, which are about 40 percent higher than theirs. I do accept new work from the better firms that contact me if they are willing to do what I recommend.

In your own practice, consider that there will always be some niches where you know it will not make sense to expend any marketing effort. If some forward-thinking companies in the niche contact you, you certainly need not turn them away. You passively accept good opportunities from the niche, while proactively seeking/making opportunities in the niches you've targeted.

THE DECISION-MAKING UNIT

Typically, firms in your target niche operate in ways that can be identified and charted. By reviewing the history of your most recent engagements with key clients, you can begin to recognize patterns of decision making on a new purchase, responsible persons and their titles, and specific processes. Review your Preferred Prospective Client Profile again (Chapter 5) for the clues provided there.

A useful concept in understanding the way target firms are likely to respond to you is to isolate their decision-making unit (DMU). A DMU may contain the following participants:

1. *The Initiator.* This is a person who tends to look outside the firm for your type of services in a need situation. In addition to being a leading-edge thinker, this person is often the one who suggests outside help, thus becoming the internal champion for your solution.

2. *The Influencer.* Influencers can be both positive and negative individuals; they are expected to give a yea or nay to the idea of retaining outside services. Since these individuals significantly affect the purchaser's decision, your message to each must be individually tailored and delivered.

3. *The Decision Maker.* This is the individual(s) who actually makes the decision whether or not to proceed with a purchase.

4. *The Coordinator or Purchaser.* This individual may not make the decision or be a primary influencer, but will be involved in the purchase, use, and application processes. Often, this person is charged with liaison responsibility with the outside service organization.

5. *The User.* This (these) individual(s) will be directly or indirectly, intentionally or unintentionally affected by the results of the services you provide.

If you have done your homework and have an insider's understanding of the niche, the process of preparing and securing appointments will no longer be the dreaded task it used to be. You are virtually paving the way for discussions with people who will want to meet with you, and you should be looking forward to those discussions.

In the next chapter, we will integrate what we have learned so far to develop and manage an effective initial-contact program.

13

Developing and Managing Your Initial-Contact Program

Your initial-contact program contains two components: the package to be sent to suspect organizations, and the follow-up telephone call. In this chapter, we will discuss the elements of the initial mailing program.

DEVELOPING THE INITIAL-CONTACT MAILING PACKAGE

Your ability to get clients is directly related to how well you execute your initial-contact mailing program. If you have chosen your targets appropriately, you will be triggering basic buying motives of several recipients.

Buying motives refers to the inner state of your mailing recipients. Buying motives are the intellectual and emotional factors that may prompt your recipients to contact you or be receptive to your subsequent telephone call.

Managing and dealing with buying motives is an important task of the client-centered services seller. If the system you're using now works for you, don't let me mess you up. If you're open to a system that works, read on.

144

Think back to the three types of need situations I discussed earlier: negative, positive, and short-term task. Let's develop a practical approach to managing and dealing with these motives.

Negative need situations involve fear: fear of failure or the unknown. A threat situation or a decision that must be made causes fear of the unknown; consequently, fear is often a buying motive. Insurance pros tell me more insurance is bought out of fear than for any other reason.

Positive need situations involve meeting the requirements of the position, feeling good, and looking good to others. *There is lots of self-interest.*

Task situations primarily involve meeting the requirements of the position. The stakes are usually lower in these situations so the buying motive is probably efficiency and/or effectiveness.

The motive is triggered when a receiver in need reads your initial-contact cover letter and properly prepared enclosure. The telephone call to make an appointment will stimulate him if you have properly prepared the scenario.

The package you mail to the targeted suspect requires only two pieces—an article that makes your selling point and a cover letter that triggers the buying motive and interests the recipient in reading the enclosure.

Preparing the Enclosure

A task in developing your insider understanding was to identify articles in niche publications that dealt with current changes, problems, and opportunities. Now is the time to turn to your file of niche articles to find one or more relating to the need situation you are promoting.

Using reprints of articles that have appeared in the niche has several key benefits:

1. It demonstrates that you are an insider; that is, you read what they read. This helps build rapport later when you contact the recipient.

2. It shows that their interests and needs are foremost in your thinking; you are a client-centered professional, not a service-oriented professional like many others who contact them.

3. You leverage on the authority and credibility of a niche influential. The article appeared because the editor was convinced it had reader interest and utility.

4. If and when you meet, the recipient already senses that this won't be a typical encounter.

There are several criteria for selecting an article for enclosure:

1. It should be easy to scan with sidebars, insets, and graphics.
2. It must address or relate to the need you are promoting in the cover letter.
3. It should be solutions oriented, unless you are selling think-tank types of services.

Once you have chosen an article, and it has cleared all the hurdles, contact the publisher. You will need to purchase professional, attractive reprints. Never photocopy the article or article abridgement. In conveys a cheap image, which you can't afford.

If the reprint is only one or two pages, the probability that your target will read most or all of the article increases dramatically over that of a multipaged article. One sheet is also particularly useful because, along with your cover letter, you can send the total package first class in a number-10 envelope at the one-ounce rate.

If you elect to abridge the original article, use as much of the first page as you can and write on the bottom of the page, "Abridged with permission of the publisher." When your camera-ready copy is complete, you have several options available: you can underline selling points by highlighting them or making marginal notes.

Your goal in using the article is to identify a central theme through the use of the hot button and then to support your position by highlighting paragraphs and sections containing evidence. If you choose to underscore any of the points made in the article, it is best to do this neatly with a light blue felt marker. Light green, light beige, and light orange are also acceptable, but blue is best because it has an authoritative hue. You may also use margin notes, arrows, or stars to highlight particular passages, but they must be done very neatly. Post-It® notes are not recommended because they can be pulled off and separated from the article reprint.

Avoid marking too many passages; usually you need only to highlight one to three sections to emphasize the point discussed in the cover letter. Remember, the purpose of the enclosure is to provide an authoritative spokesperson, to reinforce you point, to establish you as an insider, and to begin to alert the prospect about your capabilities in providing solution services.

The article you have chosen and the reprint you have prepared must attract the attention and emotions of the reader. What you have marked on the article reprint should be the focus of your cover letter. As a general rule of thumb, the more prestigious the publication, the greater impact your initial mailing will make. However, pointed, on-target articles from less prominent publications have been used to great advantage.

Let's say, for example, you are a marketing consultant to the hospital industry. Figure 13.1 is the first page of an article that appeared in the *Harvard Business Review*. This article supports several hot buttons, including downsizing, specializing, and diversifying. An attractive reprint with the appropriate article section highlighted would strongly support your new-client development program.

Preparing the Cover Letter

A good letter gets right to the point and tells why a meeting with the sender will be beneficial to the receiver. Benefits deal with improving desired situations and correcting undesired situations. Use action verbs, such as *improve, protect, reduce,* and *enhance,* to convey benefits.

The many advantages of using direct contact letters include that they:

- Are relatively inexpensive.
- Can offer a personal touch.
- Afford selectivity.
- Can be customized.
- Enhance a desired image.
- Can be controlled as to timing and content.
- Help present an organized message.
- Can be sent to many prospects at once.
- Help to boost your status, if you are already known by the prospect.

Letters, of course, can easily be ignored, may hit the wrong target, or may not be delivered at all. Some prospects may see letters as a hard sell. The communication is somewhat impersonal and one-directional (although with your follow-up calls this can be quickly circumvented). Finally, it may be difficult to differentiate your firm and its services from the scores of other businesses attempting to catch the attention of the target.

To increase the probability that your letter has impact, base the body of the letter on what I call the AIDA structure:

*In a new competitive arena,
the challenge is
to maintain both
good care and a
sound financial base*

Strategies
for survival in
the hospital
industry

Dean C. Coddington,
Lowell E. Palmquist, and
William V. Trollinger

Hospitals, besieged by new competitors and pressured to cut costs, are entering a new and unfamiliar environment. As usage declines and the government's new prospective payment system makes itself felt, hospitals are feeling the pinch. Nonprofit hospitals face competition from newer, for-profit providers of health care. These authors discuss the factors that have led some hospitals to close and forced most others to consider how they can lower costs while maintaining high-quality care. Several strategies exist to help hospitals cope with their new problems. The authors point out the advantages and disadvantages of downsizing, diversification, and joint ventures, among other practical measures that hospitals can take.

Mr. Coddington is managing director of Browne, Bortz & Coddington, Inc., an applied economic research firm in Denver, and a trustee of Swedish Medical Center in Englewood, Colorado. Mr. Palmquist is president of Swedish Health Systems, Inc. in Englewood and immediate past chairman of the Association of Western Hospitals. Mr. Trollinger is a geologist, co-owner and vice president of exploration of Marsh Oil and Gas Company, an independent petroleum producer, and chairman of the board, Swedish Health Systems.

The health care industry has joined the list of major U.S. industries facing intensely competitive environments. Hospitals, in particular, are plagued by excess capacity, many new types of competitors, and pressures to cut costs drastically.

The United States has always been blessed with excellent health care facilities and services. Now, however, revolutionary changes are sweeping the industry, and it is unclear whether most of the nation's hospitals will be able to remain economically sound while maintaining high-quality care. In this article we discuss several possible strategies to help hospitals deal with these new challenges:

Downsizing, that is, finding ways to reduce the number of beds while remaining economically viable and providing an acceptable level of care.

Becoming a low-cost provider of medical care in order to compete on a price basis.

Increasing market share.

Becoming more specialized and developing centers of special competence.

Diversifying into related health care activities so as to become less dependent on inpatient revenues.

Editor's note All references are listed at the end of the article

FIGURE 13.1. Article Supporting Hot Button. Reprinted by permission of Harvard Business Review. Excerpt from "Strategies for Survival in the Hospital Industry," by Dean C. Coddington, Lowell E. Palmquist, and William V. Trollinger (May/June 1985). Copyright © 1985 by the President and Fellows of Harvard College; all rights reserved.

Attention

In the opening paragraph or sentence, mention a strong benefit to the reader. You only have about five to ten seconds to grab the reader's attention. Here are three sample attention grabbers:

"If higher profits are appealing to you, here is good news."

"One great idea can open the door to a new era for your company."

"When is the last time your accountant's management letter really talked to management?"

"Is it time to get back to basics in your business?"

Opening with a provocative first sentence or posing a question is an excellent way to gain immediate attention. A variation on this theme is to pose a question that is actually a dilemma to the client, such as "How can anyone expect you to manage your growing firm and provide training to your staff?" Here are other possible question leads:

"Is your inventory-control system doing everything that you want it to? For instance is it . . . ?"

"Are your best clients getting the best from you?"

"How many of your top personnel really know how to . . . ?"

"When was the last time you really got something done about . . . ?"

Though we don't like to admit it, these thought-provoking questions frequently capture our attention. Another powerful way to open is to describe a favorable circumstance. For example:

"When you need expert advice and assistance with XYZ, it is useful to know whom you can call for prompt, responsive assistance."

"When your key people say, 'We just have to do something about . . . ,' it is comforting to know that help is nearby."

"You can provide your firm with its strongest defense against a sluggish economy—an effective marketing and sales training program."

The attention-grabbing portion of the letter, is its most important part. In today's competitive market, the typical executive each day receives at least a dozen well-prepared appeals and pitches. Your letter has to crash the "ho-hum" barrier.

Interest

Your letter must stress how your need-driven service solution will enable the reader to better do what she is in business to do. Thus, one of your goals is to promise the prospect that she will be better off by agreeing to meet with you. Your service solution should give her a reason for investing some time and money, and for taking the risks involved in revealing her corporate needs.

Your service must be pitched in a nonthreatening manner. This is done by linking your enclosure to your interest and ability to solve the problem. Your goal is to tap the emotions and develop interest in the mind of the target so that she will agree to meet with you to discuss her concerns.

The body of your letter stimulates interest and enhances the idea emphasized in the enclosure. First you make the target aware of a need; then you can emphasize your capability in handling it.

Desire

Next, tactfully remind the reader that she lacks the benefits you can provide, and these benefits can be discussed at a meeting with you. Offer compelling reason why she should meet with you when you call for an appointment. Since this is where buying motives are triggered, use a sentence such as:

"Getting the right training, at the right time, will enable you to take full advantage of the opportunity . . . "

"Working with an experienced bank-consulting firm improves/reduces/ protects . . . "

"Bringing in the right specialist can save you days, weeks and even months . . . "

"Hiring the best ensures that your competitive position will be enhanced . . . "

Notice how these sentences link back to the types of need situations with which you are dealing.

Affirmation

This is the part that separates the men and women from the boys and girls. Make it easy for the contact to meet with you. "I will call you during the week of the 21st to determine if you're interested in meeting." Putting the date in the letter puts the onus on you to call, which is just how you want it to be. All your work in researching the niche, finding a hot button, and supporting evidence gives you the confidence of knowing that your prospect wants to see you. This last section of your letter, which is literally the last sentence, paves the way for your call. Here are some examples of effective closings:

> *"I will contact you within five days for an appointment, so you can evaluate our ideas in terms of profit to your organization."*
>
> *"I will call you in a few days to arrange a convenient meeting."*
>
> *"I will call you next Thursday morning at 10:15 to arrange an appointment for the following week."*

Once you have offered this kind of powerful statement, you must make the call because you said you would. If you don't make it, you negate everything else of value in the letter.

Here are some additional tips on preparing an effective letter:

- Use lots of white space—nobody likes to read a long, involved letter.
- Use a you-centered focus, as opposed to an I-centered focus. Remember the Platinum Rule.
- Focus your attention on the central need and the benefit promise.
- Point out tactfully that she is not alone, she is in good company.

To learn how to recognize when you have produced an attention-grabbing letter that paves the way for your forthcoming phone call, over the next few days, save some of the letters that *you* receive from others who are trying to get your business. Which letters invite your pencil to make margin notes? Those are the ones that are most effective. Now, go back and look at your letters. What margin notes do they inspire?

Let's look at some sample letters (Figures 13.2 to 13.8). The notes at the bottom of each page have been added to indicate the positive and negative aspects of the letters. The names have been removed to protect the innocent.

First Name *Last Name*
Title
Address
City, *State* *Zip*

Dear Mr. *Last Name*

① Ensuring profitability and long-term financial security just became a lot more certain, thanks to the GETTING NEW CLIENTS Workshop.

② Where other workshops fail, this systematic approach to developing profitable new business succeeds. The reason is that it doesn't try to make salesmen out of professionals. Instead, it capitalizes on what they do best—solve important problems for clients.

The enclosed article points out the advantages of using "guerrilla" ③ marketing techniques—dominating a niche, building leverage relationships with key players in the niche, earning an insider's reputation, and staying away from fee-sensitive selling situations, all the topics covered in the Workshop.

④ The GETTING NEW CLIENTS Workshop presents the strategies, tactics and techniques to take your firm profitably into the 90s. In only three days of intensive training your professional people will be out doing the things that produce results, at a fraction of the costs ⑤ involved in traditional selling programs.

I will call you on Tuesday morning, March 16, to determine your ⑥ specific situation, and answer any questions you might still have.

Very truly yours,

———————————

Richard A. Connor, Jr. CMC
The Client-centered (tm)
Marketing Mentor

POSITIVES	NEGATIVES
2. Captivating wording	1. Not "you" oriented
3. Strong enclosure	4. "My" not "the"
5. Benefits!	
6. Aggressive	

FIGURE 13.2. Sample Letter by Dick Connor

March 22, 1991

Mr. Gary D. Kennedy, President
PRC Inc.
1500 Planning Research Drive
McLean, VA 22102

Dear Mr. Kennedy:

②

① Your marketing initiative designed to accelerate PRC's penetration into targeted commercial fields is both exciting and soundly conceived. Unlike the conventional wisdom naysayers who question your timing, my experience suggests that the time is *always right* for strategically focused action buttressed by an "obsession" with goals and commitment.   ③

Having written *the* book on niche-driven business development, plus serving some of the competitors you face, I am keenly aware of the success factors required for positioning PRC and capitalizing on its resources, reputation and relationships.   ③

④ I hope you'll accept with my compliments, a copy of <u>Getting New Clients.</u> I am sending it by separate mail.

⑤ Best wishes for a speedy and deep penetration in your markets!

The best.

Sincerely yours,

Sincerely,

Dick Connor cmc

DC:io

POSITIVES	NEGATIVES
1. "You" focused	3. Wordy
2. Specific, assuring	5. Didn't say he'd call
4. Short paragraphs	

FIGURE 13.3.   Sample Letter

Dear

① At a time when every marketing dollar must be more productive in generating new sales, our work consistently provides that critical "plus" that builds effective results for our clients.

_____ is an established advertising and promotional design firm that focuses on successfully promoting its client's *products, services* and *identities* through in-depth marketing expertise, industry ③ knowledge and award-winning design.

② We can help maximize your image in the corporate/real estate and consumer community by emphasizing your firm's flexibility and creativity, characteristics that are essential in today's competitive real-estate world. This can be achieved through successful channels of corporate communications, promotional brochures, annual reports, trade and consumer advertising, and visual presentations. ④

At present, a variety of firms uses our services, including AIG Life Insurance Company, GAB Insurance Corporation, International Commodity Services, Ogilvy & Mather, Cottage Technologies, Interior Design, Burlington Industries, and American Hospital Products, among others.

Based on our proven performance, ! look forward to meeting with you to discuss your specific needs and make you aware of our corporate and promotional-design services. I believe we can prove to be a valuable resource for your present and future projects.

⑤ I will call you in a few days to arrange a convenient meeting.

Sincerely,

POSITIVES	NEGATIVES
1. Grabber opening	3. Wordy, unclear
2. Original had attractive design	4. Too much information
5. Good close but . . .	6. He never called!

FIGURE 13.4. Sample Letter

November 12, 1991

Mr. Richard A. Connor, Jr., CMC
Dick Connor CMC
6711 Bracken Court, Suite 1000
Springfield, VA 22152   ①

Dear Mr. Connor:

All of us are aware of the importance of effective training to the success of a consult-ing assignment. ② As a fellow IMC member, you have had many opportunities to ob-serve the difference that a well-trained client team can make.

At H. B. Maynard and Company, we use our Maynard Management Institute training division to assure that our clients (and consultants) get the best training possible. We have emphasized training since our founding in 1934, and have trained tens of thou-sands in industrial engineering and management skills.

You, undoubtedly, have some of the same training needs as we do. We encourage you to contact us if you don't have your own training resource. We can accommodate your ③ training needs quickly and conveniently in our regional training centers or through in-plant arrangements.

④ We look forward to hearing from you and to assisting you in your consulting efforts.

Respectfully,

W. Terry Taylor, CMC
Senior Vice President

WTT/lk
Enclosure

POSITIVES	NEGATIVES
1. Good spacing	3. Suggests recipient make contact
2. Uses affiliation	4. Weak close

FIGURE 13.5. Sample Letter

Dear

Today's financial institutions are seeking new and innovative ways to ①
market their services to corporate and individual clients. ABC has
emerged as a distinctive new option in the design, publication, and ②
communication fields in the Washington metropolitan area.

ABC is committed to assisting your institution with the production of
superior quality print communications materials that today's intelligent
consumer has come to expect. Each of your creative promotional
programs, direct-marketing packages, and advertising campaigns
deserves the level of sophistication and style that ABC provides.

We offer a variety of services, including graphic design, production,
typesetting, copywriting, editing, and print and mail management,
which enables us to provide your institution with a host of print
communication packages, such as:

☐	Annual Reports	☐	Publications
☐	Identity Programs	☐	Signage
☐	Direct Mail Packages	☐	Advertising Promotions
	☐ Audio-Visual Presentations		

Quality control for each project is of paramount importance. Our
in-house capabilities allow us to monitor every phase of production
closely to ensure that the final product meets professional standards
and your institution's expectations.

③ Timely service, personal attention, and a competitive pricing structure
are our assurances. The brochure, folder, and stationery enclosed are
examples of the high caliber of design produced by our award-winning
creative team.

④ We look forward to showing you our portfolio.

Sincerely,

POSITIVES	NEGATIVES
Original had attractive print style on a good quality of paper. The letter made a statement before it was read.	1. Laborious Reading 2. Not Client-Centered 3. Awkward Style 4. Indefinite

FIGURE 13.6. Sample Letter

①

Dear

④
② ③ [Our company] is starting a syndicated survey of firms that we think you'll be interested in.

This new survey, [name], is designed to provide information that will help major accounting firms in the planning, implementation and evaluation of their marketing efforts.

The survey will be conducted nationally once a year among CFOs in large companies.

[Name] is designed to measure over time:

- ☐ Familiarity with major accounting firms
- ☐ Communications received from major accounting firms
- ☐ The images of major accounting firms
- ☐ Accounting firms used in the past year and would use if selecting a new firm

I've asked Jim Miller, a Vice President of [our company], to call you during the next few days to find out whether you would like to know ⑤ more about [our system]. He's our "Accounting Firm Specialist" and will be able to answer any questions you have about [our system]. ⑥ ⑦

Sincerely,

POSITIVES	NEGATIVES
2. Good use of space	1. Original had name & title wrong
3. Simple wording	4. Starts with "We"
	5. Doesn't reflect insider's understanding
	6. Responsibility passed along
	7. He never called!

FIGURE 13.7. Sample Letter

Dear

① Recognizing that your time is valuable, I will be brief and to the point.

② I would like to establish a working relationship with your firm by providing my expertise as a computer consultant to your clients. In this capacity, I would be pleased to involve and/or train your staff and share the work and fees with your firm.

③ This may be an added important resource for providing total service to your clients.

Thank you for your consideration. I will be available at your ④ convenience to discuss a specific client need or to provide additional ⑤ information.

A brief biographical summary is attached for your review. ⑥ ⑦

Very truly yours, ⑧

POSITIVES
1. Brief
2. Good grabber

NEGATIVES
3. "I" centered
4. Indefinite
5. Passive
6. Too much like a job application
7. No call for action or mention of call
8. Overly affectionate

FIGURE 13.8. Sample Letter

FINE-TUNING YOUR INITIAL MAILING

Once you are happy with your letter and its supporting evidence, carefully choose ten contacts to whom you will send a test mailing. These contacts should be representative of the target niche, but shouldn't be among you ten best prospects. You could also send one to a client, but let him or her know it is coming. In addition you should include a note on top of your grabber letter such as "Test Mailing No. 1." In other words, on this original mailing you are actively seeking input as to how to improve your presentation: You are not directly seeking an appointment or soliciting new business. However, if either occurs, you will certainly not turn it down.

When mailing, never send more that you can comfortably follow up within five to seven working days. I advocate mailing on Thursday and calling the following Wednesday or Thursday. Regardless of how well a letter is written, it is virtually useless unless followed up with a telephone call. And you must make a persuasive phone call if you want to progress with the right people.

Five days after your contacts receive your letter, it is time to call them. Your primary purpose in calling each contact is to determine the following:

- Do they remember receiving the letter?
- Is the need I have identified real and important to them? If not, will it be important in the future?
- Were they the appropriate contacts within the organization? If not, who are the appropriate individuals?

During these calls, seek opportunities to gather additional insider information and to strengthen and expand your own comfort zone. If the conversation really gets rolling, then even on these test calls, make an appointment. If your test calls were representative of the target-contact universe, and suggested a fine tuning, the time to do so is now.

If the majority of contacts felt that your hot button was not of great concern to them, you will have to reexamine your niche data base and all the steps that led to your decision to choose it.

For some reason, the selected hot button was not valid and a new one needs to be selected. You have missed the mark. Perhaps the need was quickly resolved. Maybe the article overstated the case. With very little time and effort, you will be able to make another selection that is on target. The hot button you should be using may very well be handed to you while test calling.

What if you have identified an appropriate hot button, but your cover letter lacks punch? Reread the section on preparing your letter and graciously accept any criticisms made during test calls. Remember, this is just a test; consequently, if anything requires modification, it is better to know now.

After you have restructured your letter or identified a new hot button, go to ten new contacts.

Follow up your test mailing with a call within five to seven business days or you have virtually lost your contact. Look at your own desk, and consider how much mail you get on a weekly basis. If it is less than 30 or 40 pieces, I will be surprised. Any message you send in today's junk-mail society simply has to be followed up by a human voice.

After mailing letters to your first ten contacts, choose another ten contact representative of the target niche. These should not be your best possible prospects, but should represent firms and organizations that you would like to have as clients. Then repeat all the steps previously outlined. A third, fourth, and fifth test mailing is recommended until you have a winning package.

How do you know when your contact package is ready? When the recipients of the test mailing are very receptive, keep you on the phone for a long time, are interested in getting together, and start volunteering information that adds to your insider's understanding. When you have produced a contact package that is on target, your confidence will shoot right up. Thereafter, getting appointments, and ultimately new clients, could actually become fun.

Wading Through Standard Mailing Options

If you're among the many professionals who are concerned about the speed and manner with which your contact packages are delivered to prospects, you're not along. Generally speaking, you don't need to pay for high-priced express mail services, but you do need to know the options available. Here is a brief, alphabetical description of some standard services offered by the U.S. Postal Service followed by descriptions of more extensive services to safeguard, protect, and document your packages.

Express Mail Service

This is the Post Office's fastest service, and is fairly comparable to commercial services. "Express Mail Next Day Service" provides several options for both private and business customers who require overnight delivery of letters and packages. To use Express Mail Next Day Service, take your shipment to any designated Express Mail post office, generally by 5 P.M., or deposit it in an Express Mail collection box. Your mailing will be delivered to the addressee by 3 P.M. the next day (weekends and holidays included). In many cities, Express Mail deliveries are made before noon.

There are more than 26,000 post offices and 10,000 special Express Mail collection boxes in which you can deposit your pieces. Also, your letter carrier can accept prepaid Express Mail shipments at the time your mail is delivered. The Post Office will supply you with mailing containers (envelopes, boxes, and tubes) and the necessary mailing labels free of charge.

First-Class Mail

This category is designed for letters, postcards, postal cards, greeting cards, personal notes, and for sending checks and money orders. You cannot insure ordinary first-class mail. However, additional services such as certificate of mailing, certified mail, return receipt, and restricted delivery can be purchased at the option of the mailer. If your first-class mail is not letter size, make sure it is marked "First Class" or use a green-bordered large envelope.

Forwarding Mail

When you move, fill out a "Change of Address" card in advance at your local post office. When possible, you should notify your post office at least one month before your move. First-class mail is forwarded at no charge. Magazines, newspapers, and other second-class mail are forwarded at no charge for 60 days from the effective date of a change-of-address order. Your post office has information about holding mail, temporary changes of address, and forwarding and return of other classes of mail.

Mailgram Service

"Mailgram" is a registered trademark of Western Union Corporation. Mailgram service is an electronic message service offered by Western Union that provides next-day Postal Service delivery for messages sent to any address in the United States. The messages are transmitted for delivery with the next business day's mail. You can send Mailgram messages by calling Western Union and dictating your message to the operator, or you can use your office Telex or TWX.

Priority Mail

First-class mail weighing more than 12 ounces and up to 70 pounds (with size limitations), is priority mail. The Post Office provides free "Priority Mail" stickers. Insurance (see p. 162) can be purchased on priority mail.

Third-Class Mail

Also referred to as bulk business, or advertising mail, third-class mail may be sent by anyone, but it is used most often by large mailers. I recommend that you avoid using third-class mail in getting new clients. Third class includes printed material and merchandise weighing less than 16 ounces. There are two rate structures for this class: single piece and bulk rate. Also, individuals may use this class of mail for mailing lightweight parcels; insurance can be purchased, at the option of the mailer, to cover loss or damage of articles mailed at the third-class rate.

Postal Protection and Documentation

Certified Mail

A mailing receipt is provided, and a record of delivery is maintained at the recipient's post office. You can also pay an additional fee for a receipt to indicate proof of delivery. For valuables and irreplaceable items, the Postal Service recommends using insured or registered mail.

Collect-on-Delivery (COD)

This service is useful when you want to collect for merchandise (up to a maximum amount) as it is delivered. COD service may be used for merchandise sent by first-class, third-class, or fourth-class mail. The merchandise must have been ordered by the addressee. The Postal Service includes insurance protection against loss or damage within their fee. COD items also may be sent as registered mail.

Insurance

For an additional fee, registered mail can be insured up to a maximum of $25,000; for third- and fourth-class mail and for merchandise mailed at the Priority Mail or First-Class Mail rates, the maximum amount is $500. With articles insured for more than $25, a receipt of delivery is signed by the recipient and filed at the delivery post office. The amount of insurance coverage for loss is the actual value, less depreciation, and no payments are made for sentimental losses or for any expenses incurred as a result of the loss.

Registered Mail

The Postal Service regards this as the most secure mailing option that they offer. It is designed to provide added protection for valuable and important mail. Postal insurance may be purchased, at the option of the mailer, up to a maximum of $25,000, and return receipt and restricted delivery services are available for an additional fee. Registered articles are controlled from the point of mailing to deliver. First-class postage is required on registered mail.

Restricted Delivery

Except for Express Mail service, you can request restricted delivery when purchasing return receipt service. Restricted delivery means that delivery is made only to the addressee or to someone who is authorized in writing to receive mail for the addressee. Restricted delivery mail addressed to officials of government agencies, members of the legislative and judicial branches of federal and state governments, members of the diplomatic corps, minors, and individuals under guardianship can be delivered to an agent without written authorization from the addressee.

Return Receipt

Proof of delivery is available on mail that you send by COD or Express Mail, insured for more than $25, or register or certify. The return receipt shows who signed for the item and the date it was delivered. For an additional fee, you can get an exact address of delivery or request restricted delivery service.

Special Delivery

You can buy special delivery service on all classes of mail except bulk third class. It provides for delivery, even on Sundays and holidays, during hours that extend beyond the hours for delivery of ordinary mail. This service is available to all customers served by city carriers and to other customers within a one-mile radius of the delivery post office.

Special delivery mail may be delivered by your regular carrier if it is available before he or she departs for morning deliveries. You have to call your post office about the availability of special delivery service.

International Mail

You can send airmail and surface mail to virtually all foreign countries. There are four types of international mail:

1. *Letters and Cards.* Includes letters, packages, lightweight aero-grammes, and postcards.
2. *Other Articles.* Includes printed matter, matter for the blind, and small packets.
3. *Parcel Post.*
4. *Express Mail International Service.*

Registry service with limited reimbursement protection is available for letters and cards and other articles to many countries, and insurance is available for parcel post to most countries.

14

Getting Appointments with High-Potential Prospective Clients

In the previous chapter, we examined the steps involved in developing and managing your initial mailing package, one of the two activities of developing and managing your initial-contact program. Now we turn to the second activity, using the telephone.

Popular speaker and consultant David Alan Yoho of the Professional Educators Group in Bethesda, Maryland says, "It is entirely possible for someone who dislikes using the telephone to employ it successfully in his or her work." If you ordinarily do things systematically, the phone can become one of your greatest marketing allies. This chapter presents a proven, step-by-step appointment-getting system that lets you "win at getting in."

IT'S EASIER THAN YOU THINK!

Many professional-service providers dread using the telephone for marketing purposes. Many regard making a follow-up telephone call on a par with making a cold call. A seasoned professional once confided, "Phoning for appointments is Maalox time at the old heartburn corral." Others worry it to death, and if they do make a few calls without getting an appointment, they quickly give it up as a bad idea.

I can relate to these feelings. Before I devised the approach presented in this chapter, I, too, experienced many of them. A throbbing headache and an occasional upset stomach were the payoffs for my investment. But that was before I developed the targeted-niche approach. Now I still don't *enjoy* making the calls, but they don't bother me as they once did.

Whether we like it or not, the winning professional-service marketers of the 1990s will be those who have mastered the use of the telephone.

A STEP BACK TO SEE AHEAD

Let's step back a moment and review why your targets *want* to hear from you. You have researched the niche, identified a hot button, gathered supporting evidence, developed a cover letter, test-marketed your package, refined the package, test-marketed it again if necessary, obtained feedback from test-market contacts, and, finally, produced a truly suspect-centered contact package. Now you are ready to step into the big arena and make the appointment-getting call. Contacts have received your package five business days earlier telling them you would be calling to discuss their needs.

PREPARING YOUR TELESCRIPT

I recommend using a telephone script, which is a road map to obtaining an appointment. Properly prepared, it can provide you with a proven track on which to run. Scripts enable you to adapt your rate of speech, timing and reflection, intention, and vocal expression because you have the necessary data to handle the situations you encounter. Let's look at an effective telescript format that I use, based on the best ideas I have gained during my 20 years of experience.

An effective telescript has six steps. I'll review each briefly and then discuss them later. They are:

1. *Introduction.* When the phone is answered, you introduce yourself and ask for the suspect by first name.

2. *Purpose in Calling.* You refer to the letter you mailed the previous week to see if the person remembers receiving it.

3. *Trigger the Buying Motive.* You review the grabber statement and the solution benefit mentioned in your cover letter.

4. *Trial Close.* Since your objective is not to sell the engagement, but to get the suspect to buy your recommendation of meeting with you, you determine if the contact is ready to meet with you. The trigger and trial close statements are made together.

5. *Contact Concerns and Objections.* You patiently and professionally answer your contact's questions and try again to set a date for the appointment.

6. *Confirm Next Step.* You confirm what will occur after you complete the telephone call. You'll send additional information, call again at a later date, strike the name from your mailing list, or set up the upcoming appointment.

FOR TELEPHOBICS ONLY

If you are still a bit uneasy, take heart—the number of negative incidents from making a telephone contact is very low. Are you among those who would rather do anything than get on the phone and ask for an appointment? What usually occurs is the feeling that the contact will loudly and roundly chastise you with one of the following responses:

"How dare you call me in the middle of a busy day to talk about your services."

"Are you the one who keeps calling me?"

"Don't you ever call me again—you got that, I never want to hear from you again."

"How did you get my name, because these kind of calls p— me off."

"Who the hell are you?"

"I really dislike these kinds of calls . . . "

"Where do you get the nerve to ask me for an appointment?"

"You G— D—— SO—. You salespeople are all alike. Stop bothering me."

"Why don't you take a flying leap, buddy!"

Read each possible response slowly and carefully. Now get them out of your system because you are probably never going to encounter them. And even if that remote possibility does occur and someone responds that way, it would be his problem, not yours.

The probability is medium to high that you will get a large number of rejections. However, using the client-centered approach developed in this book will effectively lower the probability of rejection because of your insider's understanding and reputation within the niche, your identification of a hot button, and your improving telephone skills. While the chance of getting an appointment is low, you must remember that every "No" brings you closer to a "Yes."

If you are concerned about tarnishing your image, forget it:

- You won't get a bad image because you use the telephone to secure appointments with target organizations.
- You are not trying to sell your services over the phone.
- You are simply trying to get the prospect to invest time meeting with you.

Many professionals still get anxious after having used the phone for 10 years or more. The anxiety stems from feeling they are interrupting someone and trying to get them to buy something.

Remember, however, how successfully you served your Key and A clients. Now, would you want to deny these types of benefits to others, just because they are not fully acquainted with you yet?

Unfortunately, the automatic response of human kind to any new suggestion, change, request, or idea is "No." The vast majority of rejections you receive have nothing to do with you, your firm, or the service need you have identified. Once you are able to depersonalize the rejection process, you free yourself to make more productive calls.

THE PROSPECT-CENTERED APPOINTMENT-GETTING SYSTEM

Let's put calling by telephone into a larger perspective and discuss the specific steps involved in preparing to make effective telephone follow-up contacts.

1. Call when it is convenient for your targets. Who am I calling and what is the best time to call? Figure 14.1 shows the best hours for calling various prospects. Again, this is where the benefit of developing an insider's understanding comes in handy—you know the ebb and flow of the contact's industry and work environment.

2. Arrange for privacy. You don't want loud talking or ringing telephones to interrupt you. Nor do you want someone walking into your office and disturbing your concentration.

3. Clear your desk of everything not associated with making your appointment-getting calls.

PROSPECT CALLING TIMES

Prospects	Best Time to Call
Chemists and engineers	Between 4 P.M. and 5 P.M.
Contractors and builders	Before 9 A.M. or after 5 P.M.
Dentists	Before 9:30 A.M.
Entrepreneurs	Before 8:30 A.M. or after 5 P.M.
Executives and business leaders	After 10:30 A.M.
Homemakers	Between 10 A.M. and 11 A.M.
Lawyers	Between 11 A.M. and 2 P.M.
Merchants, store heads, and department heads	After 10:30 A.M.
Physicians and surgeons	Between 9 A.M. and 11 A.M.; after 4 P.M.
Professors, instructors, teachers	At home, between 6 P.M. and 7 P.M.
Public accountants	Anytime during the day, but avoid January 2 through April 15
Publishers and printers	After 3 P.M.
Low-salaried people and government employees	Call at home
Stockbrokers and bankers	Before 10 A.M. or after 3 P.M.

FIGURE 14.1. Prospect Calling Times

4. Arrange your desk for action:

Put the list of names and telephone numbers you intend to make that day to your left if you are right-handed.

Place a pad entitled "Suspect Interview Notes" near the telephone to write notes. Figure 14.2 shows a copy of such a form that has served me and my clients very well.

Open your calendar to the week in which you are going to schedule appointments. Since my calendar has a tendency to close by itself, I prop it open by putting my stapler on top of it; consequently, I don't have to fumble around trying to suggest times to meet.

To assist in your calling and tracking efforts, many telemarketing software programs are available such as *Business Contacts Act* and *Telemagic*. Each has its own directions, but all of them essentially cover the basics. You call, you log in new information, and you get reports of your progress and reminders as to who needs to be called back. The learning time for these programs is a couple of hours or less. Current prices range from $99 to $495.

Otherwise, a manual system can work just as well, if you keep it updated.

Use the form shown in Figure 14.2 to capture essential information quickly while talking with prospects over the phone. It has a twofold purpose, serving as a conversation guide and data sheet. Undoubtedly there will be many holes left open following most telephone conversations. These can be filled in as you gain more information about the prospect, especially after your on-site appointment.

If you don't use this form or something similar, you will be likely to make inconsistent margin notes on any paper from your prospect files. Or, you may end up not being able to retrieve and use complete information about the prospect that would support you in subsequent conversations. As new data are added, they should be dated. Later, this form can be used to update your niche data base. Hereinafter, keep track of all prospects that you contact.

You need to determine the number of calls required to get one appointment. As we saw back in Chapter 3, these kinds of statistics help you develop your hit ratio—the level of effort necessary to generate one new client.

SUSPECT INTERVIEW NOTES

Date: ___/___/___ , ___/___/___ , ___/___/___ , ___/___/___ , ___/___/___
            1   2   3   4   5

Name of Organization: _____

Name of Contact: _____

Telephone Number: _____

Results of Contact(s):

Next Step:

FIGURE 14.2. Suspect Interview Notes

If one appointment can be gained for every four calls you make, then obviously to get 10 appointments you will have to make 40 calls. If two new clients can be generated for every 10 appointments, and you have a goal of obtaining 12 new clients in the next three months, then you will have to make 240 calls. This sounds like a lot of work, but actually breaks down to only 10 calls each Wednesday and Thursday over a 12-week period. If you have more than one person responsible for making the calls, the effort is even less so.

If you have a telephone answering machine with a two-way recording device or otherwise have access to equipment that enables you to tape your telephone conversations, experts recommend that you do so. This is important for several reasons:

```
┌─────────────────────────────────────────────────────────────┐
│                         CALLING LOG                           │
│                                                               │
│   Date:      / /                                              │
│                                                               │
│   Name: _____│
│                         (or caller)                          │
│                                                               │
│   Name of Organization: _____│
│                                                               │
│      Numbers Called           Results           Next Step     │
│     1. _____        _____        _____    │
│                                                               │
│     2. _____        _____        _____    │
│                                                               │
│     3. _____        _____        _____    │
│                                                               │
│     4. _____        _____        _____    │
│                                                               │
│     5. _____        _____        _____    │
│                                                               │
│     6. _____        _____        _____    │
│                                                               │
│     7. _____        _____        _____    │
│                                                               │
│     8. _____        _____        _____    │
│                                                               │
│     9. _____        _____        _____    │
│                                                               │
│    10. _____        _____        _____    │
└─────────────────────────────────────────────────────────────┘
```

FIGURE 14.3. Calling Log

- You may miss many of the key points the prospect is making, no matter how fast you write.
- The second and third hearing may reveal voice cues that provide additional information.
- The tape will serve as an excellent instructional vehicle for improving your telephone performance.
- Tapes of particularly effective conversations can be used as instructionals.

This is no small benefit if you've ever tried to train others on effective telemarketing. The recorded conversation gives your troops a model for their own conversations.

- Taping is a sensitive subject with many. Obviously any taping you do must be done with equipment that is unobtrusive or you are liable to interfere with the communication process between you and the prospect.

- Set up your mirror so that you can catch yourself, and keep yourself smiling. I know this sounds silly, but the very best telemarketers use one at all times. Let's leverage off the experience of others whenever we can.

Over the years, I have found it valuable to produce a personal "confidence card" that I keep by the phone. Figure 14.4 shows what my card says. Have your confidence card propped up in front of you to derive support from this technique.

Next, set your goals for the day. I set a goal of reaching three contacts before I take a break. For every conversation I have with a target, my statistics show that four out of five attempts have been made. It's a fact of life that people are busy and have become increasingly resistant to accepting telephone calls from peddlers. Too many of the executives you will be attempting to see will have been burned by hustlers who use all sorts of lies and half-truths to try to get around the contact's "peddler protection shield," his secretary, or another third party—more on this subject a bit later.

Finally, place a copy of your telescript, Figure 14.5, and a reprint of your answers to their objections within reach. Now you are ready to get into high gear.

---

1. I have valuable services that many nonclients need and that will enable them to improve their operations.

2. People are somtimes hesitant to make appointments over the phone. This does not mean they are rejecting me or my idea.

3. I have succeeded before and I will succeed today!

4. I have a perfect right and responsibility to discuss my services with eligible prospects.

FIGURE 14.4. Confidence Card

TELESCRIPT: THE OPENING LINE

Mr/Ms/Miss _____ PLEASE

Mr/Ms/Miss _____ , I'M _____ WITH _____

_____

MY REASON FOR CALLING IS _____

_____

_____

Do you recall receiving my letter?

If no: "I'm glad I called you today. If it had reached you, you'd
              know I'm calling to see if it makes sense for us to meet and

              discuss ways in which you can improve _____."
                                                    (need situation)

If yes: "Good. As you recall, I mentioned that we work with

              _____ in
                           (his type of organization)

              _____ .
                           (known/suspected need)

My reason for calling you today is to see if it makes sense for us to meet

and discuss ways in which you can improve _____ .
                                          (need situation)

If no

  Oh?

  "May I ask why?"

If yes

  Express appreciation

  Establish specifics

      Day and time
      Location
      Participants

FIGURE 14.5. Telescript

MAKING THE TELEPHONE CALL

The following in-depth discussion of the telephone contact incorporates the advice of speaker and consultant David Alan Yoho, based in Bethesda, Maryland.

1. *Introduction.* Proper telephone use for prospecting begins with a natural-sounding conversation; do not sound as if you are reading from a script or following a prepared format. We have all encountered ineffective telemarketers who begin the conversation with "Good Morning Mr. X, how are you this morning?" The conversation is stilted, forced, canned, and uninspiring. It only takes a nanosecond to determine that this is a telephone pitch: Our resistance starts immediately. While remaining polite, we wait for a break in the conversation to say, "Sorry, I am just not interested."

When the phone is answered, introduce yourself before asking for the suspect. For example, say "Good morning, this is Bill Jones calling for Ralph Winters."

If someone else has answered and tells you that he is not available, determine if the contact person is his secretary. If this person says yes, say "Good! What is the best time for me to speak to him briefly?" Get the receptionist's name, offer thanks, and call back at the given time.

If you are transferred to Ralph Winters or you reach Ralph Winters directly, say "Mr. Winters, this is Bill Jones with Star Services Inc." The reason you repeat the suspect's name is to make him feel important and to reduce the psychological distance. At all times, remember to pause, keep smiling, and stay relaxed.

2. *Reason for Calling.* "I recently sent you a letter and article that you should have received by Tuesday. Did you receive it?" If the prospect has not received it, doesn't remember receiving it, or, for whatever reason, can't make reference to it, tell him or her that you will resubmit the letter and be back in touch. Then place that prospect in the next round of calls.

In those cases when the prospect says that he or she did not receive your package and you feel particularly confident, instead of offering to remail the package, you could launch right into "Well, I am glad I called you because in the letter I mentioned . . . ," then continue on to ask for the appointment.

If the prospect has received the package, the likely reply will be one of the following:

"Yes, I got it a couple of days ago, but I haven't had a chance to look at it."

"Yes, I looked it over and then filed it somewhere."

"Yes, I know I have it here somewhere."

"I believe so. What did you want to say?"

3. *Trigger the Buying Motive.* At this point, you launch immediately into a brief review of what was in the contact package. "As we discussed in the letter and article, containing costs is a big factor in the plastics industry. Cost control is an area in which we have developed some effective methods that could be quite useful to your business. I would like to meet with you for no more than 30 minutes next Tuesday or Thursday. Does it make sense for us to get together?"

Here is another way to approach prospects: "Ms. X, a short time ago, I sent you a letter and an article that discussed the PQR situation facing organizations in your industry. As I mentioned in the letter, our firm works with companies like yours to [solve the problem mentioned in the article]. My reason for calling you today is to arrange a time for us to discuss your situation."

All the while, visualize a friendly person on the other end of the line who is seriously considering your message and the information you have sent. If you are cut off or rejected, consider that you're now one "no" closer to a "yes."

4. *Trial Close.* You'll note that the trigger and trial close are offered in the same paragraph. This is by design. You want to make the major buy decision for now—the appointment—the central focus.

5. *Handling Any Objection.* No matter how prepared you are, and even if the prospect has the need you have identified, you are still likely to encounter objections. Why might a prospect object? The number of reasons is endless, but here are a few:

Fear that your services are costly.

So busy they can't find the time to meet.

Such bad shape that the need you have identified was fifth on the list!

Already retained someone to help them with this problem.

Are skeptical of you, your firm, its services (or anyone in your industry).
Afraid that in handling this problem you will encounter many other
problems.
Don't see the consequences of not acting now.

Yoho classifies objections into four major areas:

1. *Money.* How much will it cost? Are your prices competitive? What
    is the payment schedule? What kind of return can I get on my in-
    vestment?
2. *Indecision.* Who are you? How long have you been offering this ser-
    vice? Why should I buy from you? When do I need this?
3. *Weak Desire.* This doesn't fit our needs. We already have enough. It
    is being taken care of. It doesn't come up that often. I don't think it
    is that important.
4. *Time.* How long will this take? I don't have the time. How should I
    spend my time? How long will it take to provide this service?

The following are suggested answers to the most frequently encountered objections. Your task is to rewrite them to fit your personal and
professional comfort zone.

"I'm not interested in buying anything!"

*"Ms. Griffin, I appreciate what you're saying. It will only take 20 minutes for
you to decide if my ideas are useful to you. I'll be brief and to the point. Would
Monday or Wednesday be better for you?"*

"I'm already served by ( )."

*"Mr. Watkins, you don't want to waste your time meeting with me because
you are satisfied with the service you are getting from your present accountant,
right? I appreciate your concern. In today's environment, though, I find it un-
usual for any one person to have all the good ideas about STV. My purpose in
calling you today is to see if it makes sense for us to share ideas; we'll both be
better off for our meeting. Would Thursday or next Tuesday be better for you?"*

"Tell me over the phone."

*[Laughingly] "You like to get right to the point—that's great! You don't want
to waste your time discussing something that isn't of value to you, right? Tell*

you what, let's meet for no more that 28 minutes to look at my plan for VWX. You'll be able to see how the ideas can work for you. Would Tuesday or Wednesday be better for you?"

"I don't have the time."

"Mr. McMahon, I appreciate that. We are all too busy to waste time on meeting people who can't contribute to our development. That's why I'm calling you. It's been my experience that we'd both benefit from meeting to discuss DEF. Would Tuesday or Wednesday be better for you?"

Notice that when answering an objection you close by asking for an appointment.

Veteran sales trainers regard objections merely as opportunities to gain more information about the prospect. They also serve as guideposts to making an appointment. Yoho says to use the objection to your advantage, such as, "I am glad we got this out in the open. I am going to enjoy meeting you."

If the prospect is still reluctant to give you an appointment, then thank him or her for talking with you and listening to your message. Send a follow-up thank-you note. Then file the information for future reference and use whatever information you learned to be more effective with the next prospect. If the prospect is a prominent member of the niche, you may be encountering him again.

You first contact, if it was professional and cordial, will pave the way for future discussions. Also, keep in mind that since you are developing an insider's reputation in the niche, those who won't meet with you will still be seeing your name and hearing about you from others. In essence, a good, qualified suspect remains one, even if you can't land an appointment now.

6. *Confirm the Next Step.* If the prospect agrees to meet you, you only have to establish the date and time, location, and the participants. Then, thank him and close by saying something like, "I look forward to meeting you."

Be sure to let the prospect hang up first. You don't want to convey that you are in a hurry, anxious, or happy to get this call over with.

Keeping the Momentum Going ———————————————

One pitfall of using the phone is to stop after a few calls whether or not you are getting results. When you obtain an appointment, feel free to celebrate. Stand up, stretch, get yourself some coffee. But, then get back to your *winning ways;* you have more calls to make. Don't consider the job done until you have made your quota of calls, including your callbacks.

When you get an appointment, be sure to send out a confirmation letter or fax that says, "Looking forward to our meeting on Wednesday the 7th at 2:15 at your office." Your inclination may be to skip this item, but don't. You're establishing yourself as a client-centered professional in the minds of your prospects. Hence, you make the affirming gesture, you write the follow-up note; if appropriate, you continually suggest the next step throughout the entire process. In short, you keep the momentum going between phone calls, with each appointment you secure, and with prospects you meet face to face.

If you find that you are interrupted while making calls or have trouble getting started, rehearse mentally. Visualize yourself talking with a pleasant person who is willing to listen to your ideas for improving or protecting something of value to him or her. Each call you make is new. I don't care if you have encountered six "nos" in a row; the next call may result in an appointment that brings in a high paying, long-standing client.

Most professionals prefer to call in privacy. If you are among them, make sure you are not disturbed during this time. Continue to use the supporting materials you have assembled, such as your confidence card and telephone script.

Once you begin to become adept at calling for appointments, start establishing quotas for yourself. For example, if you have decided to make 10 calls on Wednesday morning between 9:45 and 11:45 A.M., how many appointments do you intend to get? Two? Three? Pick a number and go for it.

Dealing with Third Parties

Often, you will be encountering a receptionist or secretary who screens your target-contact calls. Obviously, the higher up the person is in the organization, and the larger the organization, the more well defined the screening process will be. The best strategy for handling a third party who stands between you and your target contact is to level with him or her.

"May I ask what this is in reference to?"

(Pleasantly) "I sent her a package last week and promised to call her at this time. Is she in?"

Even if the target is not in, calling when you said you would and properly leaving a message will score you some points. The probability of the target calling back increases when he is handed a message that says you called exactly when you said you would.

Ask the intermediary if he or she could suggest the best time for you to call back. If given a time, thank the intermediary and convey the message to the target that you will be calling back at X o'clock. Then, of course, do so.

If the intermediary can't suggest a time to call back, then offer one. If you are calling in the morning, choose a time during the afternoon. If you are calling in the afternoon, choose a time the next morning.

If the intermediary is uncooperative, remain pleasant but professional. Suppose you are confronted with this type of response or one that is even less informative. "He is very busy right now and won't be available for several days. Why don't you leave your number, and I will see that he gets it." You have several options.

- You can use the technique of super seller Joe Gandolfo: State your business, using such words as "I have a message of importance." Then, issue a polite order, "Kindly put him through to me."

- You can inform the intermediary that you will be calling back on such and such a day at such and such a time. The day and time that you select should be one day after the "busy" period.

- Inform the intermediary that you will send a follow-up letter. In essence, the letter will say, "When I called you last week, I learned it was a very busy period for you. I will give you a call next Wednesday at 11:30."

Whatever you do, don't make the intermediary wrong. They are paid to do what they do and may frequently be confronted by overly aggressive, rude, or otherwise unprofessional callers. Stand your ground, remain unflustered and professional, and convey your intentions. Your professional demeanor does get back to the target person and will pay off in the long run.

Joseph Sugarman, in his book *Success Forces,* (1989, Oldcastle Books, New York) says that he can tell by the way the caller treats his receptionist or secretary whether or not he will want to get in touch. Those who behave as blowhards to the intermediary, and sugar and spice to the target, are revealing their true nature.

Figure 14.6 displays a list of telephone do's and don'ts; some will increase your effectiveness, others will decrease it.

If you follow these tips, you will easily surpass 95 to 98 percent of all professional services marketers in effective use of the telephone.

Using FAX to Bolster Your Telephone Campaign

Unquestionably, the use of your fax machine can aid in your making key connections and following up with the prospects you've targeted, *especially* if the other party suggests that you use the fax. The effective use of your fax quickens overall completion time, reduces wasted time that both parties expend trying to "catch" one another, and demonstrates your efficiency and professionalism.

Fax is best employed when a relationship by telephone is already established—never to establish one. In addition, misuse of fax transmissions for

TELEPHONE DO'S AND DON'TS

DO	DON'T
Come to the point	Ramble
Ask questions	Assume the answer
Accept the target's point of view	Argue
Compliment the competition	Knock the competition
Talk with them	Talk at them
Talk about the listener	Talk about yourself
Visualize the listener	Daydream
Sit erect (move around or even stand if it helps you)	Slouch in your seat
Control your emotions	React to their negativeness
Sell solutions	Sell hardware and techniques
Thank them	Hang up first

©1983 David Alan Yoho

FIGURE 14.6. Telephone Do's and Don'ts

marketing purposes can backfire. While regulations regarding fax transmission are currently being debated, here are some rules of thumb to ensure that your use of fax transmissions does not diminish your appointment-getting efforts:

- Don't send more than three pages to any prospect.
- Craft your transmissions carefully. Like it or not, you will be judged by what you send, when you send it, and how you send it.
- Keep in mind that a fax transmission may be a "public" document in the office of the receiver.

Unless you know who will physically remove the hard copy printout on the other end and what routing your message may take before reaching your target, take care to ensure that your message does indeed arrive safely.

15

Preparing for the Discussion

Conducting new-business discussions is expensive in terms of time and energy invested: To make them cost-effective they must be planned, managed, and leveraged. I am often surprised by the lack of preparation with which so many professionals enter a new-business discussion; too many veterans wing it instead of carefully preparing their discussion:

You never get a second chance to make a first impression.

This truism couldn't be more applicable than to marketing. Another such expression also has merit:

By failing to plan, you plan to fail.

Few professionals have been taught how to prepare for new-business discussions. Although the busy professional is told what to do, he or she is seldom told how to do it. The popular literature has not been helpful, either. Consequently, effective planning is not undertaken.

This chapter will discuss the steps involved in planning new-business discussions, and the importance of getting to the prospect's office on time and in an alert, relaxed frame of mind. In addition, it will also cover the issue of how long to wait for a prospect.

OBJECTIVES FOR NEW-BUSINESS DISCUSSIONS ──────

A new-business discussion has seven basic objectives, two of which apply in all situations:

1. Creating a favorable awareness with the prospect even if he or she does not purchase your service at this time
2. Increasing your insider's understanding of the niche

The remaining five objectives of new-business discussions are presented in Figure 15.1. Depending on the nature of the need situation, where the

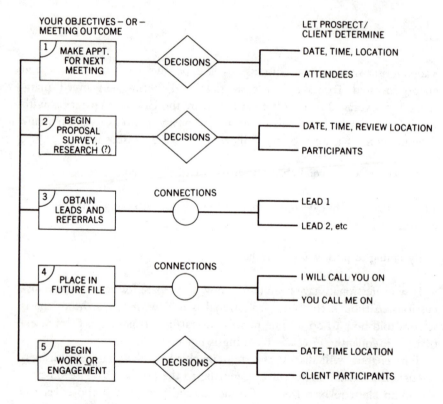

FIGURE 15.1. Objectives/Outcomes of a New-Business Discussion

discussion leads, and the level of interest and enthusiasm on the part of the contact, one or more of them may be achieved. The five objectives are:

1. *Setting an Appointment for the Next Meeting.* When the contact is enthusiastic, you have more to talk about.

2. *Beginning a Proposal, a Survey, or Research.* If the need situation is complex and required in-depth analysis to prepare your solution program, have the prospect agree to your recommendation for conducting a survey or research project. If your solution program involves a large fee, or if it is likely that the prospective client will insist on a proposal being prepared, then this would be your primary objective. This occurs as a result of a need expressed by the prospect and is a prelude to possible new business.

3. *Obtain Referrals and Leads.* As a by-product of sharing ideas regarding the target's situation, you can often obtain the names of others who may be interested in your service solutions.

4. *Place This Prospect in the Future File.* If there is currently little or no interest on the part of the contact, remember that needs can change quickly. Tell the prospect when you will call again.

5. *Begin Work.* As a result of your appointment, the prospect may actually become a client and work may begin shortly.

While making your appointment-getting telephone call, you often gain a clue as to which of these five objectives you might achieve on site. Realistically, prepare for unpredictable situations and establish a fallback or contingency objective. For example, if the contact sounded enthusiastic over the phone and practically indicated that you could begin work immediately, your objective would be to close for the commitment to begin. If some roadblocks emerge during your meeting however, try to fall back and set up another appointment.

As you review these five desired outcomes, visualize now what you will be doing to make each a reality. What information will you acquire and exchange? What attitudes will you establish, change, or solidify? What will your relationship be like during this getting-acquainted period and how might it change?

The most realistic objective for the majority of new-business discussions will be to set an appointment for the next meeting. However, expect the unexpected. For example, you and the prospect may have agreed on a particular problem area while on the telephone; on site, however, you may discover that the real problem lies elsewhere. Consequently, shift your focus to the real problem and steer the discussion toward a needs assessment and other preliminary activities.

In any case, when meeting face to face, your fundamental task is to leverage your time and proceed as quickly as possible to the next steps. In some instances, the next step may be nothing more than placing the prospect in the future file. If so, conclude the discussion in as pleasant a manner as possible. Obtain any referrals or leads that you can, and then move on. This is far more beneficial than trying to sell an engagement to a prospect who is not ready or has little interest.

I once met with the managing partner of a prominent management-consulting firm in the Midwest to discuss his new-business development needs. His firm was facing price-cutting competition that was eroding its profits. Although he agreed that the problem plagued his firm and many others in the industry, his main objection was the cost of my services. As I was about to leave, I said, "You know, Harry, you must know at least one other firm with this need that has a budget for training. How many names come to mind right now?" Like a light bulb suddenly switched on, he said, "Dave Jones, XYZ Company, Chicago." Harry set up an appointment for me using my telephone credit card number, and the referral became one of the largest engagements that I handled that year.

PLANNING FOR THE DISCUSSION

Having contemplated the major objectives/outcomes of the new-business discussion, and your plans of action once on site, let's review planning for the first meeting. By planning, you will greatly enhance your relationship with the prospect, as well as your own image and confidence. You will do a much better job because planning enables you to anticipate the prospective client's concerns and expectations. Consequently, each prospect will regard you as a confident, well-focused professional; and that is real leveraging of your time.

Here are the six stages of the interview-planning procedure:

1. *Get Totally Clear about the Need Situation You Wish to Discuss.* Although this point has been stressed in previous chapters, too many professionals begin to stray off course right here. There is a strong tendency,

even among veterans, to indicate their brilliance by discussing a variety of problem areas facing prospects in the niche and their ability to handle all of them. This tends to be counterproductive, however.

Focus on the hot button need situation that got you the appointment, and be prepared to answer for the prospective client, "Why are you bringing this need situation to me?" Your objective in answering this question is to have accumulated enough information to break through the "ho-hum" or "I-don't-need-any" barriers. *You* develop the sense of importance and urgency regarding the need situation. After all, you are a highly accomplished professional with an insider's reputation and a thorough understanding of the niche. You routinely identify need situations and bring them to the attention of prospects within the niche, often before they themselves recognize the magnitude of the need.

2. *Identify the Solution Program for the Need Situation.* Your understanding of the different types of need situations pays off here. The nature of the need and the prospect's requirements and expectations dictate the solution program you will provide. Solving a deficiency in the performance of a profit-affecting factor is quite different from assisting the prospect in making a decision. Different skills, information, techniques, and timing are required.

During this step you are doing the job mentally. You start by identifying the end products of the engagement—what they are, how they will be used, and who will use them. You identify the tasks that will be required to produce the end products, and you identify the roles the client's people will play as they assist your people in preparing the products.

3. *Assemble Existing Information about This Prospect.* This is a two-step process. First you assemble all the information you have on hand for this prospect. Then you identify information that you must verify during the meeting. As a general rule, early in the meeting you verify any information about the prospect on which you can't afford to be wrong. This is information that will affect the nature and scope of your recommended solution program.

When I conduct workshops on getting new clients for professional-service firms, I verify early on whether the prospects have provided traditional sales training programs. If they have, I know that for every 10 people forced to attend a traditional sales skills program, at least four or five still have heartburn about the experience. My solution program must be different. It must include specially developed, comfort-building modules that remove the lingering resentment brought into the training room by the reluctant and wary participants. Otherwise, they will tend to think to themselves, "Here we go again with another program that's going to deflate my technical skills and pressure me to develop a sales personality. No, thanks!"

4. *Identify Information You Must Obtain During the Meeting.* Identify the "information buckets" to be filled. Is there anything else you need to know to define the need situation and the desired solution program?

As a final check, put yourself in the prospect's shoes for a moment. What information should she expect me to have prior to the meeting? What information do I need that I can get only from this person or from someone else in her organization? If the information you need is not readily available from your contact person, help him or her to find it elsewhere in the organization.

Although all companies are somewhat different, you will get better and better at being able to obtain the needed information after conducting a few new-business discussions.

5. *Set Objectives.* Now, you are ready to set the objective for this particular meeting. What is the primary objective or end result of the meeting you want to accomplish? Remember to set a fallback objective in case the meeting bogs down.

6. *Develop Your Interview Plan.* Your interview plan should be in writing and contain the following elements:

   a. Opening benefit statement. (After saying "Hello," restate the solution goal mentioned during the appointment-getting telephone call.)

   b. Information you feel you must verify.

   c. Information buckets to fill during this meeting.

   d. At least three compelling reasons why the prospect should buy now from you.

It is essential that you present information to support your proposed solution and to justify why you should be authorized to proceed with it.

Figure 15.2 is an example of an interview plan I prepared for a meeting with a prospective client, an accounting firm located in the Southwest. Their positive need situation required instruction in identifying their clients' needs for additional services.

INTERVIEW PLAN FOR _____

1. Opening Benefit Statement—ideas for using current engagements to sell additional work
2. Verify:
   - ☐ Previous training?
   - ☐ Currently busy with ongoing engagements?
   - ☐ Leaving a lot of fees on the table?
3. Must get:
   - ☐ Number of engagements
   - ☐ Accomplished (or considered) regarding need
   - ☐ Who is for and against program
   - ☐ Desired/required specifications for the solution program
4. Reasons:
   - ☐ Have red-card system that is automatic need generator
   - ☐ Opportunity costs are staggering
   - ☐ Cross selling is retention, too
   - ☐ Firm X is 24% ahead since implementing red-card system

FIGURE 15.2. Sample Interview Guide

I frequently use the steps shown in Figure 15.3 in developing my interview plan. It builds my confidence as I identify in advance at least three reasons why the prospect needs my service solution and three reasons why my services are the best for the prospect. I also identify in advance why the prospect is justified in using my services now since I often have to provide tangible reasons for him to convince his people.

I don't list the potential objections the prospect might raise because I have a mental checklist for handling them. If a short-hand note would be useful to you, by all means jot it down. It's your plan, and it demonstrates that you are organized for action.

I've asked prospects how they felt about the way I referred to my interview plan during the meeting. The most frequent response was, "I was glad you had a plan for the meeting. It built my confidence in you as a professional."

Once prepared, review your interview plan with colleagues who accompany you, if any. Type the plan and put it in the holding pocket on the left-hand side of the writing portfolio you use to take notes during your new-business meetings.

STRUCTURING YOUR SALES STORY

STEP 1. Three reasons why this prospect needs the *type* of services I plan to discuss:

1. _____
   Positive outcome if used

   _____

2. _____
   Positive outcome if used

   _____

3. _____
   Negative condition corrected or prevented

   _____

STEP 2. Three reasons why *my* service is *the best* answer for the prospect:

1. _____

   _____

2. _____

   _____

3. _____

   _____

STEP 3. Three reasons why this prospect should buy my service *now:*

1. _____

2. _____

3. _____

FIGURE 15.3. Interview Plan

Planning for the interview and conducting the interview are not the same. Interruptions may occur, the prospect may not be attentive, the need you have identified may be the tip of the iceberg, and so on. Still, the more planning and preparation you undertake before making the on-site visit, the better.

BRINGING ALONG A COLLEAGUE

In planning for the interview, will you take along a colleague? If so, coordinating schedules could be difficult; yet, having two people present at a meeting ensures compatibility and completion of coverage.

The fundamental reason to take along a colleague on new-business discussions is to minimize the time lapse from contact to contract. If you sense that including a colleague would improve your chances of success, take several steps internally. Brief your colleague on the upcoming appointment. You will have to coordinate who leads and when; who takes notes and who follows up. If the colleague has only passing knowledge of the current situation, you may find it easier to provide three or four key questions you want him to ask in support of your presentation.

When should a joint contact be made? One answer is when a need solution requires a multidisciplined approach, or is outside your area of expertise. It is also advisable when the prospect represents a potential Key or A client. As a rule of thumb, bring a colleague when it will make it easier to communicate with the prospect.

Frequently, part of your interview plan involves asking the question, "Who is the person in my office who can most readily support this new-business quest?" Your answer will be the person to take with you. In all cases, let the prospect know that you will be bringing a colleague.

HOW TO PREPARE THE PERSONAL-CONTACT KIT

What Should Go into the Kit

The personal-contact kit includes materials that will identify your ability to solve the client's needs, such as:

- PARs (problem–approach–results reports)
- Testimonial letters from other satisfied clients
- Monthly reports
- PERT or Gantt charts
- Final reports

Other materials in your kit should include:

- Brochures or literature about your firm
- The original article containing the hot button that you first mailed to the prospect
- Any appropriate articles written by you or your staff

In determining what to include in your kit, you are really accumulating evidence and examples of "wins" in the need area. The items you include should be powerful. They should help answer the question, "Will the packet sell my services when I'm not around?" Your goal is to demonstrate through the materials that you are already an established force in handling the identified need.

If you are not an established force, and you don't have enough items to prepare a strong personal-contact kit, you can take some alternative measures. For example, you could develop a question-and-answer flyer that answers the most typical questions of prospective clients. Or you could develop a fact sheet, a one-page, typeset document that highlights the needs, current environmental conditions, and firm's capabilities.

In all instances, if you refer to clients, get their permission in advance; or don't use their names or any proprietary data that would identify them. This is crucial when you are exhibiting a final report prepared for another client.

What Should Not Go into the Kit

If you are a national firm with branch offices, some prospects will be overwhelmed by a nationally focused brochure. Don't make the mistake of coming across as a national firm with no local roots. If your personal-contact kit contains too much, the prospect may suspect that you are too big for them. Limit the testimonials you present to five; otherwise you may overwhelm your prospective clients.

The supporting materials in your personal-contact kit should show your ability to help others in the industry solve the kind of problem(s) you are there to discuss. The order in which you present these materials is up to you. What is important is that you effectively convey your firm's reputation, experience, and professionalism.

Your personal-contact kit should include such supporting items as a folder to hold a pad of $8\frac{1}{2}$ by 11-inch paper, a pen or pencil that indicates professionalism, and a professional-looking briefcase to hold everything.

PROSPECT CONTACT TIME

Once you have completed all of your pre-interview planning and assembled the personal-contact kit, you are ready to start making appointments. Use your travel time wisely. Lay out your contacts by zip codes so that you are in the general vicinity of a large number of prospects. If your travel takes you out of town, contact in advance the local chambers of commerce, economic development offices, or tourism centers to obtain maps and other pertinent materials.

Keep stationery and stamps on hand so you can leverage your time on the road. I have a tape recorder that plugs into the cigarette lighter in my car that allows me to debrief myself immediately following a new-business discussion. This information strengthens the proposal letters I prepare because they are based on facts verified and gathered during the meeting. Finally, while traveling, be alert to new suspects. Seasoned professionals called this "smokestacking."

Preparing Yourself for the Discussion

Always leave enough time to arrive at the prospect's office alert and relaxed. This is a very important step. Often, the busy professional will create inner stress by not getting to the prospect's location in time to relax. Such poor planning leaves little time for sizing up the surroundings. For example, one professional had to fight bad traffic all across town to arrive at a meeting. I insisted that he call the contact and explain that he was running late because of traffic. Instead, he argued that being a few minutes late wouldn't create a problem. Is there a problem? When you arrive on time, or when you call and say you will be a few minutes late, you maintain control and convey respect for the prospect's time.

Obviously, a car phone can work wonders if you have lots of appointments, work in a congested metro area, or easily get anxious when you're running late.

It takes time and effort to arrive at the prospect's office fully prepared to talk about new business. Get your car washed in advance of the call. If you are prone to sweaty palms, regardless of the situation, keep a towel or package of disposable premoistened towelettes in your car. How is your grooming? These may seem like basics, but every day thousands of experienced professionals ignore them. Early in the day, or if you have just eaten a mild lunch, your breath will probably be okay. However, late in the day, after a garlic-and-onions salad, or when your stomach is empty, your breath will stop a clock. The obvious solution can be found in any drugstore.

There are numerous relaxation techniques if calling on a new prospect represents a tense situation for you. You can take long, slow, deep breaths for a few minutes. Or you can visualize having a pleasant experience, meeting someone who will be warm and friendly and take an immediate liking to you. Many professionals find it relaxing to review the goals for the meeting and to visualize their desired objective being accomplished.

If you are habitually late, it is time to examine the issue. You need to ask, "Why am I doing this to myself? What am I gaining by underallocating the time necessary to arrive alert and relaxed?" Some are quick to blame a traffic jam for making them late. Traffic jams don't happen exclusively to you. You put your car in traffic that occasionally can jam up.

Perhaps the greatest relaxation technique is to acknowledge the purpose of the meeting. "I am here to create an environment in which the prospect and I think together." Your goal is to define, uncover, and articulate what the prospect wants and expects as a result of engaging you. This can only be done by getting the prospect to talk.

ON THE MATTER OF WAITING

How long should you wait? How hungry are you for new business? In general, I allow 10 to 15 minutes slack time for all appointments. However, I will politely remind the receptionist of my appointment about seven minutes after the scheduled appointment if she hasn't indicated any other prevailing circumstances. After another 10 to 15 minutes, I ask the receptionist to call the contact's secretary to see if the appointment is on the calendar and if the contact will be much longer. If I will be late for my next appointment by waiting any longer, I take out a business card and write on the back:

Mr. X:

Waited until 10:15. Since you must have been delayed, I will get back with you today to set up a more convenient time.

If you indicate that your time is too flexible or can be modified to meet a prospect's schedule, you are conveying the message that the prospect's time is more valuable than yours.

While waiting, use your time wisely. Make notes about the organization's atmosphere. Given your comfort zone, consider what may be the realistic outcome of the first meeting. Stay poised and ready to greet the prospect with a nonoverwhelming burst of energy.

We have come a long way, and our preparation has equipped us to conduct an effective new-business discussion. In the next four chapters, we'll look at the specific phases involved, and the skills and techniques for winning.

Conducting a Winning
New-Business Discussion

16

Opening the Discussion

The purpose of the opening phase is to build a bridge from the appointment-getting telephone contact to the new-business discussion.

To effectively open a new-business discussion, you must handle several important tasks, including the introductions, and communicate in a manner that builds rapport. All the while, be alert to cues from the prospect regarding his knowledge of your firm, buying motives, initial attitudes, and communication style. Now is when you establish your credentials, while your ultimate task is to find out how to proceed to the next step: defining the existing need situation. Let's examine the tasks involved in opening the new-business discussion effectively.

MANAGING THE INTRODUCTIONS

The contact is walking over to you. You stand up, exhibit an open posture—hands at your side, good eye contact. You are directly facing him. You have a smile on your face. You offer your dry, warm hand and present a firm but not overpowering handshake. In all ways, and on all levels, you offer positive vibes.

You know that in the business world, the time during which you first shake the prospect's hand is probably the most intimate you will ever have. You must manage this time effectively. In dealing with women, if they do not extend their hand, extend yours. Be careful: Many people believe the stronger the handshake, the lower the self-esteem or sensitivity to others. When you have managed this portion of the greeting properly, the contact knows who you are without feeling intimidated, bruised, or inferior; he feels there just might be something in it for him.

Just by saying, "Good Morning! I'm Elizabeth Goodwin," you establish some ground rules, including how you would like to be addressed and the level of formality. During the discussion, maintain eye contact with the prospect. Do not hand out your card at this point. If you are going to present your business card, do so shortly after you sit down or at the end of the discussion. If you bring a colleague, presenting your business cards in the order in which you are seated is both helpful and courteous.

Your briefcase is in your left hand. Your voice sounds natural and relaxed because you took the time to take a few deep breaths while you were waiting for the contact to appear. As you enter the contact's office, you get some clues about the person:

- How is the office arranged?
- Is it messy or neat?
- What pictures are on the desk and walls?
- Are there any plaques, awards, or mottoes posted?

You take your cue from the contact regarding seating. Often, the contact will head directly to his desk. If so, don't read "power game" into this act too soon. The contact may just feel more comfortable doing this. Or, he may direct you to an area used for more intimate discussions.

This point in the new-business discussion process is critical. You need to be prepared to take the lead if the contact suddenly throws the ball to you. One of the easiest ways to begin the discussion is to comment on some aspect of the contact's environment. If you have been hearing some good things about the organization you should mention it.

As an alternative opening, you may say, "How is business? Based on what we are seeing with clients in your industry, it looks like [state your observation]." This gets you down to business quickly and establishes your knowledge as an insider, provided you have done your homework.

All the while, your goal is to establish effective human interaction; you also communicate that you are easy to talk with and interested in what the contact has to say. All this should be done before proceeding to the next phase. The introduction builds a bridge from the initial phone contact to the face-to-face new-business discussion. In building such a bridge, you restate the central theme of your letter and phone call while maintaining the client-centered marketing approach. Remember, the relationship you develop may well outlast a single engagement. You want to make the contact feel unique and special. Everything about you must communicate that the contact is the focus and beneficiary of your time and intention.

If you are not met by the contact on time, follow the instructions in Chapter 15, on how long to wait. Meanwhile, make good use of this time: Review your notes; check your calendar; make some phone calls, if possible. While seated in the reception area, you can also assess the tempo of the organization, review available literature, or talk with other vendors who may be waiting. If you have to use the restroom, that is fine.

Do not make the mistake of reviewing a lot of internal notes or having to stand up quickly when the contact arrives and end up quickly gathering or spilling papers. This builds your anxiety and says to the prospect that you are not prepared or confident. The notes that you review or the paperwork that you undertake while waiting must be in a small contained area, which you can quickly and readily close up and take with you should the contact suddenly arrive.

REDUCING TENSION

The way that you communicate goes a long way toward reducing tension and building rapport. Your easy dialogue and open posture communicate that you are not a threat. The prospect has made a good decision in agreeing to meet you. It is important to try not to judge the other person, which is fairly easy to do if he does not meet your expectations. Communication specialist Janet Elsea, PhD, says "You *cannot* not communicate."

In all new encounters, the first several minutes are critical. You might get lucky and encounter a prospect who is as good at reducing tensions and creating a safe arena as you are, but don't count on it. This remains your responsibility. The better you are at reducing initial, normal tension, the faster you can build trust and rapport. The importance of arriving on time, relaxed, and alert pays off at this stage. I like to follow the three L's for reducing any residual tensions:

- Lighten up
- Listen
- Lay back

If the conversational ball remains in your court, be sure to emphasize that you have been looking forward to meeting the prospect. During this time, the contact is making a lot of snap decisions about you: You are okay; you are safe to be with; and so on. Most importantly, he is determining whether it will be easy to do business with you. Most professionals, including myself, are a bit tense during this time, especially when discussing a need that the contact person may see as a problem or threat. Remember, to reduce tension, keep it light!

BUILDING TRUST AND RAPPORT

Rapport has been defined as *being in harmony or agreement with another.* By establishing rapport early, you begin to build a relationship that is profitable to your contact. The rapport-building process continues throughout the discussion; it is facilitated by listening, accepting his ideas, sharing information and experiences, and virtually vibrating at the same frequency.

Listening and showing interest in what the contact has to say requires no less than 100 percent of your attention. Few have mastered this feat; Jacqueline Kennedy Onassis is one who has. One of her greatest strengths is that she makes the person she is listening to feel that she is interested in no other person in the world.

Besides listening, you must also indicate that you understand what the contact is saying. This can be done by offering small supporting statements such as "I see," "Hmmm," and most importantly, rephrasing what the other person has said. Another component of rapport building is respect—you must show that you accept the views of another no matter how vastly they differ from yours.

Be careful not to assume too much. For example, if there is a picture of children on a bookcase, say, "Is that your family?" instead of saying, "You have a nice-looking family." If the answer is yes, you can then say, "I have daughters, too—are you still smart in their eyes?" Any small story that touches areas of mutual interests or concern helps build rapport. The stronger the connection you can establish, the more the prospect will feel that you are alike. Then you may have access to the contact's mind and emotions and pave the way past such questions as, "How long has this person been with the company," or "What jobs did he have on the way up?"

What diminishes your ability to build rapport? Some barriers are physical, such as a poor setting in which to discuss business—noise, interruptions, and so on. A poor first impression or allowing preconceived notions to interfere with your discussion hinders your ability to build rapport. If you haven't done your homework, you will be anxious, which will be picked up by the contact. Finally, if your manner or presentation is overwhelming or threatening, your chances for building trust and rapport on a long-term basis start off behind the eight ball.

IDENTIFYING BUYING MOTIVE(S)

Buying motives are the factors that drive the contact. While I will focus on this in more detail in Chapter 17, you should be alert to what may be driving your contact's behavior.

Earlier I introduced the idea of determining the buying motives to be triggered by the initial-contact mailing program. Figure 16.1 depicts prospect buying motives. Two factors have been added—quality and price. Many of your prospects will be interested in quality, but some prospects are driven by price.

Three other factors can be used to gain further insights into the contact's buying motives.

- Short-term gain versus long-term gain
- Personal objectives versus company objectives
- Defensive posture in market versus offensive posture in market

SIZING UP THE CONTACT

Whether or not you want to, you will immediately begin sizing up the contact: it's simply human nature. However, your goal is to do it so that it enhances your chances of obtaining the engagement. First, determine how best to pitch him. You don't want to talk over his head. When you are

PROSPECT BUYING MOTIVES

Need Situation	Fear of Failure	Fear of Unknown	Meeting Requirements of Job	Feeling Good—Self-Approval	Looking Good—Approval by Others	Quality	Price
1. Negatives							
a. Fear	X						
b. Threat		X					
c. Decision		X					
2. Positive							
a. Wanted factor is lacking			X	X	X		
b. Wanted factor is in short supply			X		X		
3. Task			X		X		

FIGURE 16.1. Prospect Buying Motives

ready to bridge to the body of the discussion, you can fine-tune your approach to the prospective client's needs and communication style. An important aspect of sizing up the contact is to gauge his initial attitude toward your firm and its services.

The contact's initial attitude can be classified into one of three categories.

1. *Accepting or Interested in You and Your Firm/Service.* This is entirely likely as a result of a client-centered marketing approach to a new-business discussion.

2. *Indifferent to You and/or Your Firm/Service.* The question that immediately comes up is, "Why might this attitude be present?" One answer is that the prospect cooled to the idea of handling the need. He might have been told by his boss to curb all expenditures, and he felt embarrassed in calling you to cancel. Another reason may be that he is preoccupied with something.

3. *Hostile to You and/or Your Firm/Service.* Why is this attitude present? Since you were successful in obtaining the appointment, it is unlikely that you will encounter this attitude. I once accompanied a client on new-business calls and ran into this situation. My client was an executive search consultant who had obtained an appointment with a newly hired vice president. We were ushered into the prospect's office and greeted

Perceptive	Myopic
Risk Taker	Risk Avoider
Leader	Led
Big Picture	Nitty Gritty
Open Communications	Closed Communications
Trusting	Suspicious
Conservative	Liberal
Macho	Wimp
Suave	Earthy
Loud	Quiet

FIGURE 16.2.   Sizing Up the Contact

with verbal abuse. We even had our legitimacy questioned. The reason soon become obvious. The contact had been outplaced from his previous organization and felt a great deal of anger toward consultants. The only close made that day was the door, which was slammed as we left his office.

Figure 16.2 offers 10 additional factors for sizing up the contact. The reason you attempt to size up another is not to manipulate but to better relate to the person as an individual. Fortunately, certain patterns of behavior and communication tend to repeat themselves, and the alert professional can learn from them.

ESTABLISHING YOUR CREDENTIALS

Your task here will be to establish your credentials by qualifying yourself and your firm as a team worth knowing. This will also ensure that the contact is receptive to additional discussion. To establish your credentials, synopsize your industry experience and relate the experience to your captive audience. Offer a small bit of information on yourself and others in the firm. Briefly mention your referral sources if appropriate.

BRIDGE TO BODY OF DISCUSSION

So far you have managed the introduction, helped reduce tension, and built up some trust and rapport. Meanwhile, you have been sizing up the contact, looking for tip-offs to the buying motives. The next step is to move to the body of the discussion. This is done in two simple steps. First, you obtain agreement to proceed. Then, you reiterate the opening benefit statement. For example, you wait for a pause and then say: "Mr. Prospect, if its okay with you [agreement][opening benefit statement] I'd like to share some ideas about improving your cash flow."

You may be thinking that I'm overusing the benefit statement. Not a chance—that's why the contact is investing his time in seeing you.

The opening benefit statement represents the moment of truth. If you are a professional in the new-business development game, you have thought about your opening statement and practiced its delivery. It is precisely now that your preliminary need and solution analysis pays off.

Always, always, *always* put the prospect first by structuring the initial statement in his or her terms. For example, begin by mentioning a need, problem, or interest to the client in the form of a general statement:

> *"Many professionals are interested in improving their client-development capabilities to meet increasingly stiff competition."*

> *"Mr. Scott, since talking to you on the phone last Wednesday, I have been thinking about the way in which we have been assisting our clients in winning at the new-client game."*

Immediately after presenting your statement, observe and listen to the contact's response and classify his or her attitude toward your statement. This is a repeat of the initial attitude check. Be alert for any signs that the positive attitude has slipped.

Now you're into the body of the new-business discussion. Your immediate objective is to define the scope, costs, and consequences of the existing need situation. This will be covered in the next chapter.

17

Defining the Existing Need Situation

You have successfully opened the new-business discussion and bridged to the body of the meeting. Now it is time to prepare a very carefully developed description of the prospect's need situation. This is done by putting a picture frame around the situation so you can deliver a verbal snapshot of it at a given time. That way, you can compare the way things presently are with what is desired or required in the next step. Your suggested service solution will fill the gap.

Defining the existing need situation is a 6-step process. First you verify the *nature* of the need situation to be certain that you and the prospect are singing out of the same hymnal. Next you define who, where, when, and how. Then you estimate the *costs* to date associated with the need situation. Get the prospect to look at the probable *adverse consequences* to her and her organization if the situation is not resolved. Because you have covered a lot of ground in your definition phase, you stop for a moment to *verify mutual understanding,* to be certain you and the contact are in sync. Finally you *restate* the opening benefit statement in terms of the *central solution goal*. This goal statement serves as a bridge into the next phase where you define the desired future situation. Each of the six steps will be discussed separately, with examples to illustrate the ideas as needed.

UPSETTING THE EQUILIBRIUM

If you are doing your job correctly, you will disturb the equilibrium in the minds and emotions of the buying team. Discuss and probe the need situation so that the contact person is the one who identifies the magnitude of the problem. This eliminates the burden of having you deliver the bad news; instead, your role as the professional advocate is enhanced and preserved.

It is crucial in the new-business discussion that the prospect be the one who mentions that the current situation is undesirable. Moreover, the contact must tell you that the expectations of the management team or the organization's publics are dissatisfied in some way. This strategy also involves having her tell you the costs to date, and the consequences of not proceeding with direct action. You then, skillfully, bring a level of anxiety into play and allow the prospect to marinate in her misery. The questions or directive probes that you use will generate yes/no answers that highlight unwanted conditions or insufficient resources.

Let's step back now and examine how we steer the new-business discussion toward this desired outcome.

Verifying/Determining the Nature of the Need Situation

By the time you have sent your letter and made a telephone call, presumably the need situation you are going to discuss and define has already been nailed down. First verify that the need situation is indeed similar to that discussed in the initial-contact package.

It is possible that the need situation will have changed by the time you arrive. This has happened to me several times. The task is to determine the *exact nature* of the need situation.

Defining the Scope of the Need Situation

There is always a history to a need situation. There are always players with different stakes. Some will champion your efforts; others don't want you to succeed. You must understand the prevailing environment to be successful. This involves determining where the need exists within the organization, and what impact it has on operations.

Next you must determine when the need started. Who became aware of the need, and how? Then try to determine what has already been done to address the situation. Who has taken the lead? What kind of effort has been expended? What are the results?

Determine the Cost to Date—Extrinsic and Intrinsic

Your goal here is to get the contact to determine the out-of-pocket, as well as the emotional and opportunity, dollar costs to date. When you have caused a contact to attach a dollar figure to the need, you are then in a position to empathize with her about her difficult situation. Then suggest that the contact sum the dollar amount of the total costs to date. This can be done with a leading statement, such as, "My experience is that it costs the average consulting firm about $25,000 to $35,000 to replace a three-year supervisor. Does that square with your experience?" If she says yes, the budget for your solution program will be only a fraction of these costs.

There are several important reasons for determining the costs as early as possible in a new-business discussion. First, you gain a sense of the magnitude and difficulty the prospect has had with the particular need situation. You also convey the message, "Hey, this is getting more costly all the time." You have thus paved your way to introducing your cost-effective service solution. Moreover, the contact is less likely to be shell-shocked by your fees.

Getting the contact to talk about costs is a critical step in the definition of the existing need situation. Without a ballpark figure of the costs being incurred, you lack the ammunition to disturb the buying team's equilibrium and emotions, and to influence the recognition that this need must be addressed now. By attaching an air of urgency to the situation, you help the contact realize that it will be far more costly not to take action immediately.

Determine the Consequences of Not Proceeding

You next get the contact to recognize the dire consequences of not proceeding. In other words, saying no to your solution will be saying yes to additional costs and courting disastrous consequences. This is a powerful strategy. Approach it delicately. Express the consequences of not taking action gently, by saying, for example, "Ms. Henderson, given the widespread dissatisfaction surrounding the forced merger of the two departments, what is the probability that this situation will work itself out, without some focused and specialized attention?" Suppose her reply was:

> *"I don't see much hope of it correcting itself. God knows I've tried my best. It won't let go."*

Now you get to be the good guy and use a supporting, reinforcement statements such as:

> *"A 'no' to proceeding is a 'yes' to incurring additional costs and consequences."*
>
> or, *"You're absolutely right, Ms. Henderson, this is an important and difficult situation that is not healing itself. As you say, unless something is done you run the risk of (you mention the likely adverse consequences)."*

Let's look at the structure and power of the preceding supporting-reinforcement statement. The statement was preceded by your probing question. . . .

Dialogue

You probe. . .

"Ms. Henderson, given the widespread dissatisfaction surrounding the forced merger of the two departments, what is the probability that this situation will work itself out, without some focused and specialized attention?"

Her reply. . .

"I don't see much hope of it correcting itself. God knows I've tried my best. It won't let go."

Analysis

The probe was done in a gentle, conversational manner that led to the prospect's admission that self-correction was not probable. Because you did not mention that her own attempts have been costly, futile, or ill-advised, she did not have to defend her actions. In fact, you have been saying all along that the situation is difficult to handle because it requires special expertise.

Your replay. . .

"You're absolutely right, Ms. Henderson, this is an important and difficult situation that is not healing itself. As you say, unless something is done you run the risk of. . . (you mention the likely adverse consequence)."

You support her remark made in response to your probe, then reinforce her position and make her "right" in being there. You are not the bad guy trying to push her into something you are trying to sell. Instead, you are thinking along with her and sharing ideas in a compassionate manner.

Triggering the Buying Motive

During this step, you repeat the probe, support-reinforcement, and consequences loop until you have the situation defined. When you have the picture frame and verbal snapshot of the existing situation completed, you bridge to the next phase in the new-business discussion by restating the solution goal. Of course, you don't use the same words every time.

Verify Mutual Understanding

You have verified or determined the nature of the need situation, defined its scope and determined the cost to date. You have also helped the prospect determine the consequences of not proceeding. You have, perhaps, triggered one or more buying motives.

Before proceeding to the next phase, be certain that you are still singing the same hymn. If there is disagreement regarding the nature and scope of the need situation or of the costs and consequences, then your suggested solution will not tie up all the loose ends in the prospect's mind.

Slow down and say, "Let's see if we are both tracking this thing the same way. What I hear you telling me is GHI. Am I on target?" If not, use nondirective probes to round out or clarify the situation, such as "How is that?" "Why?" or "In what ways do . . . ?" If you two are not in harmony, slow down and ask, "Where have I gone astray?" You have to assume responsibility for the variance.

The prospect will often raise a question about a topic that you thought you had covered sufficiently. Patiently discuss the same topic using other words. Try making a sketch to illustrate a point if possible.

Verifying your mutual understanding of the need situation is a critical point in the new-business discussion. If it is achieved, your next task is to use a mutual solution goal to bridge to the next phase. (See next section.)

If you don't achieve a mutual understanding, you will have to make a decision. Ask yourself, "Does it make sense to try to get in harmony at this time? Should I suggest that the prospect restate her concerns/questions/considerations, so I can go back to the office to think through her responses?" The last option is poor because it lets the prospect off the hook, but it may be the best one in the situation.

Restate the Solution Goal

This step is as simple as saying, "Ms. Henderson, I feel comfortable that I understand the background and circumstances surrounding the fall-off of morale in the newly formed departments. Your analysis and candor really have been valuable. Let's think about the way your department is going to perform when we get the people working fully as a team."

This is a simple but powerful statement. Let's analyze it to identify the power element in it:

Ms. Henderson, (1) I feel comfortable that I understand (2) the background and circumstances surrounding the fall-off of morale (3) in the newly formed departments. (4)

In the first phrase, I was again respectful in using her name. Had she asked me to call her Elizabeth, I would have done so immediately. Phrase 2 is a personal statement of the way I work—I probe until I'm comfortable and confident that I understand. I don't wing it and risk misunderstanding the situation. Phrase 3 is a more positive description of the mess she has been living with. I didn't mind her marinating in her misery during the definition step. Now, however, I'm promising her that better days are coming. Phrase 4 refers to the newly formed departments as not being her direct responsibility.

"Your analysis and candor really have been valuable (5). Together, let's think (6) about the way your department is going to perform (7) when we (8) get the people working fully as a team." (9)

Phrase 5 rewards her for her communication style and openness. Praised behavior is likely to be repeated, so you are shaping her communications with you. Phrases 6 and 8 create the partnership that is going to enable her to win. She admitted earlier that her approach did not work. Phrase 7 is the solution goal stated a bit differently to trigger the buying motive(s) that you think are driving the prospect.

To test your mastery of buying motives, jot down the motives that are driving her behavior on the line below:

If I were conducting the interview, I would assume that fear of failure and need for approval are driving this woman's buying behavior.

Phrase 9 holds the end result of your solution program, which you have not yet introduced. At this point, she will be primed to listen and think along with you.

A skilled accountant who had attended my Getting New Clients workshop engaged me to accompany her on a number of new-client business discussions. During one meeting, the discussion focused on the accounts-receivable problem experienced by the prospect. After defining the need situation, the accountant made the following solution goal statement:

"Let's see what is involved in improving your cash flow, so you can get your organization out of the bank's pockets."

The effect on the prospect was dramatic. The accountant had activated the buying motivators of fear of failure and need for approval, a powerful combination.

Copy the chart shown on page 215 and take it with you on calls. Questions 1 through 3 relate to the points made in this chapter, questions 4 and 5 relate to material presented in Chapter 18.

After you have examined and agreed upon the nature and extent of the situation and made a bridge using a mutual solution goal, move to the next step. We will pick this up in Chapter 18.

GUIDE FOR THE NEW-BUSINESS DISCUSSION

1. What is the REAL NEED this prospect wants to discuss?
2. What is the SCOPE of the need situation?
3. Where is the need?
   - ☐ Located organizationally?
   - ☐ Felt or observed?
   - ☐ Impacting on operations?

   When did the need start?
   - ☐ Become evident?
   - ☐ To whom?
   - ☐ How?

   What has been done/tried/thought of?
   - ☐ By whom?
   - ☐ When?
   - ☐ With what results?

   Who is this person?
   - ☐ Title
   - ☐ Authority
   - ☐ Place in the decision-making unit

   How URGENT is the need?
4. What are the COSTS and CONSEQUENCES?
   - ☐ What COSTS have been incurred to date?
   - ☐ What are the probable CONSEQUENCES of not proceeding?
5. What is the SOLUTION goal?

   What is the desired/required SOLUTIONS PROGRAM?
   - ☐ Objectives
   - ☐ Solution alternatives
   - ☐ Work team—who and why?
   - ☐ Deliverables
     - ☐ What, in what form?
     - ☐ When needed?
6. Who are the other players?

   What authority does each have?

   What is their stake in the engagement?
   - ☐ Who will make the PURCHASE decision?
   - ☐ Who will serve the POINT OF CONTACT?
   - ☐ Who will EVALUATE the RESULTS?

18

Defining the Desired/Required Future Situation

In Chapter 17, we wanted to sit on the same side of the desk as the prospect to understand what he is facing. Our task was to develop the ability to see as the prospect sees and describe the need situation in his terms.

In this chapter, we will acquire new clients by helping the prospect define the desired or required future situation. If a prospect views a situation as *required*, it will be easier to trigger and reinforce buying motives.

Up to this point, we have worked with the prospect only in defining the existing need situation. We developed a carefully defined word picture of the situation today.

Now, our task is to develop a word picture of what the prospect feels is desired or required and to determine when he would like that situation to become a reality. This can be shown as the following equation:

$$
\frac{
\begin{array}{ll}
\text{DESIRED/REQUIRED} & \text{(Future Situation)} \\
-\qquad\quad \text{IS} & \text{(Existing Situation)}
\end{array}
}{
\text{OPPORTUNITY GAP}
}
$$

The best professional-service marketers always have the prospect say in advance what he expects before they suggest a service solution. Conversely, a novice attempts to find out the need and then quickly jumps in

216

with the solution. It is simple to have the prospect define specifications for the solution; he must be coached to describe what that improved situation will look like:

- What will be eliminated after the need has been addressed?
- What doesn't exist now that will?

Think *with* the prospect here rather than *for* him. You want the prospect to visualize a positive future, which both of you will create together. Rather than keep him marinating in misery, you focus on future potential. Ask him to identify the positives and negatives when you have completed the engagement.

You have yet to describe your service solution because you want as much of the prospect's input as possible to ensure that your proposed solution will be desirable, achievable, and understood.

Suppose prospect A has a restricted cash flow that is hampering operations. You walk through the desired future situation by asking him what would change if he had an adequate cash flow. First the negatives are eliminated (in discussion): The contact no longer has to be embarrassed sending out letters explaining the delay in payments; he doesn't miss opportunities to gain new business because of a lack of funds.

What are the positive developments that the contact envisions? Foremost is a checkbook with positive balance. Another is the ability to plan effectively in the short run, at least, and being able to focus on other issues confronting the firm.

As the prospect visualizes the positive conditions, his buying motives are triggered again without you selling him anything.

What if the prospect describes a scenario you know is not feasible? Actually, this is a favorable situation. Both you and the prospect want to know as soon as possible if the desired outcome is feasible.

The worst time to learn of the prospect's future scenario is when your closing statement has gone down in flames or when the prospect says, "My God, that doesn't fit what I had in mind." You get a sinking feeling in your stomach and realize that you both miscommunicated. However, there is no use blaming the prospect. The responsibility for conducting successful new-business discussions is all yours.

How can you avoid this situation? You create an environment in which you and the prospect think together. Your goal is to define, uncover, and articulate what the prospect wants and expects as a result of engaging you, or someone who provides your type of services. This can only be done by getting the prospect to talk.

Determine Solution Criteria

Now the prospect is talking and feeling a little more confident, and may even be excited. Now ask, "Mr. X, probably the easiest way to get at this is, how will you and I both know when I am doing a good job?" That is the money question. He might say, "You'll be meeting with me to keep me informed, staying on budget, and saving me money. Most importantly, you'll be building me a system that my people can handle—no bells or whistles for me!" Whatever he says, with which you agree, becomes the solution specifications; His response becomes the yardstick to measure your service.

Write down his exact words for reference later in the discussion. If you get the engagement, use his very words at the conclusion of the engagement. During a client "satisfaction" meeting, you will review his solution specifications, assure satisfaction, and seek referrals.

I remember a tough situation with a seasoned and wily managing partner of a prestigious management-consulting firm. This firm positioned itself as *the* premier firm offering its type of services. The situation was positive. The need was to fill a *lack* of required performance factors. The firm had a cadre of rainmaker partners who regularly brought in high-potential new clients. The partners-in-training, however, were noticeably deficient in the number of contacts made to actively seek new clients.

His reply to my question, "How will you and I both know when I am doing the job for you?" was instructive: "When this year's crop of potential partners is landing more work than we can handle and you're just a memory." This left me partially informed, so I returned to my notes on his existing situation and began reprobing the elements. I asked, "When you visualize the associates coming out of training, whom do you see emerging as the early leaders and why?" This opened the floodgates, and his real solution criteria emerged. He really wanted to have his preferred candidates for partners be the stars. I added that I could not guarantee this, but would devote extra attention both during and after the training to ensure the very best results possible for the high-potential PITs (partners-in-training).

Often, the prospect's response to the question, "How will you and I know when I am doing the right job?" involves some outcome that may occur in a year or two, beyond the time and scope of your solution program.

If the prospect says, "When I have a million in sales per year," and his best year so far has only been $350,000, you must assert yourself. Novices buy into the prospect's banter. The pros know how to say, "That is certainly a good long-term goal. For now, let's focus on what we can achieve in the foreseeable future." Again, the strategy is to return to the notes regarding the scope, costs, and potential adverse consequences of the existing situation, and then to focus on the "must" and "can-do" factors in the solution program. You might say, "Specifically, let's determine what can be achieved by the time we have completed out work with you." Then you might say, "I will be able to produce the new organizational plan. Will you want me to stay on to assist in its implementation? Or will you handle that?" Hence, you are literally mapping out with the prospect (who is soon to be a client) the immediate future and your respective roles. You also are conveying the message that these steps do contribute to the prospect's long-term goals; yet it is still best to walk before you run.

When you redefine the scope of work and make a stand for integrity, you are able to tower above the other professionals the prospect may have encountered recently.

DETERMINE THE TIMING

Continue to scope the future situation by probing. Steer the prospect toward a realistic time frame on which both of you can agree and in which you know you will be able to deliver. At any point in the process, you have the option of selling your services in phases or rethinking the situation if it will require a significant and continuing effort on your part. Always give yourself operating room: Don't set the time frame tighter than necessary.

I frequently have to sell in phases. The majority of clients face one of two situations: A large number are in trouble—they've lost or are on the verge of losing important clients, a rainmaker has left or is burned-out, or competition is moving in for the kill.

Another sizable number have been providing traditional sales training, earning the resentment and resistance of senior and high-potential people, and manifesting itself in missed targets. Some lament, "I'm already too busy serving the clients I have. How can you expect me to bring in more? Aren't you concerned with *quality?*"

In complex and highly emotional situations, the first phase of my work usually consists of fact finding and ego soothing. I look for opportunities to catch them doing something right. I stress that what has been done to date can be modified and can serve as a launch pad for even better performance—if the same mistakes are not repeated. This implies that I'm the new factor that will ensure success and heal the wounds.

Subsequent phases involve providing working on site with them in mentoring assignments, developing an in-house marketing director, and the like. This requires patience from the client who wants to get the problem solved yesterday and a lot of counseling and hand holding by the professional.

A managing partner of a firm whose growth had suddenly taken a nosedive asked me about my Getting New Clients workshop. He said his expectation was for me to condense the 3-day workshop into a Friday-evening-and-all-day-Saturday program, and still achieve the results of the 3 day program. His rationale was that he could not afford to have 18 participants miss 24 hours of potentially billable time, especially with a fall-off of billable hours. To sweeten the deal he told me, "I'm willing to pay you the full amount for the workshop because you'd have to push harder, and you're giving up a weekend for me."

I pointed out that the three days I allocated for the workshop was not capricious. I had developed a program that worked. He agreed that my data was sound but insisted that his needs superseded mine. I tried to reduce the scope of the program to fit his time frame, but to no avail. We wound up at loggerheads. I declined to serve him at the time.

Many professionals I have trained are concerned that the prospect may paint too rosy a picture for his future scenario. They are concerned that the prospect may ask for results that exceed their abilities. This has not happened in my experience. For those prospects who do have a grand, long-term scenario, you can be a part of the process.

One client agreed to my conducting an introductory 1-day client-centered marketing program, to be followed later with a 2-day niche-marketing program. This fit into his long-range goal of developing a marketing consciousness among all professionals in his firm prior to investing in the niche-development process.

If not handled skillfully, on occasion it may look as if you are turning business down. Or you may be setting up a situation in which the next professional-service provider actually gets the job. Continually bring the prospect back to reality. Yes, there are other professionals who promise to meet all the client's long-term expectations, regardless of how reachable they are. In dealing with a prospect's unrealistic expectations, I have often used this thought-provoking statement, "I would rather turn you down up front than let you down later." Prospects appreciate and respect this type of candor.

Your professionalism and integrity must prevail. Let the prospect feel that you are in charge and are trying to figure out the very best way to get the job done for him. What you are advocating is a realistic progression toward long-term goals by dividing the tasks into bite-size portions.

What if you know that the prospect needs a variety of services but is only asking for services in one area? If the prospect will be better off with your solution in this area, then strive to sell it. Perform the work profitably. However, make sure that the prospect maintains realistic expectations for the results of this one service.

SURFACE EXPECTATIONS

The reason professionals don't get the second, third, and fourth engagement is that the new client is disappointed. The disappointment stems from not determining with the prospective client what the desirable future scenario will be and how you will know when you have done the job correctly. Often, the final product has not been thought through or negotiated. The prospect and the professional-service provider had different thoughts on what was being delivered. This situation need not occur, and if you follow the approach presented here it won't.

By now you are chomping at the bit to tell the prospect about your service solution and the benefits he can obtain from working with you. In the next chapter, you'll have the opportunity to tell your story in a client-centered way.

19

Presenting Your
Proposed Solution

You have opened the new-business discussion and defined the existing need situation in the prospect's terms. You have thought through with the prospect the desired or required future situation. You are now about to present your proposed solution. Figure 19.1 summarizes the steps that lead up to your discussion of the proposed solution.

The need situation on the left side of Figure 19.1 includes both favorable components of the present situation, A, and unfavorable components of the present situation, B. The need situation conveys the client's uncertainty in achieving the desired situation.

How you define the problem, the approach you use, and the results you offer should lead to the desired situation, labeled C. Roughly speaking, $A - B = C$. In other words, when you alleviate the negative components of the present situation, what you create is a desired situation, C. PAR, in this figure, represents the word *par* just as in golf. The B section of the need situation is literally below par.

Continuing with Figure 19.1, the elapsed time is the time frame given to achieve the desired situation. This sets a tone of urgency and limits the scope of your solution program. After thinking through the situation, you are ready to move from point P, the present situation, to point F, the future situation. You can now offer a verbal proposal to the prospect.

Your goal is to have him think through the situation and say, "Your ideas make sense." Here, analysis ends and judgment prevails. For example, to get the prospect to think about his goals and strategies to achieve

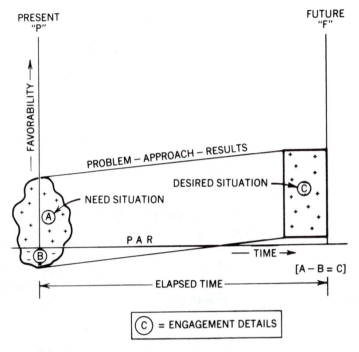

FIGURE 19.1.   Assessing a Need Situation

them, should you present a variety of options or one main solution? When the prospect is shopping around or can't articulate his wants, use your judgment, offer a range of solutions, determine the best single solution, and so on.

WEAVING BETWEEN THE FINE LINES

The existing situation is transformed into the future situation by means of your proposed solution program. This conversion process puts you on the solution track.

All the while, you are including the prospect as an active participant in the process. Instead of saying, "Let's see how I will develop your improved accounts-receivable system," you are saying, "Let's see how we can work together to improve your cash flow to accomplish XYZ." The second statement is used because it is client-centered, or more representative of the prospect's interests. The end of your conversation should be upbeat. Focus on the positives so the prospect can visualize obtaining the desired or required situation that will result from working with you.

If you feel comfortable, offer a detailed statement to move the action forward. You could say:

> "Let's see how we can work together to speed up your cash flow [a desired, favorable, future situation—the central theme of your solutions program] . . .
>
> "so you can stay out of the bank [an undesired condition] and; . . .
>
> "reduce the killing interest charges you have been carrying [the cost and consequences of the present situation]."

It's a mouthful, but if said slowly and in a conversational manner, it is music to the prospect's ears. All along, that is what he wanted to hear. Your detailed statement also tells him that you consider what he says important.

DISCUSSING SOLUTION ALTERNATIVES

If you choose to discuss a range of solutions, there is a prescribed way to do so. First, let's briefly review the potential negatives in discussing a range of alternatives. The potential for confusing the prospect is greater and mentioning alternative solutions may also provide a resistant prospect with more opportunities to argue and disagree.

Now back to discussing solution alternatives. Introduce solutions with confidence. After all, you have handled the situation before. Since the proposed solution program is the vehicle for delivering the future situation, you now want to determine how the prospect wants to travel to the required or desired future situation:

- *Rolls Royce.* Don't skimp on quality. Produce a solid, fully functioning product that will yield long-term dividends.
- *Oldsmobile.* Pay top dollar, but not through the roof, for a dependable, modest prestige vehicle (service solution) that borders on the luxurious, but is rooted in the practical.

- *Volkswagen.* Get the job done economically and efficiently; forget the frills. If it works, fine; we can always dress it up in the future.

Here is how to work with the three alternatives. Start by mentioning the Rolls Royce solution program and watch closely for signs of prospect flinch or resistance, such as facial changes, including a tightening of the lips or a squinting of the eyes.

In discussing a solution program for a firm that has never had any marketing training, I would say, "For firms that are considering installing a marketing function, I have structured my work to include the entire professional staff in some form of marketing and business development."

If the prospect remains silent, or says "I'm not interested in training everyone. I can't afford it. They wind up leaving after a while, and it's too costly," then I continue with the Oldsmobile solution: "We could limit the program to your long-term, high-potential troops and the existing partners." Again, I observe and listen to assess the situation. If this alternative fails, I wind up a bit more forcefully by saying, "Given the nature of your situation, you should get your marketing program underway by training your existing partners who voluntarily agree to the training."

If the prospect doesn't respond, or if the response is unfavorable, you clearly do not have all the facts. Refer back to your notes and verify their accuracy. The trappings of the person's office or the organization's reputation are poor predictors of how much the prospect will invest. Also, never assume that a prospect will buy or set a budget limit until given the opportunity to do so.

OUTLINING THE PROPOSED WORK APPROACH

Once you have determined the appropriate service solution, restate the goal to confirm that you are communicating effectively. Make the service solution tangible. Remember, you are still communicating on a verbal level; nothing is in writing, other than notes. By remaining in the discussion mode, you gain more information on how to prepare a winning written proposal, if required, and ensure that the actual engagement will proceed smoothly.

When outlining the proposed work approach, first discuss the methodology with the prospect. Don't overwhelm the prospect with too many details. He wants assurance that you know what you're doing. Focus on the broad tasks and the results you will achieve. Carefully explain the nature and level of assistance that you expect from the prospect and upon which the budget will be predicated. For example, what will he do, how will he do it, and what will he provide?

Next spell out what you *won't* be doing—what is not part of the engagement. This discussion will reduce misunderstandings further down the road. (Note: Try not to discuss fees in specific terms until you are convinced you have an interested and qualified prospect.)

In a similar manner, spell out exactly what deliverables will be supplied and in what level of detail as a result of this engagement. This includes sample work plans, interim reports, monthly or progress reports, and the final product. Have samples on hand; visual impact is important. If the prospect will be receiving any additional benefits, spell these out.

This kind of precision may seem tedious and unnecessary. However, it is precisely this type of effort that separates the novices from the pros in getting new clients. If is not advantageous to have vague or nebulous notions of how the engagement will turn out. Unforeseen developments occur, but in most instances, you will minimize the number of surprises if you've first thought through the situation.

Next discuss who will be leading, participating in, and supporting the engagement team. Find out who will be the engagement coordinator. Ask if bio sketches are available. It is to your advantage to have the prospect's best person serve as the engagement coordinator. This person must be a credible source, well trained, and able to serve as a continuing point of contact.

Ask, "Does it make sense to proceed?" The phrase has been carefully designed. It quietly and powerfully communicates to the prospect that from this point forward it will be a mutual decision to proceed. How you communicate during the new-business discussion educates the prospect and shapes his response to you. If you communicate that you are hungry for business or at his beck and call, many will attempt to take advantage of the situation.

During a new-business meeting with one of my clients, I was astounded to hear him tell a prospect, "I'm at the disposal of my clients; call me anytime. I'll always be available to talk to you. I'd like to have you for a client." After a long discussion about the inadvertent implications of such statements, he vowed to be more careful with his promises. You want to appear busy, but not too busy to serve them.

Viewed properly, the new-business discussion is really a miniconsulting engagement that employs the classic problem definition, fact gathering, analysis, and recommendations.

Making a verbal proposal is desirable at this time because it enables you to move in quickly for the close. If your presentation interested the prospect, you have effectively shortened your selling task and can more quickly initiate the engagement. Even if your presentation is not exactly on target with the prospect's thinking, you can still quickly regroup, redefine the scope of work, and make a second verbal proposal that may hit the jackpot.

Your verbal proposal should build excitement and confidence in the mind and emotions of the contact. She must feel that your solution program is a good purchase and that you are the best one to resolve her need.

Following the verbal proposal, test for "fit" or agreement by posing questions such as the following:

"Does this make sense?"

"Have we covered the essentials?"

And the power statement:

"How will you and I know when I have done a good job for you?"

By this time, the response of the contact should be, "That sounds about right"; or, "Yes, plus X"; or, "When can we start?" If you followed the steps outlined in this book, it would be a surprise if your verbal proposal weren't right on the mark, or at least very close.

SELLING THE SOLUTION AND ITS BENEFITS

To sell the solution and close the sale, outline the approved future picture frame of the prospect situation. Your verbal proposal puts the contact in the picture. How? You use her actual words and expressions from your interview notes. (Note: These would also appear in a written proposal.)

Stress your understanding of the many supporting elements within the prospect's organization. With these elements as anchor points in the service solution, you enable the contact to maintain her own concept, and position yourself as an advocate for improving her situation, without making her feel wrong or inadequate about retaining your services.

Conclude by stressing that the contact's positive attitude and the strength of her organization and staff, coupled with your experience and staff, will create the desired or required future situation *on time and within budget*. The benefits of this approach are that you and the prospect will be working from the same side of the fence, supplying resources to arrive at the cost-effective service solution.

20

Handling Concerns and Information Needs

You put in a substantial amount of time and effort to ensure that your services are needed by your prospect.

Yet no matter how compelling the need, no matter how precise the definitions of the desired and required future situation you develop, prospects are naturally going to have objections, concerns, and requests for additional information. Objections and concerns have been the bane of the salesperson's existence. Don't take it personally. It is a normal response to the introduction of new ideas.

Hereafter, *welcome* objections and client concerns. They give you the potential energy to close the discussion and move to action (Chapter 21). In this chapter, we will look at ways to handle objections, including the "big three" facing us all:

1. Skepticism

2. Misunderstanding

3. Stalling, indecision

To handle these objections and concerns, appear as a knowledgeable, interested insider whose only mission is to help the contact achieve his objectives and his desired or required goals. Always respond to objections with a positive attitude. Respect the prospect's doubts and view them as legitimate concerns.

ANATOMY OF AN OBJECTION

As used here, the term *objections* refers to any barrier voiced by the prospect that prevents you from moving on to the next step in the new-business discussion. The key word here is *voiced*. In the second half of this chapter, we will discuss *unvoiced* client concerns.

An objection is a reason for not buying that generally arises from a prospect's lack of understanding. Objections have a structure that enables you to analyze them and determine their cause. Happily, their structure also enables you to minimize their occurrences and cope with their effects should they arise.

As you have done in defining the existing need situation and the desired or required future situation, work with the prospect to understand the nature and scope of his objections. The information or facts you provide should be relevant to the prospect so he can understand how the service will benefit him. In short, the client-centered approach works well in handling objections.

Reasonable people often disagree. Take the lead in resolving disagreements. The sales representative who welcomes objections is communicating that the prospect's information needs are important and addressable.

A good approach is, "I appreciate what you are saying. Many of our existing clients said the same thing before retaining us." You can then build on objections by offering the following:

"Here is how we worked with them in overcoming the problem . . . "

Or

"If we can deliver it according to your schedule, would that still be a concern?"

Or

"I am glad you brought that up because it gives me an opportunity to highlight a superior aspect of our service solution. . . ."

When conducting a new-business discussion, be candid. Yes, many others will fudge and tell the prospect what he wants to hear, not the full truth. In the long term, maintaining 100 percent integrity works best. Today's consumers are far better educated and far more sophisticated than ever before. The few clients you lose will be offset by the many you gain because of your outstanding reputation for integrity.

You will not be able adequately to defuse every objection you encounter. If you listen to the prospect and acknowledge her points as being valid for her, then you have offered additional proof and justification for buying into the proposed approach.

Here are the five steps that address prospect objections:

1. *Expect* and allow them to occur.

2. *Welcome* them when they do arise because they indicate interest.

3. *Acknowledge* the prospect by restating the objection as a question to be verified. ". . . then you are concerned about XYZ?"

4. *Present* your evidence, give examples, and offer testimonials, endorsement letters, whatever relevant information you have.

5. *Support* the prospect's observation *only* if he has identified a real drawback. Then present an offsetting benefit. Say, "While your concern about DEF is justified, wouldn't you also agree that GHI more than compensates for it?"

After the prospect has brought up an objection, wait about 10 seconds before responding. Often the prospect continues talking and offers more clues as to how you should respond. If this happens, pause for an additional 10 seconds, and fully contemplate what you have just been told. Your pause also signals that you are preparing a reply to the question.

Objections signal a prospect's request for more information. Before the closing discussion can occur, you have to offer this information. By approaching objections as request for information, all your new-business discussions will proceed more smoothly. Each time an objection is handled effectively, the prospect moves one step closer to a buying decision.

Some objections are simply delaying tactics. A legitimate objection is specific and represents significant concern about your proposed solution. Such objections are based on finite resources, limitations, or other constraints, as in "It has to be finished by August 2 or we will lose several major contracts." Most legitimate objections, however, center around a lack of information.

We all use false objections to fend off others. Those who offer false objections often don't know why they do so. They may have underlying fear about acknowledging the validity of your message. If you are not aware of these concerns, you will have a hard time responding appropriately.

Skepticism as an Objection

When the prospect is skeptical about you, your presentation, or your proposed solution, it often stems from one of the following factors:

1. *"Heard you Screwed Up Previously."* The prospect may have information about a previous engagement where you encountered difficulties. Admit to any problems you encountered and why (without placing blame), and emphasize positive benefits the client gained as a result of your efforts.

2. *Qualitative Benefits.* Your explanation to the prospect may be fuzzy. He or she doesn't get it. Have you highlighted the benefits in the prospect's terms? Have your proceeded, slowly and clearly enough?

3. *Differing Favorable Futures.* What you suggest may not match what the prospect wants to achieve. Reexamine the desired or required future situation to achieve a better meeting of the minds.

4. *Insufficient Industry/Company Experience.* The prospect questions your ability to handle his situation because you haven't presented your capabilities adequately. You need to offer compelling evidence that your experience is valid and meets the demands of this prospect.

5. *Disease versus Symptoms.* The prospect doesn't think you have done the proper analysis; you found symptoms instead of the disease. For example, the prospect's initial concern is finding good replacements for key executives. If you neglected finding out why they are leaving in favor of discussing your executive search procedures, the fun part of the job, this objection probably will arise.

6. *Low Confidence.* Based on your appearance or presentation, you didn't inspire confidence in the prospect. Ask the prospect to tell you exactly what she needs to move forward. This may necessitate gathering additional information and attempting to reschedule an appointment so that you can invite a colleague or other expert to assist you.

7. *Contact's Inexperience.* The prospect may be inexperienced. Perhaps he has never worked with someone in your profession. In this case, testimonial letters and endorsements from others in similar positions will be helpful.

The preceding factors triggered the objection, can be reviewed in advance, and *prevented* from occurring. Present information and evidence designed to deactivate the trigger. The skepticism/objection rate should drop as you improve your ability to communicate in a client-centered manner.

In addition to these skepticism triggers, there may also be factors that *maintain* or *sustain* skepticism on the part of prospects.

1. *Failure to Gain Rapport.* The culprit here is not listening and responding effectively. If the prospect thinks you are offering lip service or just nodding blank approval, skepticism may set in quickly. Active listening takes work. In *Marketing Your Consulting and Professional Services,* we offer several checklists to evaluate your listening effectiveness.

2. *Not Asking the Right Questions.* The ability to ask good questions is fundamental to getting new clients. In *Smart Questions,* Dorothy Leeds says that asking good questions can be just as important, if not more so, than having the right answers. Your insider's understanding of the niche and preparation for the new-business discussion will arm you with the capability to ask the right questions. Also, by tiering your new-business contacts, you can call on low-priority suspects first to gain the insider's knowledge that will enable you to interact powerfully with your higher priority leads.

3. *Not Answering Questions.* Regard whatever the prospect mentions, no matter how trivial, as a contribution to the new-business discussion. If you duck a dumb-sounding question, the prospect may wonder what you are trying to hide. This advice runs counter to that of other authors who suggest you bypass trivial questions. As an advocate for the prospect, you can't afford to duck any questions.

4. *Defensiveness.* If you're defensive in handling a prospect's queries and concerns, you are likely to turn the prospect off. Remember, your reaction to objections is optional. As Wayne Dyer, PhD, says in *Your Erroneous Zones,* "You can choose your emotions," so choose to be responsive.

5. *Not a Client-Centered Approach.* This occurs when you speak in global terms or offer evidence that really doesn't relate to the prospect. Consider these: "We are the biggest in the world," or "Our partners get 40 hours of CPE training every year." Such statements offered at the appropriate moment can be beneficial in your marketing effort. However, avoid statements that are not client-centered nor germane to the discussion.

6. *Lack of Time Commitment on Your Part.* If you seem rushed or you haven't given enough consideration to the prospect's points, you will end up making the prospect feel uneasy. Without lingering endlessly within a

prospect's office, be willing to listen patiently and handle the client's objections within reason.

7. *Presumption*. By promising too much too soon or minimizing the unique factors of the client's situation, you are likely to contribute to the prospect's skepticism.

Review the maintaining and sustaining factors before the interview so you can plan a coping strategy. Skepticism occurs when your communication is not in sync with the prospect's. Early in my consulting career, I was too quick to respond and my answers were too pat. A partner in one of my target firms told me, "I know you're good, but don't be too quick to show and tell. You're an outsider talking to people who dislike marketing, so don't try to solve in five minutes what we've been struggling with for years."

Objections Due to Misunderstanding

Objections due to misunderstanding between you and the prospect fall into three basic categories.

1. *Inadequate Definition of the Need Situation.* In this instance, refocus on the existing situation and verify, verify, verify. Remember, defining and solving problems is your stock in trade. You earn your keep by immersing yourself in the misery of others and showing them how, by working with you, it can be eliminated. The prospect earns his keep by avoiding or getting beyond problems that affect his operations. Your task is to get the facts and promote understanding.

2. *Inadequate Definition of Desired State.* This is handled in the same manner as that of inadequate definition of need situation in number 1.

3. *Inadequate Definition of Benefits and Features.* Your task is to provide specific examples of how this prospect will benefit from your proposed solution program. It is also helpful to rely on a colleague, if present, to provide clarification and additional information.

Stalling

Figure 20.1 summarizes how to handle six situations where the prospect does not wish to proceed and stalls.

STALLING TECHNIQUES AND THEIR RESOLUTION

Factor	Resolution
1. He is not decisionmaker	Ask to meet with decision maker
Find out who makes decisions	Who do you think?
2. Not sold (uncertain/afraid of price)	Probe
Explain benefits	Explain
Probe beforehand	
3. Wants other proposals	Have client talk to others first
Ask if job is competitive	
Be last to propose	You set selection criteria
	Why other proposals?
	What info do you need?
4. Lack of understanding	Probe
Explain beforehand	Explain
Probe in previous conversation	
5. Too busy right now	When should we start?
Ask about schedule	Can he delegate?
Be prepared	Our project will ease burden
Plan	Increase scope
6. Project Not Budgeted	Cost/Benefit
Illustrate benefits	Adjust scope
Be prepared	

FIGURE 20.1.   Stalling Techniques and Their Resolution

HANDLING UNSPOKEN CONCERNS

For the balance of the chapter, we will focus on unspoken concerns of the prospect. You might ask, "How can I deal with objections that have not been presented to me?" Answer: Anticipate concerns not voiced by the client based on your insider's understanding of the niche and information gained during other new-business discussions. Through planning, you can develop strategies to deal with the unspoken client concerns and head them off at the pass.

The key to handling unspoken client concerns is to initiate a discussion about them when you sense their presence. If, near the close of a new-business discussion, the prospect appears to be reluctant to proceed or is otherwise holding back in some way, you would say, "Are there other points that we haven't discussed that you would like to bring up now?"

Many professional-service marketers prefer not to uncover what the prospect feels uncomfortable talking about. They feel that, if they skirt the issue, all will turn out well. It seldom does. Keep probing until the underlying concern is voiced. Until the humans master extrasensory perception, you'll have to get the missing information straight from the prospect's mouth.

Here are 12 specific examples of unspoken client concerns and suggested responses:

1. *You Will Not Understand My Business or Industry Because My Business or Industry Is Different.* Stress your extensive experience in industry, use client-centered language, maintain objectivity, and discuss the commonality of the prospect's problems and how you have addressed them before.

2. *Engaging an Outside Professional Is an Admission of Incompetence, an Indication of Trouble.* Emphasize that bringing you in is a positive indication that the situation is important. The mark of a professional manager is taking positive action to preclude negative occurrences.

3. *We Have Worked with Other Outside Professionals in the Past and Their Recommendations Did Not Work.* Encourage the prospect to describe the problem in detail. Then point out your experience and ability to tailor and presell solutions to ensure results.

4. *Why Are You Calling on Me Now at All?* Explain that with your insider's understanding of the niche, it made sense for the two of you to talk.

5. *My Present Service Provider Is Not, in Fact, Meeting a Particular Need.* Stress the importance of working with a professional who can meet your changing needs, anticipate them, and offer added solutions.

6. *Why Should I Do Business with Your Firm?* Emphasize your ability to help others in the industry, or others facing similar issues. Offer testimonials.

7. *If You're So Good, Why Are You Soliciting?* Explain that being good and booked to capacity are not synonymous. What entrepreneur today isn't seeking more business?

8. *Your Fee Is Less Than What We Pay Now.* Emphasize that your services are complete and cost-effective. Then cite any economies of operation or competitive advantages that enable you to offer a lower price. Don't accuse others of providing frills.

9. *If My Boss or the Higher-Ups Find Out I've Retained Outside Help, I Might Get in Trouble.* There are several strategies you can take for this one. First, mention anyone else in the same position who reaped the rewards of your assistance. Remind the prospect of the greater misery to ensue if you don't proceed. Also, ask the prospect to check it out—how does the boss feel about bringing you in? You may be surprised at the support you get from above when you offer a solution to a problem that is causing great pain.

10. *Is the Timing Right for a Change?* Encourage the prospect to focus on the costs of the status quo and emphasize that, in today's fiercely competitive climate, things rarely "just fall into place" without decisive action.

11. *Consultants (or Lawyers, Accountants, etc.) Have Only One Concern: Maximizing Their Fees.* This requires a cost–benefit analysis and discussion of how you strive to offer needed service solutions producing results that far exceed the fees involved. You can handle this using an illustration. "You know, the fee involved in tackling tough situations can look huge if taken out of context. When you look at the payoffs to clients who engage good consultants, the fees are right in line."

12. *Firms in Your Industry Have a High Turnover in Personnel and Cannot Provide the Continuity We Will Need.* Be candid about staffing and turnover, and if this is a high-potential prospect, try to guarantee that top-level staff will be assigned this job.

As a rule of thumb, any time it appears that the prospect has an unvoiced concern about something, you must probe for information. "It seems to me that you look doubtful about something I have said. Am I correct in my feeling?" Successful relationships are enjoyable, enriching, open, and perceived as win-win situations by both parties. You cannot achieve this if you fail to address unvoiced concerns.

QUESTIONS ABOUT FEES

Problems related to fees generally start in the mind of the service provider, not the prospect. Let the prospect bring up the matter of fees. If it arises early in the discussion, I respond by saying, "I appreciate your wanting to know what your budget for the engagement will be. To give you a sound answer, I need to get a little more information."

Put in perspective, fees are just a normal part of business. When the topic does come up, you want to control but not dominate the discussion.

I've made it a rule not to discuss fees until I'm prepared to justify my solution program. I never use the words *costs* or *fees* in connection with my services. The term *budget* is preferable.

To summarize, here are a couple of general principles in dealing with fees:

1. Don't make the prospect wrong for introducing fees.
2. Handle the discussion of fees on your terms—when you are ready to discuss them and in the context of expected performance.
3. Build your case based on the benefits the prospect will receive.

Getting new clients involves encountering lots of objections. Relax. Everybody faces them, but few will handle them as well as you.

21

Closing the Discussion and Moving to Action

The closing process gets blown out of proportion by many authors and professionals. The prospect is either portrayed as a tethered goat mauled into submission or a giant to be overcome by brute force. By following the steps outlined throughout the chapters of Part III, you will find that the close isn't a big deal. Rather, it is the logical end result of a successful new-business interview, an agreement to proceed to the next mutually beneficial step.

Since you are calling on prospects in a targeted industry niche, and discussing hot button needs, your close becomes much easier. In fact, the client-centered marketing approach and identification of specific needs is a powerful combination that takes a lot of the effort out of closing. If you are having closing problems, you probably need to improve the way you handled earlier steps in the new-business discussion.

It is both unnecessary and unproductive to put on your closing manner. Your personality doesn't have to change; there is no need to become anxious. Properly handled, closing is a mutually satisfying and normal wrap-up to your discussion. In many cases, the prospects will set up a closing for you by asking, "When could you get started?"

PURPOSES OF THE CLOSING PHASE

Your purpose in closing the new-business discussion is to obtain an agreement to proceed to the next mutually beneficial step, your primary goal all along. If things are not going according to plan, fall back to your secondary or contingency plan (see Chapter 20).

A second major purpose of the closing phase is to assist the prospect in overcoming inertia and resistance to change. Do this by suggesting ways to produce a more favorable future and by continuously speaking in terms of client benefits.

Three Steps to Closing

When it comes to marketing professional services, there are three basic steps to the closing process: recognizing the time to close, debriefing the prospect using a client-centered scenario, and making the closing statement.

Recognize When It Is Time to Close

Selling your service solution is the sum total of the steps you have taken from the time you first contacted the prospect until the time she is satisfied with her purchase. Everything you do during the new-business discussion is preparation for closing. For example, you observe closing signals on the part of the prospect. These occur when the prospect:

- Leans forward
- Offers more open posture, starts taking notes
- Asks another person to listen to the discussion
- Communicates her agreement with your ideas

Take a moment to recall the signals you have observed.

It is also time to close when the prospect *asks signal questions,* such as:

- Who will do the work?
- What technology would you use?
- When would you be available?

Think back to the times when you closed business recently. What questions did the contact person bring up? Also, what was there about the situation that made you know that the close was imminent?

Another tip-off to close is when the prospect *indicates requirements*. If he says, "If we are going to proceed, the start day would have to be the second Tuesday." Or, "My vacation will not be over until the 18th." Or, "Of course Mr. Walston would have to be involved in any decisions such as this. . . ."

Finally, when the needs have been confirmed, your benefits have been established by you and accepted by the prospect, and the objections have been resolved, it is time to move to the second step in the closing process.

Debrief the Prospect Using a Client-Centered Scenario

Using reinforcing statements, briefly restate the benefits the prospect can expect as a result of your service solution. Create a positive word picture of the client's desired or required future situation, calling attention to the positive purchase motivation trigger mentioned earlier.

Debriefing is truly a leverage operation! Here, you summarize your understanding of the prospect's central interest or concern. By restating benefits, you activate his buying motives with substantial leverage and encourage him to retain your services.

Debriefing begins with a statement such as, "Let's take a moment to see what we have covered so far." You communicate slowly while you leaf through your interview notes. Then you say, "If I am on target, you are interested in XYZ." Or, "You are concerned about ABC." You knew this when you determined the need situation. You then say, "Specifically, you need . . . ," and restate the solution specifications that you identified when scoping the desired or required future situation. Also include any concessions you made in response to earlier objections or negotiation points.

"As I mentioned, we will. . . ."

Then restate the actions you will take to produce the results promised and restate what the prospect must do.

"Which means that you will. . . ."

Again mention the solution goal that you used throughout the entire contact process.

You have now completed a loop: You need, we provide, you get, your need is met.

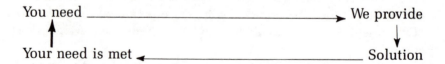

Making a Closing Statement

With the client-centered scenario established, you are ready to make the closing statement. This step moves the prospect to the final A in the AIDA process.

As you close, you make the major decision for the prospect and give him the final word on the subject by offering him options. This is also known as the "assumptive" close and is most appropriate for professional services:

"Mr. Levitt, to produce the accounts-receivable system we have been discussing, I need to get information about the current setup." You then look at your calendar and say, "Monday afternoon or Thursday about 10:30 is open right now. Which time would be best for you?"

You have made the major decision to meet again. Yet you've allowed the prospect to have the final word by allowing him to choose the date and time to meet.

If the discussion has not gone according to your plan, then make a secondary close. "Mr. Levitt, I understand your desire to be on hand if we are to proceed. Since your vacation will be over in two weeks, I will call you midweek when you return. This will allow you to go through your mail and backlog. Would Thursday, morning or afternoon be best for you?"

At this time, the prospect will suggest a meeting time or will raise some objections. In the latter case, employ the coping strategies presented in Chapter 20.

Suppose you have been having a good discussion, but you are still uncertain whether the prospect has made up her mind. You say, "Ms. Johnson, may I use your phone for a minute? Getting your marketing audit under way will require the use of our analyst Bob Richardson. I would like to make sure he will be available."

Another approach in dealing with a prospect's uncertainty is to ask him a question that leads down one of two closing paths, such as, "We need a great deal of information to start a project like this. Our people could gather it directly or we could outline the data requirements for your people. Which approach makes the most sense to you?" The prospect is bound to select one of the choices. This gives you a new vantage point from which to proceed.

Some Closing Do's and Don'ts

As indicated early in this book, a win in the process of getting new clients consist of getting a prospect to meet with you. At the conclusion of your new-business discussion, a win consists of getting the prospect to meet with you a second time, so you can move to action. If you are lucky, you might be asked outright to prepare a bid proposal or to start next Tuesday. Figure 21.1 gives tips to remember when going for the close.

SOME DO'S AND DON'TS

DO	DON'T
Stay in normal discussion mode	Change hats and telegraph that you are going to close
Include all necessary information the prospect agreed was relevant or important	Add benefits not brought up or agreed to by prospect
Remember you are not asking for the order	Pressure for a sale—continue the relationship by moving to a next step
Expect your close to "fail" due to information needs not raised and handled	Resent the failure—look on it as an opportunity to get more information
Use nondirective probes when close fails and be positive	Show resentment at stalls

FIGURE 21.1.   Some Do's and Don'ts When Closing

Leaving the Prospect's Office

After making your closing statement, you will encounter one of three responses:

1. An outright rejection of your closing options.

2. An "I'm not ready to proceed yet" type of reply.

3. An "Okay, let's get this show on the road" type of reply.

Let's examine each one in turn.

1. *Outright Rejection.* Because you are promoting solutions to important needs, the number of outright rejections should drop dramatically. Don't panic if a rejection occurs. Stop talking for a moment and then ask, "May I ask why you're saying that?" Don't sound cross or appear pushy. Ask the question in a conversational manner and listen to the prospect's answer while observing his body language. The usual cause of an outright rejection is anger; the prospect's feelings got hurt. Who knows, he may be steamed at himself for overlooking something you said you would do in solving the problem.

If you think you can salvage the situation after you have listened to him, say, "If it makes sense, let's take a few more minutes to discuss our solution goals for producing the results you want." Maintain the "we" feeling.

If it is futile to continue, then say, "Ms. Henderson, I wish that we could have worked something out. I'm glad I had the opportunity to meet you." Then shift the tone and focus of the meeting by discussing a current industry concern as you pack up and leave her office.

2. *"I'm Not Ready."* This can be handled with a simple response, such as "Oh?" or "Not ready?" Then be quiet. Since you were the last person to talk and the pressure of silence is building, the prospect will often blurt out the reason for his unwillingness to proceed. If this happens, say, "Thank you for telling me why you were not ready to proceed." Note the shift in tense from *are not* to *were not*. If the prospect lets this slide by, handle each concern in order. This is a critical point in the discussion. Your goal is not to shoot down his reasons, but to close by converting the energy behind them into justifications for moving to action.

For example, if he is reluctant to proceed because he is uncertain that a reorganization can be effective when managed by outsiders, deal with his concern by saying, "Mr. Henry, your concern about using outsiders is well founded. With a sensitive issue such as reorganization, you have to have outsiders who know how the industry works and what it takes to organize and harness the talents and temperaments of a large number of people. Frankly, it requires talent and experience such as ours, which has been developed and tested in dozens of reorganizations."

Your response should always include an acknowledgment of the prospect—he's okay, he's no dummy. Then, indicate that you've listened to his response or pose a question by using some of his words. Conclude by introducing the benefits of working with your firm and the dangers of not using the best available talent.

Train yourself to reply in systematic fashion to "not now" responses without getting into an argument or sounding to glib or rehearsed.

3. *"Okay, Let's Go."* You will encounter this response much more frequently as you build your skills and confidence using the methods discussed in this book. Attempt to schedule a start date without having to prepare a proposal. Get agreement that a confirmation letter will suffice.

Many professionals are fortunate in that they are not required to prepare proposals. They simply outline their work approach, quote budget or billing arrangements, and schedule a start date. Others are not as fortunate. The next chapter will address the techniques involved in preparing winning proposals.

22

Preparing a Winning Proposal

Following your new-business discussion, you may find yourself preparing a proposal. From your standpoint, however, the best proposal is one you don't have to write. Your time, energy, and expenses can be kept to a minimum when a confirmation letter containing the specifics of your service solution will suffice. With today's stiff competition in the service sector, proposals are increasingly required.

Entire books and training programs have been written on the subject of proposal writing. The purpose of this chapter is to present the anatomy of a winning proposal. Ernie Kosty, president of Kosty and Associates in Chicago, is an effective proposal writer, who has perfected the proposal process over the past 25 years. This chapter incorporates parts of his method with our own 26 years of experience in this area.

TO BID OR NOT TO BID

When you agree to write a proposal, one thing is certain: You *will* incur costs. So you must first determine whether you should bid. The following questions will help you make this decision:

1. Do you have a chance of getting new business?
2. Does the prospect have the money and desire to proceed?
3. Does the prospect represent lucrative, long–term potential?

4. Do you have the necessary resources to be successful?

5. Will this work be profitable and move your firm in the direction you want it to go?

6. Are you willing to do everything necessary to produce a winning proposal?

7. Are elements to be included already on disk?

8. Will you be able to use the essence of this proposal again and again?

9. Has the prospect indicated that your proposal will be icing on the cake?

Proposals don't sell the job, but they can unsell it. This occurs when you give a doubtful prospect "hard copy" justification for not proceeding.

Many professionals make the mistake of preparing proposals even when they don't believe they will get the job. Most of the proposals you write will not be winners. However, a proposal should only be undertaken when:

- There is an identifiable chance to gain new business.
- The proposal will be of use with other prospects.
- You need to propose to get your name on an authorized bidders list used by government agencies.

Preparing the Draft Proposal

A proposal has three basic purposes. First, it educates the prospective client about the nature and dynamics of his need situation. Second, it convinces the prospect that you are willing and able to deliver results. Third, it justifies the prospect's investment in terms that are useful and understandable to members of the decision-making unit.

The key to writing a successful proposal is to obtain current information on the nature, scope, and needs of the target or a particular solicitation and to present information within the proposal in a manner that convinces the target that hiring your firm represents the best way to accomplish the task. Yet, *writing a superior proposal will never substitute for effective personal selling.*

In producing a proposal, I recommend first writing a draft. This allows for prospect input. Let's discuss the steps to preparing an effective draft proposal.

1. *State the General Theme of the Proposal.* For example, "To describe how (your service) will enable the client to counteract the negative effects of previous indebtedness and maintain a positive cash flow."

2. *Develop a Written Outline.* Determine the major elements/sections to be included. Most proposals contain the following sections:

    A. Introductory paragraphs

        Indicate broad nature of job

        Cite meeting that occasioned proposal

        Indicate how proposal is organized

        May have some kind words about client

    B. The present situation, or our understanding of the problem

        Expanded definition of problem

        Details of problem (includes "you are concerned. . . .")

        Confirms our understanding of the situation

        Includes our thinking through the implications of what the prospect told us

        Puts the problem in context

    C. The objectives and scope of the work

        Objectives to be met

        What we will do and not do

    D. Our approach to solving the problem

        A prediction of what the assignment will involve stated in such detail that prospect appreciates and understands our approach, without committing us to an inflexible course of action

    E. How we would work with you

        Work closely with key people

        Draw upon the creative thinking of client people

        Hold frequent progress meetings

    F. Anticipated benefits/end results

        Stated from top-management viewpoint

        Implicitly justifies why client should hire us

        May be stated as final product of proposed outcome of project

G. Estimate of time and charges

Time charges stated either in range (e.g., $15,000 to $17,000) or an appropriate dollar figure per month

Reimbursable charges stated separately

H. Starting date

Typically gives two-to-three-week period for assignment planning

Frequently close with, "We await your approval to proceed."

I. Closing paragraph

Statement of interest in doing work for prospective client

May include generalized statement on benefits

J. Qualifications statement

Not in all proposals

State why we are qualified to do job

Background of principals

Corporate history

Facilities

K. References when appropriate

Normally provided only on request

Often submitted by separate letter or attached to proposal letter.

3. *Organize and Distill Your Interview Notes.* Include other related client data for each section.

4. *Review Each Section from the Prospect's Viewpoint.* Identify omissions, points that require proof, and nonessential redundancies. Winning proposals have deliberate redundancy in regard to benefits, experience, and the consequences of not proceeding.

5. *Write the Initial Draft.* Let it sit for a while before reviewing it.

6. *Type the Proposal in Semifinal Draft Style.* Leave lots of white space for notes by either your or the prospect.

7. *Stamp the Words "Working Draft" on the Cover.* Schedule an appointment with the "champion" in the prospect's company to review the proposal.

What Makes a Winner ————————————————————————————

Even if you have followed to the letter the items listed for developing a written outline (number 2 in preceding section) some additional elements will make your proposal stand out:

1. *Introductory Paragraphs.* You want to provide introductory comments that are warm, are tailored to the audience, and exude confidence that a mutual understanding will be achieved. Don't be overly solicitous, using such statements as, "We are grateful for the opportunity to propose. . . ." The prospect is not doing you a favor by asking you to prepare a proposal. Indeed, if you do the job correctly, he is going to derive value from it. Some prospects obtain proposals so they can do the jobs themselves. We will talk about avoiding that trap momentarily.

2. *The Present Situation or Understanding of the Problem.* Winning proposals provide a balanced description of the situation. This section is written to avoid embarrassing the reader and to avoid undue criticism from significant others. Take great pains to positively present the need situation and prior actions. Then you convey your prospect's concerns and interests and how they relate to the present situation.

3. *The Objectives and Scope of the Work.* The solution objective, the benefit that will accrue to the prospect, and supporting goals are spelled out in this section. You must also spell out precisely who will do what and what will be included in the solution program.

4. *Our Approach to Solving the Problem.* This section discusses what the solution engagement will involve. Winning proposals generally follow this structure: (1) The tasks required to produce the future situation are listed; (2) The products of each task, including the deliverable and intangible factors such as morale, confidence, and so on, are identified; (3) The benefits statements are fully defined for each task. Your task is to offer just enough detail to make the prospect appreciate and understand the approach, without committing your firm to an inflexible course of action.

For example, I've figured out the process involved in formulating a strategy and positioning a firm in its niche. Instead of giving away the store, I write,

> I will personally work with you and your key people in determining the current and preferred strategic posture for your firm. The posture will contain a definition of the current strategic direction, an analysis of the

scope and service mix, and recommendations for using this analysis to position your firm as a leader in the niche.

5. *How We Would Work with You.* Surprises are the enemy of good relationships. Your proposal should pinpoint the submission of early and frequent progress reviews. This is especially necessary if the engagement is complex or of long duration. Your goal at all times is to avoid the nagging question, "I wonder what the professional is up to now?"

Give the client credit for having a competent staff, with which you can work and communicate well. Offer such statements as "We will draw upon the experience and creative thinking of your people to . . . " Build a relationship between your firm and the organization's employees. Keep the prospect's confidence level high.

6. *Anticipated Benefits/ End Results.* In an eye-catching manner, state in specific terms what you will strive to produce given the resources and time constraints. For example, "As a result of the reorganization of department XYZ, management can expect a substantial improvement in morale and personal performance." Also implicitly justify why the client should hire you, using statement such as, "Using our unique approach . . . " or, "We will rely on our 15 years' experience to produce a . . . "

7. *Estimate of Time and Charges.* You should state the amount that you will charge in a range. Remember, this is a draft proposal and chances are you will modify what you have written. If the norms of your profession dictate an alternative way of presenting estimated charges, then use it. Any reimbursable charges (i.e., out-of-pocket expenses) should be stated separately.

8. *Starting Date.* Your availability to start is an important selling point, a fulcrum on which the action proceeds. You need to strike a balance here. If you are available on too short notice, the prospect may wonder why you're not busy: "No good?" On the other hand, having to wait six to eight weeks can cool off a hot prospect. Even if you are working flat-out, you can still find a half day to get the engagement started.

9. *Closing Paragraph.* Your closing paragraph should re-emphasize your interest in doing work for this prospective client. "Working with you and your staff to (solution goal) will pay dividends to (name of prospect). We await your approval to proceed."

10. *Qualifications Statement.* Depending on how familiar the prospect is with your firm, it may not be necessary to include this section in your

proposal. The qualification statement outlines the general capabilities of your firm and why you in particular are qualified to do the job. The key point here is to ensure that you are a known quantity to all members of the decision-making unit.

11. *References (When Appropriate)*. Don't underestimate the power of a previous client's positive comment on a job well done. The support and endorsement offered by someone outside your firm can be the deciding factor in your ability to gain a new client.

Proposal Preparation Hints

Use graphics when needed, but don't overdo the dramatic. Consider making the proposal look more like a report by using sidebars and headlines. Your goal is to have it read. If it looks inviting, it will be. Start each section on a separate page because it allows you to make changes easily and facilitates easier reading.

Review the language you have used and make sure your proposal contains a majority of active verbs. If you have included a qualification section with biographical sketches, make sure they appeal to the prospect. Use exceedingly friendly charts, such as shown in Figures 22.1 and 22.2, to help the reader. Every one is busy today—a good chart or table *is* worth a thousand words. Your proposal is literally a sample of your professional skills. Moreover, it is the most tangible product you will offer the prospect until the promised results are delivered.

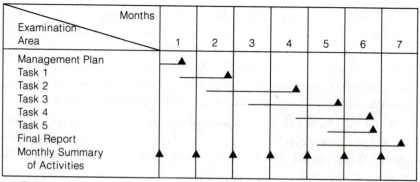

▲ Deliverable

FIGURE 22.1. Monthly Work Plan

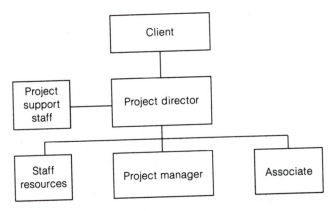

FIGURE 22.2. Typical Project Organization

A winning proposal blends technical and managerial competence to deliver a cost-effective result. It must demonstrate your firm's professionalism loudly and clearly. The checklist in Figure 22.3 can be used to examine your proposals.

PROPOSING WITHOUT GIVING THE JOB AWAY

I wish this section were not necessary, but some prospects ask for proposals just so they can learn how to do the job themselves. To avoid this problem, follow the principle of going long on benefits to accrue, and short on how you are going to produce them. For example, instead of telling how you assemble a market-focus study group, describe what you will do. You could say, "After forming a focus group designed to capture the full range of buying dynamics for your type of product, our interviewing team will ask six to eight questions, which, based on our extensive experience, will yield the information you need to make the go/no-go decision regarding product X."

PROPOSAL DELIVERY

I believe in directly presenting the proposal to the ultimate decision maker(s). Seek to be present during the review with the decision-making unit.

CHECKLIST FOR PROPOSALS

	ITEM RATING			
S = Satisfactory Q = Questionable U = Unsatisfactory N = Not Applicable	S	Q	U	N
Does it cover the underlying purpose of the proposed job?				
Does it refer to the client's own expressions of concern about the situation?				
Do we sincerely believe and express the importance of the matters to be studied?				
Is the work we intend to perform covered in sufficient detail?				
Is there a detailed work plan (whether included as a part of the proposal or letter of understanding) that clearly describes the work we will do and the estimated time required to do it?				
Can a client, employee, or executive who is to participate in the project understand what he or she is supposed to do from reading the proposal?				
If problems were to occur during the engagement because client personnel failed to perform, would the responsibility be evident from the proposal language?				
If there any danger that the client could misunderstand the extent or depth of our study—in terms of procedures and records to be reviewed, divisions or departments to be included, and persons to be interviewed?				
Have we included provisions for informing affected client personnel about the project? Who will inform them?				

FIGURE 22.3. Checklist for Proposals

CHECKLIST FOR PROPOSALS				
			ITEM RATING	
S = Satisfactory Q = Questionable U = Unsatisfactory N = Not Applicable	S	Q	U	N
Have we covered the procedures to be used to keep the client informed of our progress? How will the client be able to periodically review our findings and recommendations?				
Who will be assigned to the engagement from our firm?				
Have we expressed logical reasons why *we* should be engaged to do the work?				
Does the engagement plan, as expressed in the proposal, enable a reviewer to determine whether the committed dates are feasible?				
If references are made to previous client engagements, has approval been obtained?				
Are fees and expenses clearly stated?				
Has an executive, other than the person writing the proposal or letter of understanding, reviewed the technical approach?				
Has the proposal been reviewed by an internal executive to ensure good style, organization, and clarity?				
Did a partner or principal sign the written document to the client?				

FIGURE 22.3. Continued

If this can't be done, try to meet with at least two or three members of the decision-making unit prior to the decision. Other-wise, it may be best not to propose because you effectively are telling the prospect he is in charge of the project. This may sound harsh and may not be your standard practice, but I urge you to reconsider your position.

When you present your proposal to the decision-making unit, nothing is lost in the translation. You are able to answer questions and provide immediate feedback to the contact persons. Perhaps your being there may inhibit full and open discussion, but this can be overcome, especially if you have developed an in-house champion who will work and sell on your behalf.

PREPARING THE FINAL PROPOSAL

If the draft is accepted, ask your new client to write the words, "Accepted as noted," and the date on the bottom of the draft. You can sign it and send him a copy. This becomes your engagement-detail-confirmation letter.

Larger organizations typically insist on a finished, final draft that is letter perfect. To paraphrase Confucius: When you have to prepare a final proposal, do the best possible job because it is visible evidence of your ability to deliver a useful and informative product on a timely basis.

If the draft proposal is not accepted, you have to determine why it died. Otherwise, you run the risk of repeating the same mistake throughout the niche.

A continuing question asked by professionals is, "How do I follow up on an outstanding proposal without being perceived as pushy and hungry?" I don't have the answer; I don't think there is one answer. I send a note to the contact person thanking him for his efforts. If I haven't heard from him in a week, I call him and find out what is happening. Does he need any additional information? If he says he does not, I ask him when the organization will be making a decision. Should I call him shortly after that time?

Remain focused on the prospect you have been tracking. If you don't hear from him in a few weeks, send him a letter saying you're still interested in working together, but you will not be able to guarantee a quick start-up time because you're getting into your busy season. Much like spending too much time waiting in the reception area, you must consistently demonstrate that your time is valuable.

One consulting engineering firm calls its marketing team together to assess its proposal preparation and presentation. The team leader asks each member to answer the following questions:

1. What was the "tie breaker" in each winning situation?
2. What percentage of submitted proposals won in each of the functional disciplines? Was there a consistency in the wins for each area?
3. To what extent did the oral presentation play a role in the situations in which they did not succeed?
4. Is the competition doing something new or different?

Lively and penetrating analysis then ensures.

CONCEPT PAPERS: A SHORTCUT TO THE PROPOSAL PROCESS

We addressed concept papers in our companion book, *Marketing Your Consulting and Professional Services,* but it bears major mention here. The concept paper is a marketing tool and significant aid in moving the client further along in the selling process. Concept papers are relatively easy to prepare, inexpensive, and most importantly, well-received by clients. They lie some place between offering a client or prospect a full-blown proposal and making an informal suggestion about services you can provide. It is a valuable marketing tool as it helps you to "test the waters" before committing more substantial resources in pursuit of new business development.

A concept paper should define what you perceive as the prospect's or client's problem and offer a methodology or approach that will provide an effective solution. If favorably received, it can lead directly to a professional service engagement or to the development of a more formal, detailed proposal.

Putting It Together

Generally, the concept paper ranges between three and five pages, preceded by a one-page cover letter. It should convey that these are your initial thoughts after spending some but not an inordinate amount of time on the problem. Regardless, a well-developed concept paper should indicate that you understand and have expertise in handling the client's problem. The concept paper should be developed as an *end product;* it is not intended to be modified, revised, or otherwise reworked. However, the concept paper does not deal with the scope of work, project management, or project cost.

Five-Part Approach

An effective format for concept papers consists of the following approach:

- Cover letter
- Statement of the problem
- Objectives
- Proposed methodology or technical approach
- Summary

Cover Letter

The cover letter begins with a short paragraph confirming your interest in helping the client solve a specific problem. This is followed by a second paragraph that alludes to the concept paper that follows. This paragraph also informs the client that the concept paper is a document designed to stimulate discussion and perhaps further examination of the problem areas.

The third paragraph of the cover letter thanks the client for expressing interest in your firm and for the opportunity to submit the concept paper. It never hurts to mention that you look forward to working with the client, as this helps foster an atmosphere of team work and cooperation.

Statement of the Problem

This section should not exceed two paragraphs or roughly one-half page of double-spaced typing. It succinctly states the history or background of the problem as well as any present considerations. The information contained in this section should be derived largely from what the client has expressed to you or what you have learned in close observation of the client's problem.

Objectives

The objectives section should be brief and to the point and can be completed ably by bulleting three to five major project objectives. These objectives may encompass what you believe to be important in addition to what has been expressed by the client.

Proposed Methodology or Technical Approach

This is the longest and most involved section of the concept paper. It includes a task-by-task description of your proposed approach in undertaking to solve the client's problem. Normally, two to three pages in length, it should convey your proposed methodology or technical approach in specific terms in chronological sequence. Project organization, staff allocation, and other charts and diagrams, however, are not necessary and are not recommended for inclusion in a concept paper.

Summary

The summary need not consist of more than a one-paragraph wrap-up that restates the client's problem and highlights or emphasizes the effectiveness and benefits of your proposed methodology or technical approach.

Whether or not you can get by with a concept paper, anytime you can land the engagement without producing a full-blown proposal, you have leveraged valuable time and resources.

23

Reinforcing Your Client's Choice

When it comes to actually making the "go" decision a reality, many professionals get heartburn. They eagerly wait to hear that the client is going to proceed but then hesitate to follow up to garner a decision to proceed. The rule on following up is simple: Do it early and do it often, because a variety of engagement killers can creep up at any moment:

- The prospect might be going out for additional proposals now that you have brought your solution approach to his attention.
- The prospect may be getting into hot water internally, facing budgetary concerns, office politics, and so on.
- The prospect may vacillate because you vacillate.

The key to effective follow-up is always to offer something to share or have something to check up on every time you make contact. For example, say you called to get some information you need to develop computer software. Listen for clues that the opportunity may be hanging by a thread:

"It is going to be a while before we can get started because . . . "

"Are you really certain that you will be able to . . . ?"

"We need to discuss this further. I was talking with . . . and he raised the issue of . . . "

"Unfortunately, that's been moved to the back burner" (a euphemism for never).

Any of the preceding responses demands your immediate attention. Review the techniques for handling objections and client concerns. If you sense that face-to-face discussion is necessary, arrange another appointment and be sure that essential members of the decision-making unit will attend.

However, if you've followed all the steps, at this point in the process, many of your marketing efforts will begin to pay off. And why not? You've positioned yourself in the eyes and mind of the prospect as few other professionals ever have.

HANDLING POSTPURCHASE CONCERNS

You know how it feels. Tonight you are going to pick up a new gizmo that you just bought. You mention your purchase to a good friend who says, "Gosh, I wish you would have let me know before you did that. I could have saved you a ton of money and gotten you a better deal."

Now you are having second thoughts. This postpurchase concern shows up in many ways, but mainly by worry:

- Did I really make the right decision?
- Have I been taken?
- Will I look like a fool?

No matter what the purchase, the bigger the price tag and the more closely it affects your personal and professional life, the greater the level and intensity of postpurchase concern. Experienced professionals are aware of this phenomenon and take a number of steps to manage and minimize its consequences with their clients:

1. They call the new client with a bit of good news. "I was just reviewing the work plan, and thought you would be interested in knowing

that Bob Henry is going to have more time to work on the project. This means that you will have our best manager handling your project."

Joe Gandolfo, who is listed in the *Guinness Book of World Records* as the world's most successful insurance salesperson, says, "You would be surprised how much a brand-new customer appreciates a phone call saying how much you appreciate having the opportunity to do business with him." Gandolfo makes it a point to send a handwritten note, such as:

Dear Mark,

Tonight does not seem too soon to congratulate you on this afternoon's decision about _____. This is certainly a major step in establishing _____. I hope that our meeting was the beginning of a long and enduring relationship.

Sincerely,

Joe Gandolfo

2. They send something that relates to the upcoming engagement. This could include a relevant article, a previous PAR summary, or some other item that solidifies the initiation of the engagement.

3. They schedule a lunch appointment with the new client and with another client for whom the same types of services were performed.

4. As soon as possible, they send someone from the professional-service firm to visit the client firm and be seen in action. Your visibility on site will calm the client.

As the engagement is about to begin, look for additional opportunities to reinforce the new client's decision to retain your services. There are many things you can use as reminders of your services:

- The schedule you'll maintain for getting results.
- The new measure of internal control that will ensue.
- The nature and volume of work you'll be tackling.
- The contribution your staff will make.

In short, successful professionals reassure the purchaser that he made a good decision to proceed.

The subtle message that you are conveying to your new client is, "You chose the right firm to do the work. Consequently, the results will be forthcoming, and your organization will get the benefits they need and are paying for. You will be safe and well regarded."

You will have many more opportunities to make the "go" decision a reality by using the niche-marketing approach presented in this book. You made a good choice when you bought it. Jeff and I have enjoyed presenting it to you.

Glossary

Affinity Factor   The behavioral characteristics and communication style of your best existing clients that enable you to feel comfortable in relating to them.

AIDA Process   Creating a favorable *awareness* (A), sharing *information* (I) to develop an interest in seeing you, conducting need-driven *discussions* (D), and building a desire to proceed to *action* (A).

Alert, Yellow-Red   The zone of unacceptable performance of a factor deemed to be important in the operation of a prospect's business.

Benefit   The satisfaction your client receives from your service solution.

Buying Motive   The internal force that activates and directs the behavior of members of the decision-making unit to accept your recommended solution program.

Champion   A member of the decision-making unit who wants the company to purchase the solution you are proposing.

Client-Centered Marketing   The continuing process of developing and enhancing relationships with clients and other receptive people who are or can be useful to you in using, retaining, and referring you and your services.

Client Referral   An existing client that has provided you with leads, introductions, and/or has vouched for you.

Clones   Nonclient suspects in your niche that have many, if not all, of the positive characteristics of your best existing clients.

Close   The self-initiated step designed to obtain commitment to move to a mutually beneficial next step in the new-business development process.

Comfort Zone   The range of effective, self-initiated behavior in an activity area; the area of professional behavior where one is productive, confident, and forthright in communications and actions.

Confidence Card   A list of positive statements used to keep the professional on track and motivated while making follow-up telephone contacts.

Critical Success Factors—CFSs   The five to seven areas of performance in a prospect's business where things must go right for survival and profitable growth.

Data Base   The accumulated information about the niche that can be entered and accessed in a variety of ways.

Decision-Making Unit   The members of the prospect's organization that are involved in the purchase and use of your solution program.

D&B   The things you do and provide to prospects that are perceived by them as being *different* from and *better* than others who attempt to serve them.

Industry   All clients, prospective clients, and suspects in your practice area having the same 4-digit SIC number.

Infrastructure   The clients, prospects, suspects, nonclient influentials, competitors, and others who serve and affect the niche in some way.

Initial-Contact Mailing Package   The cover letter and enclosure that are prepared and mailed to suspect organizations in your niche.

Initial-Contact Program   The mailing and telephone follow-up contacts made in relation to a need-specific mailing program.

Insider's Reputation   The favorable awareness of you and your firm by members of the infrastructure.

Insider's Understanding   Your in-depth knowledge of how the niche works, what it takes to make a profit and compete successfully.

Integrity   An unfailing consistency between what you promised and what you actually delivered.

Leveraging   Concentrating on the smallest number of clients, prospects, niches, and targets that will produce the largest amount of profitable revenue; a multiplier type of activity that produces a cascade effect of results.

Market   The postal ZIP codes that comprise your practice area for a specific SIC; a defined geographical area.

Menu of Needs   The list of hot-button, recurring, and emerging needs identified as a result of developing your insider's understanding of the niche.

Motive—*see* **Buying Motive**

NCI's   Nonclient influentials, people in the infrastructure who can assist you in meeting your marketing objectives and goals.

Need   A generic term referring to an existing unwanted situation, a desired situation wanted and in short supply or lacking, and a task to be completed.

New-Business Discussions   The face-to-face meetings with prospective clients to define the existing and desired situations, and the solution program for delivering the required results.

Niche   An abbreviated term for industry-market niche.

Objectives, Closing   The primary decision you make and seek to obtain from the prospect to move to a mutually beneficial next step in the new-business development process.

PAR Report   A report that summarizes the *problem* statement, *approach* used by your firm, and the *results* achieved for a given engagement.

Players—*see* **Infrastructure**

Potential Clients—*see* **Suspects**

Preferred Prospective Client Profile   The list of desired characteristics, and the factors that "knock out" a suspect from being considered for attention in your niche.

Preliminary-Need Scenario   A worksheet prepared to get in sync with targeted suspects for your need-specific mailing.

Probes   Purposeful questions with a specific structure and desired outcome.

Promotion   The process of informing, persuading, or reminding targets of opportunity and influence about your firm's ability to meet selected needs in the niche.

Proposal   A document designed to describe the firm's ability to perform a specific task(s). Indicates that the firm has the facilities, human resources, management experience, and track record to assure successful project performance and completion.

Prospect   A former suspect who has met with you to discuss a need situation and has not yet purchased your proposed solution program.

Prospecting   The activities involved in obtaining appointments with qualified suspects.

Referrals   Clients and nonclients who mention your name to others and provide you with introductions and leads to new-business opportunities.

Scenario   A word picture describing the outcomes of your application of resources.

Scope   The range in which something occurs.

Services Delivery Program   The activities and work steps involved in delivering and installing your recommended solution program.

Services Promotion Program   The activities and worksteps involved in bringing a need and proposed service solution program to the attention of suspects in your niche.

Solution Goal   A statement describing a favorable outcome.

Suspects   Desirable nonclient organizations possessing suspected opportunity who have not yet agreed to meet with you.

Standard Industrial Classification (SIC)   A 4-digit number assigned by the U.S. Department of Commerce to identify commercial entities.

Target Niche—*see* Niche

Targets of Influence   Nonclients such as attorneys and bankers with whom you do not yet have a referral relationship.

Targets of Opportunity   Existing clients with needs and budget, prospective clients, and suspects in your niche.

Telemarketing   Using the telephone for marketing purposes, especially to obtain appointments with prospective clients to discuss potential new-business situations.

Telescript   The written guide used by professionals in preparation for and making follow-up telephone contacts.

Value-Added Service Solution   Service deliverables/products and activities that fully create the desired/required future situation within the agreed-upon time and dollar budget and exceed expectations.

Visualization   A technique for doing a job in your mind to identify the outcomes, and so on.

Resource Guide

Bacon's Publicity Center
Bacon's Media Directories
332 S. Michigan Avenue
Chicago, IL 60604
   A quick, convenient guide and desktop companion to newspapers, periodicals, radio, and television.

Business & Financial News Media
Larriston Communications
Box 20229
New York, NY 10025
   All of the business and financial newspapers, periodicals, radio shows and networks, and television shows and networks, available in a ring-binder and on disk.

Facsimile User's Directory
Monitor Publishing Company
104 Fifth Avenue, 2nd floor
New York, NY 10011
   A comprehensive directory of fax numbers as well as addresses and phone numbers of government, industry, and service firms, that would take months to compile on your own.

Federal Executive Directory
Carroll Publishing Company
1058 Thomas Jefferson Street, NW
Washington, DC 20007
   The definitive listing of everyone in government including name, address, and direct-dial phone number, update every two months. Indespensible if you market to the government.

Gebbie's All in One Directory
Gebbie Press
Box 1000
New Paltz, NY 12561
    An information-packed highly useful directory of newspapers, magazines, radio stations, and television stations.

Market Keys®
Dick Connor, cmc
6711 Bracken Ct.
Springfield, VA 22152
    A DOS software program that enables you to select targeted industry–market niches, classify your clients by their potential, and automatically identify targets of Opportunity, Attention, and Influence.

Newsletter Yearbook
Newsletter Clearinghouse
44 Market Street
Rhinebeck, NY 12572
    A bible of the newsletter industry, offers a wealth of information on more than 10,000 newsletters including circulation, page count, target market, subscription information, and so forth.

Power Media Selects
Broadcast Interview Source
2233 Wisconsin Avenue, NW
Washington, DC 20007
    A large, detailed guide to the nation's most influential media in a handy three-ring binder.

Sharing Ideas
Royal Publishing Company
PO Box 1120
Glendora, CA 91740
    A bi-monthly, coveted magazine loaded with tips, leads, and insights for achieving a successful consulting, training, or speaking career.

Successtrax
Successtrax International
202 Summer Walk Terrace
Mechanicsville, VA 23111
    An entertaining and enlightening cassette series available by subscription offering the latest insights on personal effectiveness, marketing, managing, personal finance, and achievement, by experts in their respective fields.

Tradeshows & Exhibits Schedule
Bill Communications, Inc.
633 Third Avenue
New York, NY 10017
A bible of the meetings industry and de riguer if you attend or exhibit at trade shows.

Yearbook of Experts, Authorities, and Spokepersons
Broadcast Interview Source
2233 Wisconsin Avenue, NW
Washington, DC 20007
A key resource in which you can be listed that is regularly used by journalist, writers, and reporters, and radio and television show producers in need of experts to interview for their respective publications or shows.

Zip/Area Code Directory
Pilot Books
103 Cooper Street
Babylon, NY 11702
A small, handy book that enables you to figure out zip codes if you know the area code.

Postscript

Information about Dick Connor's software program, *Market Keys*® and a series of marketing guides can be obtained from him by phone (800-383-0958) or by fax (703-569-2566). To get in touch directly with Dick Connor write or call him at:

Dick Connor, CMC
6711 Bracken Court, Suite 100
SPRINGFIELD, VA 22152
1-800-383-0958
Fax 1-703-569-2566

For more information on having Jeff Davidson speak at your next convention or meeting call Linkie Seltzer at Speaker Source International in Dallas on her direct line: 1-214-783-9111, or FAX 1-214-783-9111.

For questions or comment for Jeff Davidson write to him at the following address:

Jeff Davidson, MBA, CMC
2417 Honeysuckle Road
CHAPEL HILL, NC 27514

Index

Index